From Murder Incorporated To the PGA Tour

The Remarkable Untold Story of Charlie "The Bug" Workman

& His Son PGA Pro Chuck Workman

Chuck Workman

With

Peter Cimino

Copyright © 2018 Chuck Workman with Peter Cimino
All rights reserved.
No part of this book may be reproduced or transmitted in any form or by any electronic or mechanical means, including photocopying, recording, or by any information storage and retrieval system, without written permission of the publishers and authors, except where permitted by law.
ISBN-13: 978-0-692-18235-2
Published by: "the Combination"
Publisher Number For Title Management: 1905860
First Edition
*****
All pictures made available by Chuck Workman's personal collection.

Cover Design: Elyse Draper
Edited by: Brett Ellen Block
Proofread by: Toni Anne Hyde
Manuscript prepared and formatted for e-book and print by: Elyse Draper

DEDICATION

It is with great love, admiration and respect that I want to dedicate this book to Gyp DeCarlo.

Other than my Dad, there is no man that meant more to me than him. He was my mentor, my voice of reason, my protector and so much more. Other than my parents he was the one person who I wanted to make proud and did not ever want to let down. It was the least I could do, after all he did for me.

It has been 45 long years since Gyp left this earth. Yet, every morning, when I get up to shave, I think of two people: my dad and Gyp.

Thank you Gyp for everything. I hope, with all my heart that I made you proud.

I will love you always and will see you on the other side.

~ Chuck Workman

IN REMEMBRANCE OF:
ARNOLD PALMER

In memory of the greatest ambassador to golf that ever lived. He revolutionized the game and transcended the industry. He made golf what it is today. An incredible golfer and most importantly a marvelous man.

CONTENTS

	Acknowledgments	i
	Foreword	ii
	Introduction	5
1	Man of Honor	7
2	Charlie "The Bug" & "Handsome" Charlie	16
3	My Mother My Hero	25
4	A Horse Named Chief	39
5	Dad's in the Navy	47
6	Reality	63
7	It Was Mostly the Italians	76
8	The Kid Who Plays Golf	86
9	Respect the Game	96
10	How Did I Get Away with That?	104
11	Gangsters and Golf	120
12	The Art of the Hustle	126
13	Radical Changes	137
14	Am I a Good Guy or a Bad Guy	147
15	That's Not All Your Dad Was	157
16	Above the Law	167
17	Truth and Acceptance	192
18	Lucky 16	200

19	No One to Blame but Me	212
20	The Garment Center	220
21	The Dark Side	230
22	Put a Candle in the Window	239
23	She's with Me	246
24	Stop the Nonsense: Do What You Love	253
25	Charter Oaks: Back in Business	264
26	The Kid is Back for Good	270
27	Rest in Peace	280
28	Bethpage The Patch	289
29	The New Bethpage	294
30	End of an Era	305
31	The Sr. PGA Tour: Fulfilling a Boyhood Dream	314
32	The Tour	327
33	Florida: Just When I Thought I was Out	337
34	K.O.	343
35	He Still Watches Over Me	350
	Memorable Participants	358
	Our Story	367
	Update on the Authors	369

ACKNOWLEDGMENTS

In loving memory of my Mother and Father

It took me many years to fully realize that everything my parents did, they did with me in mind. They put me first, no matter what.

I know, without question, during those many difficult years they always did what they thought was best for me. And although, I did not understand it and did not come across as being grateful, when I was young, I sure am today.

They kept me protected. They kept me busy. They surrounded me with people who took care of me, did things for me and with me, not out of obligation, but out of love.

They taught me what unconditional love is and how powerful it can be. They taught me that family always comes first. They taught me the true meaning of loyalty and respect. They taught me that everyone deserves a chance, no matter what walk of life.

Without them, I would not be the man I am today. I hope that I have made them proud.

FOREWORD

Jean Bartholomew – *LPGA Professional*

I'll never forget the first time I walked into Chuck Workman's Bethpage Pro Shop, when I was just 13 years old and had just gotten the golf bug! It was like a wonderland of everything golf. Clubs, bags, shoes and so many sweaters! My father had to drag me out of there because I wanted to touch everything.

I didn't meet Chuck officially until a few years later after playing around with his wife Elyse. She told him she played with a girl who hit it farther than him and he just couldn't resist playing golf with me. I won't say who hit it further, but from that day on, I can't imagine my life in golf as an amateur, an LPGA touring professional and now a teaching professional, without Chuck being part of it.

Chuck taught me so many things about the game. He taught me how to play for money. I can't count the number of times we almost killed each other when we were partners, because I was giving tips to our opponents!

Chuck got me a place to practice, found me my first group of sponsors and even helped me with my first teaching job. My life in golf has been so much better because Chuck and his family took me into their lives.

Chuck's knowledge of the game and all other things tied to it really helped me have a long-playing career, which continues to this day. I can't thank him enough for being a part of my life and for all his help and friendship. I still go see him regularly and enjoy him yelling at me on the practice tee. He is one of a kind guy and I am so lucky to know him.

Bob Toski: *PGA Pro & Hall of Famer*

I have known Chuck Workman for about 40 years, during which I had the opportunity to play many rounds of golf and watch him teach the game to all types of players. What impressed me was how well he played the game and his knowledge of the golf swing.

Since then, we became close friends and have shared stories about his and my career. When he asked me to write a forward for this book, I then felt he was a true friend.

The book, "The Hitman & the Kid Who Plays Golf", is unique and different. One must understand the background of his association with his dad and why he wrote this interesting story of golf and life as he experienced it.

I've always said that "Many are called, but few are chosen." Chuck and "yours truly', were lucky to be the "chosen ones" in our field. "We have lived to learn and learned to live."

I hope all of you enjoy this book and get to know the real "Chuck Workman"!

Jerry Coats: *PGA Member - Former President of the PGA Metropolitan Region*

I met Chuck Workman in the golf business in the Metropolitan New York area. We played together in several Metropolitan PGA tournaments and had a chance to visit with each other at PGA meetings.

Chuck's desire to be a member of the PGA of America was very evident in our discussions. I know he deserved to be a PGA member. His good qualities led to his induction into the membership in the PGA of America and I was glad to be a part of it.

Joseph Moresco: *Golf professional*

After several years, when Chuck Workman was denied membership into the PGA of America, he was eventually admitted and became Director of golf at Bethpage Golf Club on Long Island New York. Through his vision and efforts, the golf courses and facilities were enhanced greatly; particularly the famous, "Black" course.

Chuck was successful in convincing the state of New York officials under former Gov. Pataky to propose that the U.S.G.A. awarded the US open golf championship to the restored Bethpage "Black" Course. His efforts were successful and so was the ensuing tournament which was won by Tiger Woods. Thus, began a new era of venues for the U.S. Open at public facilities.

During this time Chuck had great successes with his own game competing on the PGA Senior tour. He even won several local events including the Met PGA Senior championship.
Chuck's legacy goes far beyond his contributions at Bethpage. It is one of dedication to the game and unshakable integrity. He and I go back some 50 years and one is hard-pressed to find a better partner in golf or in life.

Glenn Rodermann: *Attorney at Law*

My opinion of Chuck Workman is probably very different from the others that have chosen to write about him. I totally respect him and like him. I consider us very good friends, this started from the "get go", simply because of who he is and who I am. I am a criminal defense attorney who has been in the criminal justice system for well over 40 years. I chose the prosecution side from the beginning of my career other than the mobster side that was first offered to me by my Uncle Tony who was a mobster. Much like Chuck, I took the high road in law and he took the high road as a golfer. We both did well in our choices and have proven to be right in the success we have had in life. He has been a golf pro since his twenties, playing on the PGA Senior Tour for almost 10. He still gives lessons and helps so many golfers.

I have been in the courtroom about 17 years longer and we found the reward we set out for at the beginning. Chuck is an upfront guy who tells it like it is whether you like it or not. He either likes you or he doesn't and lets you know from the get-go. If he is your friend, then he is always there for you and always has something to offer that is truly genuine. His life story is amazing, and his author has truly captured the history, facts and details, that make this story so fascinating and imaginative. Congrats on a great story of a great guy!!

Alfred Wolfson: *President of Charter Oaks Country Club*

Chuck Workman is "a man of all seasons": a fantastic golf pro and close friend. A man who can spot a problem in your whole form, address, whether in your swing, hands or feet. Taking the right club for a pitch shot into the hole. His way of explaining it in easy, concise English that you remember and take it to the golf course to execute it to become a low reliable handicapped "hole-in-one" player.

I love the game of golf and it meant so much to me to have a "Pro" like Chuck Workman in my life who took a genuine interest in me – it was great! You can't ask for anything more.

INTRODUCTION

My given name is Solomon Workman. I was born on March 23rd, 1935. However, my real name is Chuck Workman. It is not Charles or Charlie.

A gentleman by the name of Charlie "Lucky" Luciano gave me that name at Flower 5th Avenue Hospital, while they did the Honors officially making me a Jew. He not only gave me that name, he was named my godfather. I have never been called or answered to any other name other than Chuck of Chucky.

My father is Charlie "The Bug" Workman, a loyal, honorable, respected yet, dangerous, ruthless banger and hit man for the Mafia and Combination Mob from 1925 through 1940. He is most known as the man who took out Dutch Schultz on the orders of Charlie Luciano and Meyer Lansky in October of 1935. That may very well be what the media and most people know him for. However, that is not what his legacy is. His legacy as you will see is the antithesis of that.

I was born and raised in a different era. An era, when honor meant something. When family came first. When being a gangster was just a profession. When respected mobsters were also honorable caring, generous men, who took care of their own. When the Mafia and Combination Mob was about making money, with ultimate visions of getting into as many legitimate businesses as possible. It was a time when those who were involved with that life, did or threatened to do anything to jeopardize the end game, paid the ultimate price.

Yet, innocent people were left alone. Everyone was given a chance to make a living. And the most generous and caring of these people were the wise guys themselves.

This is the heart and soul of my life's journey. A journey that has led me to pay homage to men, who put the fear of God in most anyone, but who helped me get to where I am. For as long as I live and probably beyond, I will never forget them. When it came to me, my mother and my father these men were straight up and would do anything to help us. And they did this because of the type of man my father was: a man of honor and respect.

This is where my incredibly, unique and almost unfathomable

life begins.

It is time for the truth to be told.

What you are about to read is my story. There are NO liberties taken or "creative licenses" used. This is all the 100% truth, as I remember it.

~ Chuck Workman

1
A MAN OF HONOR

1964

They're dead.

They're all dead. They were dead the moment they picked up the phone and heard a familiar voice telling them to come to a last-minute sit-down, dinner or meeting. They were already dead. They just didn't know it.

They didn't see it coming. It comes from someone they are close to. That's how it worked in the mob. The last thing that passes through their mind is the regret of what they know they did wrong.

I was no mobster, but I knew the "score" and the "rules of the road". I hung out with gangsters my whole life. They told me stories that would send shivers through any man's body. To them, it was always justified.

My father received a phone call like that. But, you've never met my dad.

They say people who are afraid to die are the ones with regrets. My father didn't have any nor was he afraid of anything. But, that night as we crossed the Brooklyn Bridge in my blue Ford Thunderbird, I thought for sure there had to be fear in him somewhere.

I didn't see it. That worried me.

My father sat in the passenger seat facing straight ahead, stoic as usual. His tailor made, Brooks Brothers, charcoal, pin-striped suit fit him like a glove. A silk navy blue tie, perfectly knotted, and the tip of his navy handkerchief that rose out of his lapel pocket accessorized his suit. His silver tie clip glinted in the passing headlights. His black alligator, Fergamo shoes were shinier than a soldier's military boots.

"Where exactly are we going?" I asked, music playing softly on the radio.

Expressionless, he replied. "I told you. Don't worry about it. It's dinner with some old friends in Jersey City."

I knew what "old friends" meant – his former mob associates.

His call came only a few hours earlier. I don't know who made the call, nor did I want to know. He was called to a dinner. It was an order. Good mob soldiers follow orders. No questions asked.

When a guy arrives at a specified location or gets into a car to go for a ride there are familiar, friendly faces all around with smiles. He is put at ease - relaxed, unsuspecting and guard down. In the blink of an eye it's over. Gun blast to the head. An icepick through the back of the skull. That was how it worked for knock-around guys. You live by the sword and you die by the sword. You don't follow the rules of the road, you die.

I knew enough about my dad by now to know he was loyal to the core and he always did what was right by his employers. But, with these guys…. you just never know.

"You're driving too fast," he said. "You in a hurry?"

Dad adjusted the crisp cuffs of his shirt and patted his perfectly groomed gray hair into place. He'd been out of prison for just two weeks after serving 24 years for what should have been a 12 ½ year sentence for the murder of Dutch Schultz. He still carried this undeniable aura, one of respect, honor and distinction. I could only hope that someday I could pull that off. At 29 years-old, I had his intense eyes, the sharp angle of his chin and his strong shoulders, but I had a long way to go.

My dad's name was Charlie Workman. His friends dubbed him "The Bug," a key member of Murder Incorporated and a high-ranking member of the Combination Mob. He was famous. He was infamous. He was my father.

I had learned a lot about my father during his time behind bars. The media and people who feared him never had a nice thing to say. However, anyone who really knew him had nothing but praise for him. This was in all his circles: the mob, the neighborhood, legitimate people, even cops. He was a walking contradiction. It tormented me for the past 17 years.

I had no idea what to expect. What exactly was this all about? I just drove and let the music fill the silence. I had a feeling we could be headed into an ambush.

Since my dad went to prison back in 1940, the mob had changed drastically. The original old-school mob bosses were falling by the way side one by one. Greed for money and power had gotten out of hand. Killing anyone who was a presumed threat had become the norm.

"I don't like this, Dad. How do you know this is not a set-up to whack you?"

Cars hurtled by on either side, blurred by motion as if we were standing still and the whole world was moving except us.

"If they were going to kill me, they would have done it 25 years ago."

I knew he was right. But, I still didn't feel right.

I drove up to the street where the hotel was. A car facing us about fifty yards ahead flashed its lights.

"Flash back in the same sequence," my father ordered.

"If they're going to get you, this is the perfect time."

He didn't say a word. He didn't even look at me.

I drove forward slowly, closer to the other car. A big, burly guy dressed in a suit knocked on my window. For the first time during the whole ride, dad finally looked at me. All he gave was a nod.

I rolled the window down tentatively and held my breath.

"Follow me please," the guy said politely.

I parked in a lot next to a hotel that bore signs saying it was closed for renovations. The looming windows were dark. My father and I got out and walked toward a set of heavy double doors. The guy, who had to be a body guard or banger, opened them. Inside was a grand lobby a beautifully decorated hallway, with gilded mirrors and marble floors that still managed to gleam in the dusky light. There were fresh cut flowers everywhere. It smelled like a florist, mingled with the scent of Italian food.

My pulse was pounding. I knew better than to glance at my father to search for anything in his gaze other than confidence. His stride wasn't that of a convict but one of a dignitary, easy and unhurried. I scanned every dusky corner for a sign of trouble. The quiet foyer was completely empty.

"This way." The guy ushered us towards shimmering white double doors.

I shivered as if a ghost walked right through me. Everything unfolded in what seemed like slow motion. I knew behind those doors were the most notorious mobsters in history. My thoughts raced, and my comprehension could not catch up.

Charlie "the Bug"? "Handsome Charlie"? Who was I going to dinner with? I know what people told me. But, was it real or just lip service? Nothing but mass confusion smashed in my mind. I still was not convinced this wasn't a trap.

The large man opened the doors and led us into a grand ballroom lined with floor-to-ceiling picture windows adorned with off-white, silk drapes. At every window, there was a guard facing out, not in, watching the street for all movement.

Above us were about a dozen massive, glistening, glamorous, chandeliers with dripping crystals. The likes I had never seen before. In the middle of the room sat a long, rectangle table with a bright white table cloth and place settings. The table looked like it was set up for a President – extravagant.

The nerves that had been hounding me dimmed. This was not the set up for a hit.

As my father walked in with me hard on his heels, every single man stood up and gave him a standing ovation. It was thundering and long. Some of them were pounding on the table in celebration.

I was stunned. My fears had immediately been replaced with awe-inspiring pride.

When he approached the table, he was instantly greeted with warm hugs and kisses by everyone, starting with Angelo "Gyp" DeCarlo, who was my godfather at the time.

Most people knew Gyp from his association with Frankie Valli and the Four Seasons. He owned them and protected them. He also made a lot of money through their success. However, Gyp was the most powerful mob boss in New Jersey. Jersey was his. Although the hierarchy stated he was under the DeCavalcante Family, who supposedly ran New Jersey for the Genovese Crime Family in New York, he reported to no one. He didn't have to. He always did the right thing as La Cosa Nostra goes. He knew the rules and never broke them. He was an old-school, hardcore, traditional Sicilian mobster. He knew it. Was proud of it.

"I'm a hoodlum. I will always be a hoodlum. I will die a hoodlum. It's that simple. I don't pretend to be anything else." This is what he told me on several occasions.

It was a who's who of the Sicilian Mafia. Frank Costello was Charlie Lucky Luciano's right-hand man and partner since the beginning. At one time, only two mobsters reeled more power: Luciano and Lansky. He was called "The Prime Minister of New York". One of his key roles was to get members of law enforcement to "buy-in", when it came to the Mafia and Combination Mob. He made sure these men were taken care of, from the beat cop all the way up to the top, including politicians.

His aura was not one of a typical mobster. He carried himself with class and dignity, always smiling, shaking hands, holding babies, saying hello. He represented Luciano's Family now known as the Genovese Family. Although semi-retired, he remained a Mafia elder statesman and advisor. Vito Genovese, the new leader of the family, was in prison at the time, still trying to rule his family.

Sam Giancana was the boss of the "Chicago Outfit". At one time, he was regarded as the most powerful mob boss in the country. Powerful enough to rig a Presidential Election for the Kennedy's. Sam got his start as wheelman for Al Capone. He made his bones and became an incredible earner during Tony Accardo's reign. Once Tony A stepped down, Chicago was Sam's. He earned it.

To put it nicely, he was as unpredictable as the path of a tornado. You never knew what you were going to get. He was without question vicious and yet there was a soft side to him that most never saw. He had close ties to the C.I.A. and F.B.I, working with them to take out Castro. So, he had just as much on them, as they had on him.

Santos Trafficante ran Florida and Cuba during the Fulgencio Batista era. But, once Fidel Castro came into power, that all went away. That did not diminish his power in the southeast. He was smart though. He followed Meyer Lansky's lead and ventured into many legal businesses.

Carlos Marcello; boss of New Orleans and Texas. If there was one gangster who had it out for the Kennedy's it was Carlos. He was investigated, but never charged. They put him through hell, including deporting him to Guatemala. He ruled his world with an iron fist. Fear of him, was his greatest alley. He had his hands in everything in two states, building up an unmatched cache of wealth. Although his English was very poor, it didn't stop him. His actions did the talking for him.

It looked like a table for the mob's last supper. Besides these powerful Sicilian Mafia Bosses from across the country all five New York Families were represented by their leaders. Genovese (Formerly Luciano) Frank Costello. Colombo Crime Family: Boss Joe Colombo. Lucchese Family: Tommy "Three Fingers" Lucchese. Gambino's: Carlo Gambino, now regarded as the "capo de tutti capi", the boss of bosses. And of course, Joe Bonanno, of the Boss of the Bonanno Family. Joe had already played a major role in my life.

In some respects, it was a last supper. Most meetings of Bosses in both the Mafia and Combination mob were held to resolve beefs and sometimes to decide on who should live and who should die. The tension involved with these gatherings could be hair raising. But, not today. It was nothing but smiles. A celebration. Laughter. Cheer.

I received several nods and handshakes but was quickly escorted to a small table set off in the corner of the room, where I sat by myself with my own waiter, captain and bus boy, who eagerly catered to my every need. Although separated, I could see everything and was able to hear some of what was said.

Gyp sat at the head of the table. Frank Costello was at the other end. On the right side of Gyp was his right-hand man, Cy – I never knew his last name. My father sat to Gyp's left, which had a special meaning. It was the chair closest to Gyp's heart.

All these men knew they could no longer be around my dad due to his probation. If he was seen with any of them, he would be in violation of his parole. Hence, the secret location and last-minute preparations.

I was motioned over to be part of the toast given by Gyp, who stood and adjusted his tie as if he needed more air to say what had to be said. "Charlie, we'll probably never get to see each other again. But you will always be with us."

Everyone raised their glasses. Some followed with Sicilian words that I did not understand. Others said, "Salut!"

Waiters bustled around serving food while wine flowed non-stop. Gyp gave me a look that told me to return to my lone table. I was Charlie's son, but I wasn't one of them. I could be there, but not in the way they were, not totally.

Course after course of extravagant entrees came out and the more food the men ate, the more they drank. Voices got louder and even more cheerful. Their talking was the only noise in the room.

I watched my dad closely. He was not a man of emotion. Of course, he smiled, laughed a bit and conversed when he felt he needed to. But, most of his communicating was done with his facial expressions and nods.

He whispered frequently to Gyp. That was more like my dad. It was as if every thought or feeling he had was a secret and should be conveyed that way. But, when another boss came over he turned towards them to show respect. He went to stand a few times but some of the most powerful men in the country would wave him off, saying, "No, Charlie. Please. Sit."

As dessert was being served, Frank Costello, walked over with his famous Du Maurier cigarette in hand. The noise softened for a second and as he looked at my father squarely, I wish Charlie (Luciano) was here to see you finally come home. He would have been so happy."

Luciano passed away two years before my dad came from a heart attack at the Naples airport on January 26th, 1962

"On everyone's behalf I want to know that we will all be forever grateful to you for what you have done for us. You are a true man of honor."

My dad took Frank's hand with both of his. "I wish he was here too. He passed much too early." He paused as if giving a moment of silence. "I want you know how much I appreciate all that everyone has done for me and my family while I was away."

Frank grinned. "Charlie, for as long as this thing of ours is alive, your legend will live on. Most importantly, you and your family will be taken care of."

With his hands still on Franks, my father nodded. "I'm not too good at Sicilian, but grazie mille. We have been family for a long time. It will always stay that way. It was and still is my honor to be your friend."

"One more thing." Frank added. "Tell the Kid Who Plays Golf to do what he does best and make us proud."

My father glanced over at me and our eyes met. For a second, it was like the whole party went mute and heard him as clear as a bell. "I will pass on the message."

They were talking about me. Here was a man who I loved but didn't understand and barely knew. I was his son, Charlie "The Bug" Workman's son. The meaning of that was lost on me for more years than I could count. However, the honor was not.

Hours later, the grand gala finally started to come to an end. I don't remember who the first guy was to stand up, but it seemed like a domino effect. One after another all the guests lined up like a wedding precession in front of my dad.

One by one, they walked up, gave him a hug, a kiss and said something to him. I heard a lot of "I love yous" from these guys. It became very emotional. Every man handed him an envelope. I was not privy to, nor was I told what was in those envelopes, but rest assured every single one of these bosses handed him one. They could not and would not ever see him again. This was goodbye in the grandest way, a show of sincere respect from the most powerful and reviled men in America.

Rest assured, this dinner had very little to do with what my dad did for the mob. It had to do with who he was as a man.

As I was walking behind my dad toward the door, Gyp pulled us aside. "Charlie, if you need us for anything, just send Chuck. We will take care of whatever it is."

Gyp patted me on the back as I passed him then two bodyguards escorted us to my car.

My father fell silent again. But, I was busting at the seams. I had a million questions.

I kept glancing at him waiting for him to say something. Anything. He acted as if the event never took place. I waited until I couldn't take it anymore. I had to say something.

"Dad, who was that guy sitting a few seats over from Frank Costello?"

"I don't know."

I wouldn't give up. "Dad, you know Carlos Marcello?"

He didn't blink. "Who's that?"

I pushed on. "I can't believe Sam Giancana came all the way from Chicago just to see you."

"I don't know who that is," he replied flatly.

I tried a few more times to no avail. Then like a slap to the back of the head, it hit me. In his eyes, and in the eyes of the men who came to pay tribute to him, that dinner never happened. It was a moment in time now gone but not forgotten. Just unspoken.

As I continued the drive home, back over the Brooklyn Bridge I could not shake the conflicting feelings I had inside of me. Who was my dad really? Was he the stone-cold killer, "The Bug"? Or was he "Handsome Charlie" the man revered in all his circles as a man of respect and honor.

I still needed answers. I had heard about so much of his good side, but I could not let go of "The Bug" references; they were everywhere.

I knew the only way I could try to find out who exactly I was, and who I was supposed to be, was to find out who this guy Charlie "The Bug" Workman was. It was the missing piece to my identity puzzle.

2
CHARLIE THE BUG AND HANDSOME CHARLIE

When you have an opportunity to play golf with Dean Martin, you don't say no.

I was drinking an espresso in the corner of the clubhouse at the old Dessert Inn in Las Vegas at around eight in the morning. It was a golf hustler's heaven and I was probably better than the rest of the other golfers hanging around. Only they didn't know. And that was the way I preferred it.

Bo Winniger, a PGA Tour Player, was the pro there. Tall and lean with wavy dark hair, he was a pro for a reason, winning multiple times on the PGA Tour. He spotted me in a secluded booth and came over wearing a smile and said, 'How are you fixed?"

I had been playing golf since I was 15 years old. It all started at the behest of my father who demanded I take golf lessons. I hated it in the beginning, but I got hooked. Before I turned 20 I was hustling and winning money.

"I'm holding pretty good," I told Bo. "Got about $800 in my pocket."

"We have a game today. Ten-sharp. I'll set it up."

He told me the game we were playing. I figured I might lose $500. I could cover that, so I told Bo, "Let's go."

Bo nodded toward the two men sitting at the bar. The man most people didn't recognize, tanned with dark hair and dominant nose was Paul "Skinny" D'Amato. Skinny was Frank Sinatra's real manager of record. He was heavily connected. Most people didn't even know he was affiliated with Frank. His connections went all the way back to "Nucky" Johnson in Atlantic City.

Sitting beside him, looking dapper in crisp slacks and cigarette in his hand, was Dean Martin. Our paths crossed a few times when I played in Vegas. I'd usually get sent out to Vegas for set up matches through my connections. They'd set up a few at a time over the course of a few days, to make it worth our while. Sometimes I'd pick up a few extras on my own.

Dean knew who I was because of my golfing. He also knew who my father was. Every time we'd bump into each other, he would always ask how my dad was and say to send him his best.

If Dean Martin knew who my dad was, why didn't I? I knew what he did. But, I didn't really know him. There seemed to be two Charlie Workmans, one the complete antithesis of the other. This haunted me for years, and still did. What did Dean know that I didn't? Or anyone else for that matter?

My father, Charles Workman, was born on September 15th, 1908. He was raised on the East Side of New York right in the heart of the Jewish and Italian neighborhoods, the epicenter of mob activity.

He left high school before he graduated, as young men commonly did to help provide for their families. He and my grandfather started the Baker's Union to make a living, not as a member of the mob, so his initial connection to gangsters like Louis "Lepke" Buchalter and James "Ghurra" Shapiro was quite innocent.

But, my father was tough through and through. He knew how to take care of himself and his interests and was not afraid to do so. That got him noticed by mob bosses. Eventually he started running with "The Bug and Meyer Gang". These guys held up banks, hi-jacked trucks, and stole cars. Soon, he became the "go to man" on the east side of New York. The money was good, too hard to turn down. Lepke used to say he had so much guts that he was "bugs." The nickname stuck. Allie Tannenbaum called him one of the best killers in the country. The press dubbed him: "The Bug, the "The Powerhouse" and "Handsome Charlie." But, I just called him "Dad." And until I was 12 years old, I had no idea what my father did for a living. Not a clue.

Bo headed over to Skinny at the bar. They talked in a whisper directly into each other's ear. Bo, then turned back towards me and gave a nod. I offered one back. Nothing needed to be said. It was game on.

We met up with Dean and Skinny at the first tee. The sky was cloudless, and the sun was beating down on the freshly cut grass. Dean strode over to Bo and me, looking every bit the movie star that he was, in dark shades while Skinny followed behind him. Then

Dean broke into a big smile. "Are you okay with the game?"

I smiled back, a bit in awe. "Yes. It's hundred dollars Nassau with automatic two presses."

Skinny added, "We play progressives."

I wasn't quite sure what he meant, but I didn't want to sound cheap or dumb in front of them. "That's fine. I'm okay with it."

"Good," Dean said with a wink.

He was about a nine handicap and Skinny was about a five, so they gave me three shots.

When I am on the golf course, I am all business. I catch on to whatever the "set-up" is, especially if I don't put it together myself. This one was about me being better than they thought. So, I had to play it cool from time to time.

What very few knew about my golf journey was my first love as a sport was baseball. I was a baseball player all through my first few years in college and a very good one at that. Up until I was 15 years old, no one could have ever convinced me that I would not only play the game, but I would turn into one hell of a player. One thing about me, when something becomes a passion of mine, I need to be the best. I always have something to prove.

One hole on the course had a picturesque, crooked creek framed by palm trees, which crossed the fairway. Something about the way the sunlight was coming through the leaves suddenly reminded me of pictures of my dad from when he was in Hot Springs, Arkansas. Growing up, I just thought it was a vacation spot.

I guess you can say it was.

As I became wiser to the mob world, I found out Hot Springs, Arkansas was a safe-haven for all mobsters, especially bangers, a place renown in the Mafia where members could lay low after a job.

What I didn't understand until later in life was that professional hit men weren't just paid handsomely. They would receive a weekly retainer, from one or perhaps several organizations then they would be paid extra for whatever work they were ordered to do. Once the job was done, the banger would immediately go into hiding and disappear for a long stretch of time to evade capture.

I am not nor; will I ever deny what my father did for a living. I am not condoning his wrong doings. I am not denying or sugarcoating his crimes. He was what he was. But, for most of my life, I didn't have the slightest clue what his nickname "the Bug" meant.

For the first 12 years of my life, that nickname, "The Bug" meant nothing to me. I knew some people called Ben Siegel "Bugsy" – but never to his face. To me he was Uncle Benny.

"So, everything's good? You? Your dad? Your mother?" Dean asked as we watched Skinny tee up a shot. There was respect in his voice.

"All good," I told him. Less was always more when you spoke of people who were connected, let alone family. Dean's deference was obvious, and I knew he didn't expect a long-winded answer, just wanted to show he cared. Then he launched into some joke, making himself the brunt of it while Skinny quietly played the straight man.

The four of us leisurely went from hole to hole, talking, laughing and having a good time.

As we turned the corner and headed to the back nine, Bo and I knew we couldn't lose. My competitive juices really began to flow. We poured it on. As much as I admired Dean, I needed him to know how good I really was.

By the time it was over, Bo shot 66. I made four birdies, two on stroke holes. We'd blitzed them. Dean and Skinny were good sports about the loss and when we went back to the club house lounge. Everyone ordered a beer, I had my standard coke. Skinny dished out the $800 I'd thought I won.

But then the hundreds kept coming. And coming.

I wound up with four grand! For the life of me I couldn't figure out why. But, I kept my mouth shut.

After paying us, Dean gave me a huge, mega-watt grin and shook my hand firmly. "It was a pleasure to play you, Chuck. Please send my regards to your parents." Skinny did the same, and they both walked away happily, even though they'd just lost thousands.

"This has gotta be a mistake," I said to Bo after Dean and

Skinny were gone. "How come I have $4,000?"

Bo elbowed me hard as he swigged his beer. "Don't you know what progressives are?"

I'd hustled some of the best players from coast to coast. "Of course, I do. Each press is $500 and repeats itself down through the match."

"You can't be that dumb. Progressives are double each time plus the original bet."

I almost fainted. If I had known we were playing for that large of an amount, I probably would have choked.

Bo could not stop laughing. I wouldn't have been able to pay if we lost and that would've caused a major problem. I don't care who you know or are, you're supposed to pay if you lose and collect if you win. What a lesson I learned that day.

I'd grown up getting respect from strangers. I suppose I took it for granted without comprehending where it stemmed from. And I certainly didn't know what the Combination Mob was back then either.

The "Combo" as they called it, included other ethnicities like: Jews, Irish and others. You had to be Sicilian to be in the Sicilian Mafia. But, there were many gangsters, like my father, Meyer Lansky, Benny Siegel, Louis Lepke et al, that were considered invaluable to the cause. So, the Combination was created after the Sicilian Mafia was officially born in 1931.

When Charlie Luciano held the original commission meeting that year, all the heads of the original families were there: Joe Bonanno, Tom Gagliano, Joe Profaci, and Vincent Mangano represented New York City. Al Capone stood up for the Chicago outfit. The seventh boss was Stefano Maggadino of Buffalo.

As it was told to me, there were only three Jewish gangsters at this meeting: Meyer Lansky, Ben Siegel and Charlie "the Bug" Workman. That's how revered my father was in that life. Charlie Lucky was my first godfather. He was the only person who held me in the temple during my bris

The Sicilian bosses considered his input invaluable. He was

much closer to the people that were the "higher ups" than the ordinary street thug. He was not only privy to the decision making, he was involved with it. The reason was, he was referred to as a "specialist". Rusty Rastelli, a high-ranking boss in the Bonanno crime family, adored my dad. He once told me, "If I had five Charlie Workmans, I could run this country!"

The most honorable and respected "bangers" honored never sang or ratted out their associates. They are loyal to the core. They would rather go to prison or die than sing. That was my dad. Unfortunately, he was one of the very few who lived by these rules.

Dad handled the more difficult things – physical punishment or retribution. He knew ahead of time when the orders were handed out to other people. So, he had to be part of the decision-making process.

From what I have learned about the hit on Dutch Schultz, it was a Commission decision. Dutch wanted to whack Thomas Dewey, because he was coming down hard on the mob, and one of his original targets was Dutch.

Taking out Dewey or any government official, would have brought terrible heat on everybody. If the Dutchman would have done what he threatened to do, kill Dewey, it would have had a major negative impact on mob business. Neither Luciano, Lansky nor any other member of the Commission wanted or could afford that.

A special meeting was held. My father was there. The answer to the Dutchman's request was an emphatic "no" by both Luciano and Lansky. Their reason is exactly what I stated above. Plus, it was commission rule to never harm members of law enforcement.

This did not sit well with Dutch. As legend has it, he slammed his fist on the table and yelled. "If you won't take care of this, I will."

That brash, reckless statement sealed his fate. He had to go.

The Dutchman, as far as what I was told and learned, was a complete nut job; wacko and psychopath. He'd kill a guy over a newspaper for a nickel. If Luciano and Lansky had not stepped in, Thomas Dewey would have been killed. That you can take to the bank.

The contract to take him out was given to my father.

There were six guys in The Palace Chop House in Newark that fateful night, including Dutch. Supposedly, dad and his partner Mendy Weiss, did them all, while the driver, a young kid called Piggy, waited in the car as the story is told. The bartender is the only person who survived. As soon as they walked in the door, he ducked down behind the bar.

The story goes my dad found Dutch in the bathroom taking a leak. He took him out with one shot that ripped through the Dutchman's midsection mortally wounding him. Supposedly, my dad rummaged through his former boss's pockets and took whatever money he found. That was his M.O. and his perk to do so.

Schultz did not die immediately. It took 22 hours before he finally succumbed to the deadly wound.

When dad came out, Mendy and Piggy were both gone. Furious, dad took off running for miles, eventually finding a safe-haven at an associate's house. He immediately put out a "beef" on both Mendy and Piggy to his boss, Louis "Lepke" Buchalter. At the time Lepke was the CEO of Murder Incorporated.

A sit down was held. In the end, he was told to let it go. He did. It was over.

He got rid of a bad man. He did what had to be done. That's the way it was.

What people fail to recognize or acknowledge is the Commission and my father saved Thomas Dewey's life. And this was the guy who was driving hard to get rid of every gangster he could!

What is truly disturbing is, this Special Prosecutor and fast rising politician knew it. He wasn't stupid. He just didn't care, as you will soon learn.

What happened, happened. As I had been told so many times by so many close friends of my father's "It was a long time ago. It doesn't matter. Let it go."

I never knew, nor did I meet "The Bug"

I understand its origin and why his mob associates gave him that nickname. But, that is not a person I ever knew. I only read about him. No one in that life ever talked about what my father did; ever.

Even with knowing all of this, I still struggled with the dichotomy that was my father. It seemed like every time I focused on his career, someone would turn me the other way.

Contrary to popular belief, whenever my father walked down the street regular people didn't avoid or run away from him. They did the opposite. They'd approach him with a warm hello hug and a kiss; be it women men and even kids he knew. He was more generous in the community than anyone ever realized. His suits might have been flashy, but he wasn't, not when it came to taking care of his family and his community.

A friend of dad's, Frankie Fask, who owned Montrose Motors, told me, "If it weren't for your dad and his generosity, I would not be here."

It turned out my father was part owner of Montrose Motors, a very successful car dealership, up until he went away. He turned it over to Frankie just before he turned himself in. He asked for nothing in return other than to make sure my mother received a new car every few years.

A neighbor, who was a legitimate guy, told me, "Your dad is the most generous man I know. He got me a job in the garment district and put food on my table when we had no money."

The reverence people showed my dad was in turn showed to me too. I'm the first to admit I was treated like a prince. But, I can say with confidence that it wasn't because people had to or because they were afraid. It was because they wanted to.

Would you believe me if I told you that my father was revered by Supreme Court Judge, Eddie W. Well, that is one-hundred percent true. After my father got out of prison I took dad to see the judge. They sat together secretly had coffee and spoke about old times.

He had nothing but the highest praise for my dad as a man. He told my dad, "Charlie, I probably won't be able to ever see you anymore, but I am so glad you made it through this bit and that you are finally home. I'm sorry that we couldn't help to avoid this whole thing."

The famous Cardinal Spellman – who I hold in even higher regard than a Supreme Court Judge - was another. He stepped out for my dad numerous times. He was close to my dad and liked him a lot, even though my father was Jewish.

These are the type of guys that stepped out for my dad at one point or another. Some even went so far as to become good friends. These were straight, legitimate and well-respected men of the community.

So, who was my father really? The Bug? Handsome Charlie?

He was a killer, yet well-liked and respected by most who knew him including legitimate people, law enforcement and men of the cloth.

I think he was both. However, it was the suave, caring, generous and giving man that so few acknowledged or knew, that really defined him.

If that's not who he really was, I don't think my mom would have married him and stuck with him until the very end.

3
MY MOTHER, MY HERO

I handed my ticket to the Yankee Stadium attendant at the gate. I was so excited, I thought I was going to spring out of my shoes. This wasn't just any old baseball game – because I had been to lots of games - this was game seven of the 1947 World Series, pitting the Brooklyn Dodgers against my beloved New York Yankees.

In one deep breath, I could smell everything. There was nothing like it in the world: hot dogs, peanuts, pretzels, even beer. The hustle and bustle of over 71,000 fans buying scorecards, food and trying to find their seats was unforgettable. I'd never seen so many smiles in one place at one time.

Even the way everyone dressed seemed to be a bit sharper than usual. It was like going to church. Women wore their finest dresses while the men looked like they were working for the government or something. Stylish wool suits, of all colors with matching trench coats and fedoras were everywhere. Some even had on derby hats like Babe Ruth used to wear.

The kids dressed a bit different. Most had on nice pants and shirts with a hat of some kind. Me, I had on my Yankee cap. I never went to a game without it on.

Suddenly, I felt a hand on my shoulder. It was Jewy Ribbentrop, a friend of my father's, who had taken me to see the game. I didn't know much about him. I didn't even know his real first name. I was told he was involved with the Wurlitzer Jukebox Company. What I did know was that he was very nice to me and very sweet to my mom. She trusted him.

"Come on, Chuckie," Jewy told me. "Let's go find our seats."

He guided me through the crowd to our gate entrance. I walked up the ramp and got chills. No matter how many times I had been to Yankee Stadium, I could not get over how magnificent it was. The first thing I saw was the amazing white façade that made the stadium not only unique, but it looked like a cathedral. I guess in a sense it was. The house the Ruth built, as they called it.

Our seats were in the front row, near the Yankee dugout. This was normal to me. Every game I went to was no further back than the 3rd row. Jewy stepped aside and led me to my seat while he sat on the aisle.

My head felt like it was on a swivel. I could not take in the scenery fast enough. It was one of the greatest spectacles I had ever seen. And I was a part of it.

Ralph Branca was the starting pitcher for the Brooklyn Dodgers. Spec Shea, who won 14 games for the Yankees that season was on the mound for the Yanks. Johnny Lindell, the starting left fielder for the Yankees, stepped out of the dugout and turned towards us. He locked eyes with me right away then gave me a wave with a wink and smile. I couldn't believe it. It was like he was my friend.

Earlier in the season, Spunky, who usually took me to baseball games, had introduced us. It turned out, they were good friends. I'll never forget how larger than life he was, a big strapping guy with a California tan and warm disposition.

I was in heaven. My heart was racing. I could not wait for the game to start.

"You want something to eat kid?" Jewy asked politely.

"Yes, please. May I have a hot dog and a Coke?"

He quickly flagged down two vendors. Within seconds, I had my food and drink in hand. Now, I was ready.

Jewy tipped the vendors, all decked out in their Yankee attire. They gave him hearty thank-yous. I watched as he put his money back in his pocket, a huge wad of cash. Though it was nothing I hadn't seen before. I was far more interested in the field.

We all stood as they announced the singing of the National Anthem. I took my Yankee hat off and put it to my heart. I looked at the flag in centerfield but could not get over the grand spectacle of it all. When the Star - Spangled Banner ended, the roar from the crowd was deafening. Chants of "Let's Go Yanks!" filled the air. Spec finished his warm up pitches and stepped off the mound. The lead-off hitter for the Dodgers, second baseman, Eddie Stanky stepped into the batter's box and dug in, waiting for the first pitch.

"Having a good time, Chuckie?" Jewy asked, giving my

shoulder a squeeze. He was one of the many men my mother entrusted to take me places. He watched me and watched out for me.

"The best," I told him.

My mom was my everything. And I had no concept of everything she did to keep me safe and on the straight and narrow. She had grown up on the lower East Side of New York, with her three brothers. They were a close-knit family. Her brothers took care of her and protected her throughout her entire life.

Back then, the lower East Side was a hot bed of gangster activity. She was surrounded by mobsters. Even though she was Polish, she understood what that life was about. Many of the boys she grew up with wound up being in the mob should as Johnny Dio. From an early age, she came to know most of the big-time bosses. She was very friendly and respectful to everyone, both inside and outside the mob life. These guys never forgot that. She grew up street wise. As mobsters would say, "She knew the rules."

Everyone loved her. No one ever had a bad thing to say about my mother. I often think that she may have been more loved and respected than my dad, and that's saying a lot.

Any friend of my mother's was a friend for life. She made it her business to check in on everyone and make sure they were taken care of. She stayed close to all her good friends, going all the way back to grade school. They played cards together. They'd have lunch or dinner together. They never severed ties. They did everything they could to keep the friendships going. My mother also had a soft spot for those in need. Whether someone was sick, in need of money or a job - she always managed to find a way to help. She did it because she wanted to. As a result, she was dearly loved and respected by so many.

Although she barely stood five feet tall, she was larger than life and carried herself like a movie star, with grace and dignity. Newspaper reporters and writers even compared her to Lana Turner and Katherine Hepburn. Whenever she went out, she caused a stir. Those that knew her always doted on her. Even those that didn't know her turned their heads. She was something special

She had a reputation as a beauty, a class-act and of course, as

Charlie "The Bug's" wife. It was well known that she could get help with a single phone call, no matter what the situation. She always knew who to reach out. If she made a call, when the person on the other end of the phone heard her voice, it was always, "What do you need Katie?" Followed by, "We will take care of it right away."

If she had to go see someone face to face, it was never some low-level, street hoodlum. It was usually a boss or very high-ranking guy. Those guys would then send people to take care of whatever the situation was. One thing is for sure, all situations would be straightened out very quickly.

It would be easy to say it was just because of who she was married to. But the truth is, the respect my mother had wasn't only because she was the wife of The Bug. It was for who she was and for how she carried herself.

So, when Katie Workman asked somebody to take care of something, it wasn't just going to get done. It was going to get done right.

Whenever dad came up for parole, we had to pay the lawyers to represent him at the meeting. The money for the lawyers came from several high-ranking Jewish mobsters, one of which was. Farvel Spick. I had just found out the truth about dad, so I really didn't know much about how it all worked.

One night my mom took me to the Latin Quarter at around ten o'clock at night. She was told that Farvel would be there. We found him in a booth. His cigar had to be three feet long. He was sitting there with two showgirls on each arm. I walked over with my mother and I immediately get an erection with the showgirls there. These women were amazing.

Farvel greeted mom. "Katie, it's nice to see you."

Mom shot back. "Get rid of the broads."

The girls jumped up in their skimpy outfits and took off.

"Charlie is coming up for parole." She reminded him. "We need some help."

"Katie, things are terrible, things are bad right now."

My mom went nuts. "Whoa! Things are bad? That's a bottle of

Dom Perignon, isn't it? Am I or am I not in the Latin Quarter? Waiter! Get me a milk crate. Go to the kitchen and get me a milk crate!"

Farvel had this puzzled look on his face. "What do you want with a milk crate?"

"I want to stand on a milk crate and tell everybody in this place how bad things are. And then I'm going to tell Charlie how bad things are."

"Oh no! Wait a minute! It's okay. How much do you need?"

"He's up there doing time, and you're here? Things are bad, huh? We need a couple of thousand -dollars. Pony it up. Now!"

That was that. I couldn't believe what happened. She had a mission, and she got what she came for. No was not an option.

"You need anything, Chuckie?" Jewy said. "Another hot dog?"

It was the second inning and the Dodgers had two runners on base. I was riveted to the game. "No, thanks. I'm good."

Yankee manager, Bucky Harris, wasted no time and pulled starting pitcher Spec Shea for reliever Bill Bevens. Unfortunately, Spider Jorgensen greeted Bevens with a double that scored two runs, giving the Dodgers an early 2-0 lead.

The Yanks got one back in the second. In the bottom of the fourth, they took the lead for good when Bobby Brown singled to drive in two runs. The tension in the crowd was so thick I could feel it on my skin. The minutes ticked by so slowly it was like I could feel every second passing by. By the fifth inning, Bevens was replaced by relief pitcher Joe Page, who started mowing down Dodgers one after another. He was in a zone. And so was I. It was truly mesmerizing to watch.

Then came the seventh inning and the Yankees were up by a score of 4-2. I was so focused on every detail of the game I couldn't hear or see anything else. Suddenly, my heart jumped when two Bronx cops pulled Jewy right out of his seat by his coat, jerking him into the air.

"Mr. Ribbentrop, you are under arrest!" A tall, lanky policeman yelled as he took out his handcuffs.

Instinctively, I stood up, but was ordered to sit back down by the other policeman

Jewy tried to reach into his pocket as they grabbed his hands. "Keep your fucking hands where I can see them." The other cop yelled.

"Let me give the kid some change so he can call his mom for a ride home!" Jewy yelled back.

"Don't make another move or I'll beat you down right here and now," the first one said in Jewy's ear.

Everyone in the stands nearby was staring, distracted from the intensity of the game by the cops manhandling Jewy, who was struggling under their grip. "Goddamnit! The kid needs a ride home. You can't leave him here! What the fuck is wrong with you?"

The tall cop snapped, "He's not our fucking problem."

The other finally slapped the cuffs on Jewy behind his back. I was frozen in confusion.

"You can't be serious! He's 12 years old for Christ's sake! You can't fucking leave him here!" Jewy continued to shout and fight.

"Our job is to arrest your ass and that's it! Now let's go, you piece of shit!"

As Jewy was dragged up the steps, he glanced back at me, a desperate and angry look in his gaze. "Call your mother!" he insisted. "Find a way to call her!"

The cops scared all the vendors and the ushers away. The onlookers who'd been gawking at the scene now intentionally turned away. I was all alone.

But, this was game seven of the World Series against the Brooklyn Dodgers, with Jackie Robinson about to step to the plate! I had a choice. I could go find a phone and try to call my mom, like Jewy told me to do. Or I could keep watching.

So, I turned back towards the field and continued watching the game.

For 24 years, while my father was away, Mom raised me on her own. Yes, my dad's influence was there through her visits with him while he was behind bars. But, when she left the visiting area of those prison walls, it was all on her. She guided me with a firm hand, making sure all my dad's instructions were followed, especially when it came to me and his mob associates.

The fact was, she was smarter than my dad. And he knew it. My dad said on several occasions, "She is smarter and tougher than I ever was."

I think he was right. And my dad was no slouch, especially when it came to the streets and the mob.

My father realized he had created this whole situation and it was going to be hell on my mom. In the 48-hours he had before turning himself in, he made sure she would be taken care of. He did everything in his power to make at least some things easier for her and to have some fun. I can only imagine how many meetings he had during that time, how many associates he called on for assistance. No matter who he asked for a favor, out of shear respect and reverence, it was done. No questions asked.

My mother lived by the code, "You pay your way." She was not a taker. Before my dad went away she was not comfortable receiving things "on the arm" or for free. It was not her way. She was the complete opposite. She was a giver and a care giver. She took care of more people than anyone could possibly imagine.

However, with her husband behind bars unable to take care of the family financially, she had to do what she had to do, even if it went against every fiber in her being. She knew she couldn't do it on her own. Who the hell could?

Because dad was held in such high esteem, mom was afforded to live a good life. Every mob associate or friend my father called upon stepped up. They not only delivered. They went overboard.

From what I was told, a few days after my father went away a Mafia Commission meeting was set up. The sole purpose of this gathering was to handle how my mother and I would be taken care of financially.

She was offered two generous offers. This first was to accept a very large one-time sum of money. I believe the number was $50,000. The second option was to accept a much smaller amount on a weekly basis. This would be hand delivered to the house and it would last throughout dad's incarceration.

To be honest, I would have taken the large sum, but that shows how smart I was – not very. My mother did not hesitate. She took the weekly amount. And like clockwork, every week, an envelope was delivered to our house. How much was in it? I have no idea. It was none of my business back then.

It was the right move. Sure enough, every week some guy would bring the money right to our door. As the cost of living went up she'd get an extra amount of money. Not only that, I thought it was supposed to end when dad came home. It just kept coming every week. Even after dad passed, I was told by certain people, "Katie we hope you live to be 100 the only change is that Chuck has to come and get the money in a particular spot in New York or Queens.

Like everybody else, I respected my mother, even feared her a little – she was my mom, after all – but even with Jewy's words ringing in my ears, I just couldn't tear myself away from the game. It finally ended with Joe Page tossing five shut-out innings for the Yankees to lock up the win and a World Series title! I watched in awe as the team celebrated and the fans swarmed the field. I was jumping up and down screaming my twelve-year-old lungs out, alone but happy beyond belief. The roar was deafening. People I didn't even know were hugging me. It was incredible! In those moments, I completely forgot that I was a kid all by myself.

Eventually, the players went into the dugout and into the clubhouse to continue their celebration. The fans slowly filtered out. That's when it hit me. I was in the Bronx and we lived on Long Island. And I had no way home.

Nervous and a little bashful, I found an usher and tapped his arm. "Excuse me sir."

The tall man turned, looming over me. "Yes, young man. What can I do for you?"

"Can I borrow a nickel? I need to call my mom to get a ride home."

"You're by yourself?"

I shrugged. "Yes, sir."

Concerned, he asked, "What kind of parent leaves a young boy like you alone in a big place like this?"

"Oh no, sir. I was with a friend of my mom's but…he was escorted out."

The usher squinted. "You were with that man that was arrested by the police?"

"Yes."

"What happened there?"

"I don't know. I just need to call my mom."

He reached into his pocket and pulled out a nickel. "Here you go, son. There are no pay phones in the stadium. You will have to go outside to call your mom."

Relieved, I clutched the nickel tightly. "Okay. Thank you."

"I can't imagine your mom is going to be very happy about this."

"Oh no, sir. I don't think she is going to be either."

I ran out of the stadium and quickly found a pay phone. The second she answered, I blurted, "Mom. I need a ride home."

Worry flooded her voice. "Chuck! Where are you?"

"Yankee Stadium."

"Why are you by yourself?" Her tone took a turn. "Where's Jewy?"

After I explained, she took a deep breath. "You mean to tell me the policemen did not arrange for you to make a call or get you a ride home?"

"No. They told Jewy I wasn't their problem."

"Oh, is that right?" There was a moment of silence, of dead air. I was just grateful I wasn't the one who my mom was mad at. Because that silence meant something. Something serious. "You stay right there. Don't you move an inch! I will have someone there in a few minutes."

When my mother said she was going to do something, there was no hesitation, no thinking it over. She had the strength of more than a few mobsters put together. She had to.

As the twelve-and-a-half-year sentence dragged on to what amounted to twenty-four years, the help from father's friends and associates continued. My mother accepted it on both of our behalves gracefully and respectfully.

Dad's stomping grounds had been the garment center and before he left, he made it known to everyone: "My wife does not pay for anything."

She'd go shopping with my aunts or friends and always go see a guy named Louie Weinstein. He absolutely adored my mother and loved my father. They were dear friends. He was one of the biggest dress manufacturers in Manhattan. No matter how hard she tried to pay, she was never allowed.

"Your money is no good here, Katie." She would be told time after time. "Please give our regards to Charlie."

He would walk them through the entire district to get whatever they needed.

I remember one time she came home with my aunt Anna. The car was so full she couldn't see out the back. She could have opened up her own store!

As it turned out, most of the clothes were gifts for other people. She figured, if she had this luxury of free clothes, she should share. That's just the way she was.

Mom was escorted to Broadway shows and movies all the time. She went dancing at the best night clubs. However, she was always escorted by bodyguards and family. If any guy wanted to dance with her, they had to get through a line of men protecting her, including her brothers. If she needed a vacation, she was taken up into the country for a stay at a cabin. Louie Weinstein, not only took care of her in the garment center, he took us all to Florida on several occasions. He would call my mom and say, "Katie, do you want to go to Florida next week?" He'd get us down there and set us up in the swankiest hotels and rooms.

Before dad went to prison, he had also been a partner of Montrose Motors with Frankie Fask. When he went away, he gave the dealership to Frankie. The one condition and only favor he asked was that Frankie give my mother a new car every year or so, whenever she wanted one. That was it. He didn't ask for any money. All he said was, "Just take care of Katie."

But, when Frankie tried to renege on the deal, he must have realized the she could be as hard-nosed as my father. She had taken me with her to help pick out the color for our new car when Frankie said, "Katie, things are bad. They're really bad. I had to fire the chauffeur and learn to drive. I let go of the upstairs maid. You know, business is tough."

My mother stared him down. "Should I tell Charlie that you fired your chauffer and the maid? And that you have to learn how to drive a car, even though everyone knows how to drive a car these days. Should I tell him that?"

Frankie thought about it. "No, Katie, come tomorrow. Pick up your car."

There was no arguing with my mother. Because she didn't need to argue. She just told you what was going to happen. Then it happened.

One time, a new guy came to deliver mom's weekly envelope of money. We had never seen him before. My mom was immediately suspicious. She took the envelope and instinctively sensed it was short. She dropped the envelope on the ground like it was on fire then turned around and went back inside,

She didn't say a word. Not to the guy. Or to me. She just made a phone call.

The next day, she took me to a meeting with high ranking mobsters at Twin Brooks Country Club in Watchung, New Jersey. This was a golf course where some nice people were involved. Ray "Gyp" DeCarlo told me to bring mom and meet him there. We got into a golf cart and drove all the way to the back into the woods. There were four or five other guys in carts, who I did not know. Ray was in one of them. He was waiting under the trees. My mom got out and they greeted each other with a hug and a kiss. I was a few feet away.

"Katie, we understand there was a problem with the envelope," one of them said as I listened from around a corner, safely out of sight yet listening intently.

"It was short." She snapped.

"What did you do with it?" He asked with a curious look.

"I dropped it on the ground and went back inside," she replied, glaring at him.

"Good. Now we got him. Here is the envelope. Not only is everything going to get straightened out, but you are going to get a raise for your troubles."

The following week, that same kid came back and apologized profusely. He did everything to get on her good side, short of kissing her feet. He not only gave her the envelope he gave her an extra $100 out of his own pocket.

This kid wanted to see how strong he was by taking money. He took money from the wrong person. For us, that would never happen – not to Katie Workman. I also think it might have been a test to see what my mother would do.

It was a bit of an unplanned test. But, she knew just what to do. The amount never changed from that point on. The amount might have gone up a little bit, but never down.

My mom never let on to her sadness about dad being gone, at least not to me, or the fact that she missed us being together as a family. It wasn't until after dad came home that she let it out. She broke down at one point. It was one of the only times I saw her cry almost uncontrollably. It was tears of happiness, combined with what probably had to be the weight of the world lifted off her shoulders. She told my father so many times. "We will get through this." She was right. But, dad and I both knew it was all her. She was the pillar of the family and the cement that held us together.

I knew those 24 years were tough on her. But, I was never able to get my brain wrapped around it until that moment. She just kept saying. "We are a family again."

Even with all the luxuries and comforts that my dad set up for her, 24 years of being a single parent while her husband was still alive, took its toll. But, that all changed when he finally came home. She was her old bubbly self. Her steps were lighter. Her smile was more radiant, and she seemed relieved. She no longer had to do the heavy lifting.

The thought of how strong she had to be on my behalf brings tears to my eyes.

As I stood outside Yankee Stadium and waited, the crowds thinned. I kicked rocks into sewer grates to pass the time. It was as if the excitement was cooling and drifting away, leaving me feeling even more alone.

Minutes ticked by. But within a half hour, my Uncle Red and two guys I did not recognize pulled up in a swanky, black car. The brakes squealed they stopped so fast.

"Chuckie! You okay?" Uncle Red said, rushing out of the car toward me and honestly, I was glad to see him. He led me to the car, saying, "That was a mistake."

"Me calling Mom?"

"Naw, kid. Not you. Those cops. But don't you worry about it. Hop in and we'll get you home."

It wasn't until a few years later that I found out Mom told my father what happened when she went to see him the following Sunday. My dad hit the roof. I have no idea who was called or how it was done, but those two cops were shipped out of state. They never worked in New York again. Someone even told me they ended up in Alaska. I don't know if that's true or not, but it would not surprise me.

I can't begin to tell you how many of my dad's associates asked me about the incident and told me it was taken care of. "You won't see them no more." It was like I was their son and it happened to them. That's how devoted all these people were to my mom, my dad and me. It worked both ways.

One of my mother's most admirable traits was her loyalty, especially when it came to my father. Mom stuck by him the entire time he was away. My father told her on several occasions. "Katie,

Divorce me. You don't need or deserve this."

Her response was always the same. "You are my husband. We got into this thing together and we will get out of it together. I'm not going anywhere."

My mom never missed a visitation day with my dad; except once when she was very sick. Not once in 24 years! No matter where we were, even if it was on vacation or on a trip, she made sure she was back in plenty of time to visit him.

All children are supposed to love and respect their mother – at least I hope so. But, to me my mom was more than a mother. She was a father for 24 years. She was my protector. She was my pillar of strength. My shoulder to cry on. She was my world.

I cannot possibly begin to comprehend what she went through during those 24 years. I wish I had half of the unbelievable qualities that she carried. If there was anyone on earth that I idolized, it was my mom. It was always that way. From as far back as I could remember.

4
A HORSE NAMED CHIEF

Out of nowhere, the phone rang. I was not expecting it. I barely got hello out of my mouth...it was dad.

"Get dressed up, Chuck," He ordered with a strange edge to his voice. "Smitty is taking us to Belmont Park."

Smitty was the guy who was responsible for taking me to all the boxing matches when I was a kid. That was 15 to 20 years prior. At 30 years old, I didn't see him quite as much anymore. I still loved the guy though. He remained close to me and the family even after dad came home.

Belmont Racetrack?" I questioned.

"Yeah, Belmont Racetrack. You have a problem with that?"

"Dad I've never been to a racetrack. I don't like watching horses race." I explained, holding back the real reason why.

"You know who Diane Crump is?"

"Yes, I know who that is. She's the famous female jockey. So, what?"

"That's why Smitty is taking us."

"You want me to go watch horse races for the first time to see Diane Crump?"

"That's right." He answered with a little less edge to his tone.

"Do I have to?"

"I want you to. It'll be a good time. Plus, how long has it been since you've seen Smitty?"

"I haven't seen him in a while. But, I still don't know why you want me to go pop"

'Because it will be well worth your time. Trust me." I had no idea what he was talking about. Reluctantly I said, "Okay. I guess I'm going to Belmont."

Honestly, I was not happy about this day out with dad. Seeing horses brought back wonderful memories. However, the sadness that came with it far outweighed the happiness. Because it reminded me of that day back in 1940, the day I wish never happened.

It was a warm summer afternoon and we were cruising down Ocean Parkway in his 1939 Dodge Luxury Liner Sedan with running boards. I was probably around four years old. It was a four-lane road divided by a center median that had park benches on it. Usually, mothers would take their strollers and they would stroll along the road and congregate on the benches. But that day, there was a big crowd at a stoplight. As we got closer, I could see that they were all circled around a horse. Somehow, it had gotten its hoof caught in a storm drain. The men were trying to get it out. They couldn't do it no matter how hard they tried. I don't know whose horse it was. It was not a police horse that's for sure because those horses were all dressed up a special way with police colors on them.

Dad pulled over and out of car to help. Through the open car windows, I overheard them talking about having to put the horse down and I started to cry. I loved animals. We had a dog since as far back as I can remember. He was my best friend. I simply had an affinity for all animals.

Even without seeing my tears, my father starting shouting at the handlers of the horse. "Do not shoot that horse!"

He reached into his pocket, pulled out a wad of cash and handed a bunch of money to them, purchasing the horse on the spot. Then he paid one of the onlookers to go to the corner candy store to make a couple of phone calls.

The crowd that had gathered continued to grow. I sat with my chin on the open passenger side window as more and more of my father's men showed up, some in coveralls, many with equipment. They started to dismantle the whole storm drain. Sparks were flying as the handlers tried to calm to nervous horse.

Within an hour, the horse was free. The crowd cheered and clapped, patting my dad's guys on their backs as if the horse was theirs. But that day, the horse became mine. We named him Chief.

Not far from Ocean Parkway there were stables where we boarded Chief and a bridle path that ran from there all the way to Coney Island. I went to the stable with my father every Sunday morning. We rode the horse around or sometimes we'd just walk with him. Those were some of my fondest memories of my father, spending time with him and Chief.

That pathway is where I learned how to ride a two-wheeler and where we intended to ride the horse. But, I couldn't really ride it where people were pushing strollers.

One Sunday, we went to the stables but couldn't take Chief out because there were too many pedestrians. I was disappointed, but as usual my father wasn't going to let anything stand in his way.

He called a couple of his guys as well as a few policemen to come over. They cordoned off the entire road, so I had it all to myself to ride Chief. That was unheard of. Closing off that thoroughfare was like shutting down Broadway. Only a man with my father's influence could ever pull off something like that.

It sounds crazy and outlandish, but it was normal to me.

Pulling up to Belmont Park, I was anxious, but I couldn't help but feel the electricity in the air. The grandstand held more than 100,000 spectators. Everywhere it was a sea of green, from the track to the clubhouse to the stands. Smitty met us with warm embraces, his ink black hair slicked back, his navy suit pressed so immaculately that it seemed to shine.

I was never told how my dad met his friends and loyal associates, but one thing was for sure, Smitty had major connections. It was always the best of the best with him. He led us to a private box, where we had our own server and a betting window only a few steps away. As has always been the case I felt like a prince.

From infancy through age five, I was treated like royalty. One thing is for sure when I was a spoiled little kid. I was an only child, so I guess that was to be expected. Everything was about me. My mom and dad made sure of that. My whole world was my mother and my father. Their whole world evolved around me. To me it was normal. I thought everybody was treated like this.

I was also surrounded by some of the most dangerous mobsters this country has ever known. These guys were part of my family. That's what I was told and that's how they treated me. You can say this started from birth. My Godfather – the man who held me during my bris at the temple – was none other than Charlie Luciano. Charlie Lucky and my father were very close friends - along with Benny Siegel and Meyer Lansky, who both from what I have been told.

They were around when I was an infant. I obviously do not remember because I was a baby.

Many other big-time mob leaders were always around: Abner Zwillman and Jacob "Jewy" Ribbentrop. The list is endless. I had no idea who these men were, what they did or how powerful they were. I called almost all these notorious men, uncle.

They treated me like a little Prince, all showering me with gifts: a toy, a baseball, a mitt, a football, a TV set, a bicycle, bubble gum (which you could not get during the war). I wanted for nothing.

Every summer as far back as I can remember, we went to the mountains with the Yoey Glickman and his kids. Yoey was dad's partner in a trucking business at the time. We used to go to Lapidis Bungalow Colony on White Lake.

I remember distinctly, my dad had a mahogany wooden speed boat called the Coca Cola. We were on or in the water all the time. The Coca Cola was my dad's toy. He liked to drive out into the middle of the lake alone, dock it and just lay out there.

I have such wonderful memories of going to White Lake. We were always doing something. We never really sat around. We swam a lot, did archery, went bike riding, had camp fires and roasted marshmallows. You name it. I always had great summers with a lot of fun.

These times were no different than any other kid, as far as I was concerned.

I did not know it at the time but Yoey Glickman was one of the biggest bookmakers on the east coast.

"So, what race is Diane Crump in?" I asked just to get into the conversation.

Smitty laughed. "I thought you didn't want to come, Chuckie?"

That was how it was in my father's world. Everyone pretended not to know anything, yet they always knew everything. You couldn't hide a thing from these men. I could either be intimidated by it or in awe of it. More often than not, it was both.

Smitty passed me a soda after busting my chops. "She's in one of the feature races. I'll let you know."

On February 7th, 1969, Crump shot out of the starting gate and into the all-male world of horse racing. In a mere fifteen months, she turned the Sport of Kings upside down. She was the first woman to ride in Hialeah Park, Florida in Miami. She was the first woman to run a Pari-mutuel race, which is a special one on one race with special betting. And she was the first woman in the Kentucky Derby in 1970.

As I leaned back in the seat of our private box at Belmont Park, my dad and Smitty talking quietly behind me I knew the horses would be led out soon. It made me anxious. I wanted to see them, but I didn't. It was as if the memories were waiting to flood back too fast.

I used to go with my dad to help groom Chief on either Saturday or Sunday. I would have to stand on a step ladder to reach his back. Chief was the biggest thing I had ever seen besides a bus.

He loved apples. I used to gently feed him with my palm flat, careful of his enormous teeth. Brushing him, riding him, just being with him alongside my father, those were magical times for me, moments I cherished. Not just for myself but because Chief was also an escape for my father.

He loved to ride him. Maybe more than I did.

"Okay Charlie. This is big one now." Smitty gripped my shoulder.

The horses were being walked onto the field, their jockey's mounted. The crowd murmuring in anticipation, all eyes glued to racetrack. My father whispered something in Smitty's ear and gave him a stack of cash. The only other thing I heard was, "Yeah, for Chuck too."

I didn't take a dime out of my pocket. I just sat in anticipation for the reason we were here – Diane Crump.

When she and her horse were announced the roar of the capacity crowd was deafening.

Soon afterward, the bell went off and the horses charged out of the gate. In a flash, the horses flew, gone in the blink of an eye.

Smitty was already out of his seat yelling. "Come on Diane! Come on Diane!"

As the horses barreled down the back stretch and headed

towards the far turn, it was like everything went into slow motion. The horses out front seemed to pull back in unison. Out of nowhere Diane came charging through a thick pack, passing every jockey and taking the lead. The crowd exploded with cheering. I watched in amazement as she crossed the finish line winning the race.

Belmont Park was bursting with the energy of her triumphant win, clapping, shouting, and hollering. The place itself was alive with the win. I was excited for my dad, Smitty and everyone who'd bet on Diane. But, I could not take my mind off Chief.

We had Chief for about a year, when that fateful day came. The day my dad left to turn himself in to the police; two days after the police officer came to the door with a warrant. I was only five at the time and was completely shielded from reality. That was what my parents wanted. I didn't know where he went or why. All I knew was that he was gone, and thus ended our special bond with Chief

What followed a few months later was devastating. One thing after another. All I knew was things were changing and I didn't really understand why. First dad was gone. That was hard enough. Then we moved into a new house, with new neighbors and surroundings. Then my mom sat me down at the kitchen table and said, "We just do not have the time, the means or the space to take care of Chief. I am so sorry, Chuck. I really am."

I was 6 years old. It felt like a piece of my heart was being taken out of me. I broke down and started to cry. I didn't stop crying. Not for days. I was never told who Chief was sold to or when. It just happened and not another word was spoken of it. I didn't understand why my father wasn't with us, but I did understand that losing Chief was another form of losing my dad.

Ever since that day, I could not look at a horse without thinking of Chief.

"I told you she'd win!" Smitty was going nuts, jumping up and down like a kid.

Dad looked at me with a sly grin. "Told you it would be worth your time."

"Every horse pulled up going down the stretch," I shot back. "They let her win."

"Charlie, he's still a little slow with these things, but eventually he catches on," Smitty quipped.

I glared at Smitty then my dad. "So, this was a set up?"

Dad looked over at Smitty, who replied, "Let's just say it gives us a chance to win some money. Speaking of which, I'll be right back."

"You brought me here because you knew Diane would win?" I asked my father.

"No. I just wanted you to see the races. If you win a few bucks, good for you." That was it. As usual, he stopped talking and never said another word about it. It was like it never happened.

Smitty came back a few minutes later with a huge amount of money. He sat down with dad and they started dividing it up.

"Here, I placed a little bet for you." Dad handed me some serious money. I don't remember exactly how much it was, but it was somewhere close to a thousand dollars.

I cherished these new times with my dad. I was grateful to have him back in my life. As now I saw him in a whole new light; quite differently from early childhood and his prison years.

My dad never spoke much about emotions or things that happened in the past. It was just not his way. What's over is over. However, after 24 years behind bars he was desperately trying to make up for not only lost time, but the pain and torment I went through during those painstaking years. He didn't speak about it. Instead, he let his actions speak for him. Typical dad.

In this case, he knew how much letting Chief go hurt me. I truly believe in his mind, this was his way of trying to heal that wound and help me think positive about horses again. That, and of course seeing Smitty and winning money.

The reality of it was, the mob influence was still there and the power and influence my father still had, because of his real career, were still very apparent. As they were even before I found out who he really was and what he really did.

You see, up until age 12, I really knew nothing about what my father really did for a living. I was told he was a salesman. I don't remember exactly what type of salesman. I think it had something to do with trucks and cars.

I was also told that part of his job was helping other people get jobs. It made sense to me because my dad's brothers worked normal jobs at the Daily News. My dad and my mom from the very beginning kept me completely away from the other part of my father's life.

They all just went with the flow and made my reality as normal as possible. To them, this was the right thing to do, especially at a very young age.

Regardless of how my father made his money, he never had any reservations about spending it, especially on me. Later in life, I realized and began to resent that my fortunate childhood was not the result of my dad being a salesman, as I had been told, but because he had a different career altogether.

Looking back at it now however, I would say undeniably, growing up the son of a renowned mob hit man came with its privileges and problems. I am not condoning anything my father did while he was engulfed in that life. This is just the plain truth.

Regardless, there is no question that Mom and I were his whole world. He never wanted us to want for anything. He wanted us to live a good life, have everything we ever wanted, go on nice trips - all of that. I guess you cannot begrudge a man for wanting the best for his family.

The lie about what my father did for a living, how he made his money and who these men really were, would not be the first nor the biggest untruth I would have to deal with. For seven years, from age five through 12 my whole childhood would turn into an historical, theatrical performance of deceptions, cons, shams and ruses involving more people than anyone could ever imagine. It is without question something movies are made of. But, I was kept so busy I never had time to think about it. I thought my dad was a hero fighting a secret war – doing all that secret stuff for our country.

The war started in 1941 and ended in 1945; so him going away in 1940, before the war started had to be secret stuff. I believed it and didn't believe.

I began to have my little doubts. But the charade was on.

5
DAD IS IN THE NAVY

When you tell a lie often enough and long enough, it becomes reality and the truth. This was my reality for seven years.

1940

There was $100,000 in the briefcase. Where the money came from was unknown and not important. Carrying it was a guy named K.O. He took orders from high-ranking bosses from the Combination Mob and Mafia.

His errand was simple. Go to the D.A.'s office in downtown Manhattan and place the briefcase on a certain desk then leave. K.O. did as he was ordered.

What happened to that briefcase, I honestly don't know. I was told, it was a pay-off, as part of an agreement to lay off certain gangsters. This was during Thomas Dewey's quest to take down the entire syndicate, starting with Murder Incorporated.

How do I know this? K.O. told me himself.

His real name was Harold Konigsberg and he was one of my father's dearest friends. He'd gotten his nickname from his boxing background. But like my dad, he was a hit man and a bone breaker. A mean one. That was his reputation. I knew a totally different side to him.

He would call the house regularly just to see how I was and how mom was. Harold taught me things and told me many truths, like this story. He wanted me to know the score, what was what and why.

Back in the 30's and 40's, Thomas Dewey was hell-bent on making his mark as a prosecutor. He portrayed himself as an honest yet tough lawman, dead set on taking down the mob. Dewey didn't just want them in jail. He wanted them all executed. Nailing gangsters would be his ticket to the top of the political tower structure – the Presidency. And it almost worked.

He was devious, conniving and manipulative. His ambition was relentless. In my mind, he abused his power. To me and people in my circles, he made Mafia family leaders seem like saints.

What made Dewey worse than any mobster was that he was a hypocrite. Real gangsters never claimed to be anything but what they were. This guy was a fake and a phony. The things he did, along with Burton Turkus and Bill O'Dwyer, throughout my father's whole ordeal, would probably be grounds for arrest today.

On the morning of March 23rd, 1940, I heard a knock at the door. My dad looked through the small window in the door, then opened it. It was a police officer. I found out later, from the East Side.

I looked up at dad. He winked and smiled.

The officer whispered something to my dad directly into his ear. I had no idea what he said, nor did I think much of it. It wasn't the first time a policeman had come to our house. At five years old, I thought they were just being friendly stopping by. It made me feel safe.

My dad nodded, then whispered something back. In a flash they were both outside and the door was closed behind them.

What I did not know, and would not find out for quite some time, was the cop came with a warrant for my father's arrest.

From what I have been told, my father said something to the effect of, "I need a couple of days to get my affairs in order. Just give me that and I will come in to the station on my own at nine o'clock in the morning."

Contrary to what most believed, my father was respected and liked by many police officers, including captains and chiefs. He was regarded as a man of his word. They trusted him. As did this police officer, who agreed to give my dad the two days he asked for.

My mom came out of her room and started talking quietly to my father.

Sally, a lovely young woman, who helped take care of me and the house, had moved me quickly into a small room where we would play. She knew I should not be privy to the conversation.

A few minutes later, my mom came in. "Sally, why don't you take Chuck to the park. It's a beautiful day."

That was my favorite thing to do. I jumped up! "Thanks mom!

Come on Sally. Let's go."

"Okay. But, you have to get your coat."

I ran to the back door and grabbed my coat. I looked back to say good-bye to my parents, but they went into their bedroom and closed the door – nothing unusual. To me, it was just another normal day.

Little did I know, that knock at the door turned our entire lives upside down.

At that moment, with only 48-hours grace time, my parents were faced with making some very difficult decisions, especially when it came to me. These decisions would affect me for the rest of my life. Together, they decided to do what they thought was best for me at the time. That was to keep the truth from me for as long as possible. By any means necessary.

Two days later, one day after my fifth birthday, March 25th, 1940 my dad said good-bye to me the same exact way he did every day with a hug and a kiss. He acted as if nothing was wrong. It was the day after my fifth birthday.

As promised, at nine o'clock in the morning he showed up at the Clinton Street Police Station. The same cop, who had come to our door two days before, met him there to take him in. There is a famous picture of Dad sitting on a bench in the police station with his overcoat covering his cuffs, which the cop was nice enough to put on in the front, rather than behind, like most common criminals.

It was a small gesture but a kind one and in a strange twist. Fifty years later that policeman's son became my doctor. That was how small and tightly knit my world was whether I understood it or not.

Little did my dad or anyone else know the day he turned himself in would be the last time he would see freedom for almost 24 years.

I guess you can say my dad was "arrested by appointment." It was a testament to how well he was thought of. This is contrary to what has been written about him in countless books, newspapers and magazines. They either didn't bother to find out or they knew and refused to explain the whole story. To this day, that really pisses me off. Too many authors have dramatized him as a notoriously hot-tempered tough guy and hit man. They made money off my father's back without ever telling the whole truth.

I've got news for all of them. Charlie "the Bug" Workman was much more than that. He was also "Handsome Charlie," a well-liked, honorable, respected and extremely giving person. However, he was a tough guy if the situation called for it.

The original warrant for my dad's arrest was vagrancy. This was a trumped-up charge by District Attorney, Bill O'Dwyer and Special Prosecutor Thomas Dewey, simply to get him into custody.

The next day, they held a press conference and told the media he was being held as a "material witness" for another murder. They were keeping him under protective custody for his own protection. They claimed if he was set free, he would likely be killed by his mob associates because he knew so much about the inner workings of Murder Inc. They were acting as if they were protecting my father. It was all a sham.

Their weak attempts to make my father look like a "rat" didn't work, nor did their feeble insinuations that my father was in danger. Nobody in my father's circles bought that bullshit. His reputation as a stand-up guy far outweighed their lies. My dad would never sing. Everyone knew it.

And he never did. He took it all to his grave.

A few days later, O'Dwyer and his cronies indicted my dad for the murder of Arthur Flegenheimer, also known as Dutch Schultz. At the time, Dutch was one of the highest-ranking Jewish mobsters in the country, one of the leaders of Murder Inc.

From the moment I said goodbye to my dad on the morning of March 25th, 1940, I began living in a fantasy world – a world continuously fed by lies, deceptions and crazy tales – each designed to keep me protected from the truth.

About a month after my father left, I began to ask where he was. It wasn't unusual for him to go on trips and not come home for a while, but I started to become curious. I finally asked my mom, "Where's daddy? When's he coming home?"

That's when it truly began.

She replied nonchalantly, "Well, your dad went to work for the government to do all kinds of hush-hush stuff. He is traveling around the world, like a secret agent."

I instantly became excited. I imagined these incredible visions of my dad being a super-spy. Though I was young, I felt genuine pride that my father was doing something important, maybe something that would change the world.

Soon, I began getting letters and postcards from far-flung places, like Buenos Aries and cities across Europe. Every note was signed, "Love, Dad."

Shortly afterwards, we moved from Brooklyn to a house in Queens. My mom's brothers, my aunts, and cousins moved in with us. The reason they said was to be close to the family and to help out. Why? Because Dad was in the Navy.

It took over a year for Dewey, Turkus and O'Dwyer to get ready for the trial. It began on June 2nd, 1941. By then, my father had been in jail for over a year. He'd pleaded innocent as the result of a frame-up. There was no hard evidence. There were no eyewitnesses. He was convinced he could beat the rap.

Unfortunately, things went wrong after just eight days of the trial.

My dad suddenly changed his plea from innocent to non-vault or no defense. He did this to avoid the electric chair. It took years for me to learn exactly what caused this sudden change of heart. Let's just say a few canaries started to sing. But, what really convinced him to change his plea, was when they threatened to throw my mom in jail for being a material witness. All of this for just saying hello to my dad in the court room.

With his new plea, came an automatic life sentence, which in New Jersey back in 1941 was 12 years and six months.

A few days after Japan bombed Pearl Harbor, my father was sent away to serve his life sentence. I remember, because my mom told me that my dad would now be gone even longer, due to the war officially starting. Little did I know that this outrageous, ingenious ruse, to convince me that my father was in the Navy serving his country, rather than serving a life sentence for murder, was being master-minded by the top men in the Mafia and Combination Mob, along with a list of family members and friends. This hoax lasted seven years. That's how unbelievable – or should I say believable – it was. Not once did I question it.

Why were all these people so willing to help my parents? It wasn't out of fear. It was because they loved them. From in-laws to neighbors to casual acquaintances, my mother and father were sincerely respected regardless of the company they kept. The lengths people went to were proof of that.

This scam became so elaborate that to this day, I still can't believe how well they covered all the bases.

The mailman was in on it. Every time I would get a letter from my father, he'd come running over, hollering, "Hey Chuckie! You got another one from your dad!"

When I'd question why the postmark said Trenton or Rahway, he'd tell me, "That's a stopping point for all mail from the military."

The Good Humor Ice Cream man, another friend of my dad's, was clued in to what was going on. I'd go out to the truck to buy a Popsicle or two and he'd give me a third one for the dog. "Tell your mom I gave you one for the dog and give her one too."

Some of the teachers in my school were in the know as well. I was nine years old and my sixth-grade teacher, Mrs. Pribie, always jumped in every time she overheard something being said or going on.

The lengths everyone went to keep this ruse alive was astounding. They were creative. They were theatrical. Some were downright outlandish. And yet, there is only one organization that I know of that could pull off something like this: The Mob.

The kicker is they all took their direction and instructions, not from my dad, but from my mother! As he always said, "She is smarter than all of them!" She always knew what to do, who to contact, when and how. She was an amazingly smart and strong woman. She carried as much honor and respect as my dad.

The one thing my mom was most afraid of was some kid spilling the secret, either in school or out in the street. She was right to worry. It did happen quite a few times. They'd say, "Your father's a racketeer," or "Your father's a hoodlum." Fortunately, I didn't even know what those words meant at that time.

Usually my mom, Uncle John or Uncle Red would pay a visit to the kid's house and talk with their parents. Every time the parents cooperated, and the name-calling stopped. This had less to do with threats and more to do with the fact that most of the neighbors were dear friends of my parents. They were aware of where my dad was, and wanted to help, so they would immediately put their kids in line.

I was constantly doted on, kept busy and spoiled by everyone. The idea was to keep me happy, so I wouldn't think about my father. It worked.

For those seven years the top mob bosses of both the Combination Mob and Sicilian Mafia: like Luciano, Lansky, Siegel, Costello and Anastasia didn't come around the way they used to. This was my mom's doing, to avoid slip-ups about my dad. She figured the less I saw of these guys, the less likely I would be to catch on. They all agreed it was the right thing to do. However, there can be no doubt that these men of incredible power were working for my benefit behind the scenes.

I was taken to different places, sporting events and to do things by several of my dad's Jewish gangster associates, all who were part of the Combination Mob: Frankie Katz, Jacob "Cuppy" Migden, Yoey Glickman, and guys named "Spunky", and "Smitty". Each one of these guys was assigned specific tasks when it came to me.

The Combination Mob was created and run by the Sicilian Mafia, with Charlie Lucky Luciano leading the way. Only Sicilians could be members of both the Combo and the Mafia – never the other way around.

The boss of the Combination Mob boss was Meyer Lansky. However, that entire organization reported to the Sicilian Mafia and Luciano. In other words, at that time, Luciano called the shots for both the Sicilian Mafia and the Combination Mob.

Rest assured, my godfather, Charlie Luciano, made sure everyone did what they were supposed to do, when it came to my well-being. Most importantly, all these mobsters took care of me and my mother out of devotion.

Frankie Katz was an intimidating mob tough-guy; often used as a union strike breaker. He was loyal to the core. He was a dear friend of my dad's since childhood. Frankie's job was to be attentive to my mother and make sure she had everything she needed. He took her to see my dad every other Sunday in the beginning, then every Sunday. He also took her wherever she needed to go afterwards. He was also responsible for passing messages from my mom or dad to the Combination mob or to whoever.

Jacob "Cuppy" Midgen, also called Jack, like most mobbed-up guys started out as a hit man. He was a member of Murder Incorporated. He did a stint in Sing Sing for murder. He later became involved with many mobbed-up businesses.

He was another guy who was around all the time. When we needed him, he was there. He often took us out for dinner to nice restaurants and took us shopping.

Yoey Glickman was a big-time bookmaker in Brooklyn. His reputation was nationwide, and he was under the protection of the Sicilian Mafia and the Combination Mob.

He always took me and my mom up into the mountains on vacation. He rented several bungalows right next to each other for my entire family. Whenever he went away on a trip he made sure we were involved.

Spunky, also known as Maxie, spent twelve years in prison, but never told me why. Later, he became involved with all kinds of union business – all run by the mob.

Spunky's job was to take me to baseball games. He always wore a New York Yankees hat. We sat in the best seats, went to the biggest games, the play-offs, the World Series. He even took me to Jackie Robinson's first game as a Brooklyn Dodger on April 15th, 1947 at Ebbets Field in Brooklyn, against the Boston Braves. For a kid, it was heaven.

One of my favorite memories was the day I met Babe Ruth. Spunky got us seats in the owner's box right next to the Yankee dugout, in the first row. The date was April 27th, 1947. Babe Ruth's last appearance at Yankee Stadium before he passed away. It was his farewell speech.

Before the festivities started, we were leaning over the railing watching all the Yankee players. The Babe came out of the dugout in his long tan wool coat. For some reason, like it was planned he turned right around towards us. I couldn't believe it!

He waved. "Hey Spunky. How are you?" His voice was gruff. You could tell he was very sick.

He came right over and shook Spunky's hand. "Hey Babe. Good to see you. Thanks for stopping over."

I was ready to jump out of my skin! Spunky and Babe Ruth knew each other!

Spunky looked at me. "Babe I would like you to meet a very dear friends of mine's son. This is Chuck Workman. Charlie Workman's son."

The Sultan of Swat extended his enormous hand to me. "Hey pal. Nice to meet you."

I reached my hand out and shook his hand, but I could barely speak I was so star-struck. "Very nice to meet you too Mr. Ruth."

"Oh no. You call me Babe. That's what my friends call me."

"Okay. Nice to meet you Babe."

Ruth reached into his coat pocket. "Here, I have something for you kid." He pulled out a baseball and a pen. He signed the ball and gave it to me.

"Thank you so much Babe!"

"You're welcome kid. I gotta go. You enjoy the game."

He shook Spunky's hand again. "Take care Spunky and take care of the kid."

"You too Babe and thank you again."

Ruth waved and walked away.

Spunky looked at me, "You save that treasure, you hear!"

Smitty, last name Smith, was married to Jacob "Gurrah" Shapiro's sister. Gurrah was Lepke Buchalter's partner in everything.

Lepke was the CEO of Murder Incorporated. Unfortunately, Gurrah was killed in prison when some unknown persons injected air bubbles into his veins. Who do you think did it?

His job was to take me to the fights. For the life of me, I couldn't figure out why everybody was so nice to me? Why did I always sit ringside? To me, that's just where we sat.

I met and saw some of the greatest fighters of that era: Chico Vejar, Willie Pastrano, Archie Moore, Tony Janiro, Will Pepp, Sandy Saddler and Charlie Fusari.

I was ringside for all three Rocky Graziano versus Tony Zale fights — two of them were in Chicago at Soldier Field and one in Newark at Ruppert's Stadium off the Pulaski Skyway.

At the time Rocky was banned from fighting in New York, because he was supposed to fight a boxer named Cowboy Rubenshank but didn't. There was also evidence of a supposed fix in the fight. So, his boxing license was pulled. The promoters wanted the New York crowd, so they moved it to Newark near Pulaski Skyway, so fans could get there easily

Rocky was the middleweight champion of the world at the time. Rocky got TKO'd in the third round and Zale took the title back.

As soon as the fight ended, Irving Cohen, who was Graziano's manager of record, took us to the fight and was sitting right next to us. Out of nowhere he slid off the chair like he was having a heart attack. People started screaming for help.

I didn't know what was going on.

"Mom! What's wrong? Is he dying?"

"No, he's probably just in shock. It's okay Chuckie."

She pulled me away from the fray to shield me from what was going on.

Within minutes, medics came out with a stretcher, accompanied by a doctor.

"Mom, where are they taking him? He's dead isn't he?" I questioned in a state of panic.

"It's okay Chuckie. He just can't walk right now. He will be fine."

Graziano walked to the dressing room while the medics carried Cohen.

Because he drove us to the fight, he was also our ride home. Mom fully expected someone to come out and get us to take us home.

The entire arena was empty, and we were still waiting.

"Mom. Why are we still here? Everyone is gone."

"Well, we are waiting for our ride home. Why don't you go into the dressing room and see what's going on?"

I took off to the locker room. I slowly opened the door. The first thing I saw was Irving lying on a table with an oxygen mask on. He turned his head towards me and waved me over. "Come here kid." He ordered in gruff voice.

I hesitantly walked over.

"Don't worry. I will be fine."

He managed to reach into his pants pocket, pulled out his keys and handed them to me. "Here's the keys Chuckie. Give them to your mom. She can drive you home in my car."

I took the keys from him. "Okay. I will tell her."

As I made my way towards the door I heard Graziano. "Don't worry Irving everything is fine"

We went back to the car and got in. My mom froze. "This is a stick shift. I don't know how to drive one of these." She was furious! She said things I have never heard her say. If Irving were there, she probably would have knocked him out!

She had no choice, but to give it a try. We left Newark at around 12:00 midnight. We didn't get home until 4:30 in the morning. It was start stop stall, start stop stall the whole way home.

The fight was on Friday night. My mom couldn't wait for Sunday, so she could tell dad what happened. When she did, he was enraged.

The next day after I came home from school at around 3 o'clock in the afternoon. Irving Cohen, Whitey Bimstein (Rocky's cut man) and Rocky were sitting on my front step. I asked, "What are you guys doing here?"

"We're waiting for your mother."

In front of the house was a big Devega Sports Truck.

"What's the truck for?" I asked curiously.

"Oh, there's some gifts in there for you kid." Irving chirped.

"Gifts?" I questioned.

He got up and opened the truck. I couldn't believe it. Inside was a boxing ring, boxing gloves, speed bag, heavy bag - everything needed for a full-sized boxing gym. To top it off, there was a television set.

I asked. "What is this all for?"

"Tell your mom we're sorry. Please call off the dogs."

Rocky and I became good friends after that. I gave him golf lessons and I called him Shirley. He couldn't hit his way out of a paper bag. My wife and I would see him from time to time at celebrity golf tournaments. He would run over to give us a hug and a kiss.

He was beloved by so many. I was very fortunate to have him in my life.

I got to know a lot of other boxers because they gravitated to the guys I was with, who were all knock-around guys. They were all incredibly nice to me.

I became such a huge fight fan that I was at a boxing card almost every night of the week. Mondays we'd go to Ridgewood Grove. Wednesday's it would be St. Nicholas Arena. Thursday's nights it was Sunnyside Gardens. And to top it all off Friday night would be Madison Square Garden.

One a Wednesday Smitty took me to Nicholas Arena. I was watching Chico Vijar vs. Chuck Davis, a southpaw from England. We were sitting next to Steve Ellis the radio announcer who was doing the blow-by-blow for radio.

I heard Steve say: Vijar hits him with a left; Vijar hits him with a right; Vigar hits him with everything but the ring post. I couldn't believe what I was hearing.

"I turned to Smitty and said. "Is he watching the same fight we are?"

Smitty turned to me and said. "You're not too smart kid."

He told me that Ellis owned half of Chico Vijar and they were setting him up for a title fight.

Vijar looked like he was in a war. The other guy looked like he was in a dance.

Boy, was I disappointed. I finally learned the truth about the insides of the fight game.

Time passed, and the ruse went on, becoming truer in my mind with every year. In 1944, a movie came out called Destination Tokyo, starring Cary Grant, John Garfield and Alan Hale. My mom took me to see this show on Jamaica Avenue in Queens where the theaters were.

The movie was about a submarine called the USS Copperfin. The sub snuck into Tokyo Bay to get information for the first air raid over Tokyo. They placed a spy team on shore to conduct surveillance and take pictures in preparation for the bombing. I remember soaking up every second of the film, picturing my dad's face in place of the actors.

A year later, a memoir came out about a submarine called the USS Silversides, based on the true story about the crew, called the "fighting underwater team" which consisted of sixty men, led by Lt. Commander Creed Burlingame. My mother told me that my father was on that submarine – the USS Silversides. She also claimed that even though they called the sub the USS Copperfin in the movie, it was really about the Silversides. She even pointed out the guy who supposedly played the role of my father. I was elated, envisioning my father as a hero worthy of the big screen. The more they fed me, the more I ate it up.

My Uncle Stevie was part owner of Sunnyside Gardens. I don't know how, who or why this happened, but he got to Lt. Commander

Creed Burlingame of the USS Silversides. Somehow, somebody was able to convince him to help and add some reality to this great deception. He agreed to come over to our house just to see me.

I was sitting in the kitchen with my mom. I heard the front door open. Uncle Stevie shouted. "Chuckie! Come here. I want you to meet somebody."

I ran to the front door and stopped dead in my tracks. In front of me was this impressive looking, tall, clean cut man dressed in full Navy regalia. His jacket was filled with ribbons, buttons and stripes. I couldn't believe I had an actual war hero in my living room.

He approached me with a huge smile and stuck out his hand for me to shake. "Hi Chuck. I'm Commander Creed Burlingame of the USS Silversides."

My jaw must have been on the ground. I took his hand and gave him my best firm handshake. His hands must have been five times the size of mine.

"Do you know who I am?" He warmly asked.

"Yes sir. I do. You know my dad."

"Yes, son. I sure do."

I beamed! Finally, someone who knew about all the things my father had been doing was here to confirm it. And my goodness did he ever.

First, he handed me a bunch of gifts: Japanese flag; samurai swords; U.S. Navy jackets; secret codebooks. Then he sat down next to me on the sofa and started telling me stories not only about the USS Silversides, but about my father: what he did what his job was on the submarine, on and on. I was completely mesmerized. All I kept saying was, "Wow!"

How they convinced a Naval Commander to do this is completely beyond me, but I believed and hung on to every syllable. Maybe I wanted to believe these tales. Or needed to.

During the war, it was customary to put flags with blue stars in the windows of the houses that had family members serving in the military. So, I asked my mom. "Why can't we put one of those flags in our window, the one with a blue star on it to show that dad is off fighting too?

"We can't because he is on a secret mission," she told me. "No one is supposed to know about him."

Again, I believed her. It pacified me for what seemed like forever. I remained very proud of my dad for what I thought he was doing. I truly thought he was on one long secret mission.

Despite the distractions, I would still regularly ask "Where's dad now?"

The answer was always the same. "He's in the secret service. We really aren't sure exactly where he is. Don't worry about it. He's fine."

I continued to receive letters that had a return addresses on them from the Navy. Many times, my mom would tell me, "Write your daddy a card." Whether it was a Father's Day card, a birthday card or just a note, I'd send these letters to whichever prison he was in at the time: Rahway or Trenton State. I still remember the Trenton address: Lock Bag R, Trenton, NJ. I was always told that these were places where letters were collected for all men in the military. Doubt never crossed my mind. Why would anyone lie to me?

How far the mob's reach went to help keep me convinced is mind boggling. The famous author Arthur Conan Doyle, who wrote Sherlock Holmes and "Fabien of Scotland Yard" the television series even got a call to help.

Again, somehow, someway, somebody – convinced him to come over the house and tell me stories about my dad being a secret agent. I already believed the whole ruse, but this was like the icing on the cake. I was completely sucked in.

Bells and whistles started blaring on a hot August day in 1945 while I was away at summer camp at White Lake. I was only ten, but I understood that whatever was happening wasn't just big. It was huge.

It was V-J Day. Finally, the war was over. The camp counselors as well as the children started yelling and celebrating. The first thing that popped in my head was: Dad is coming home!

I was ecstatic and ran as fast as I could to the camp telephone.

But, the line of kids seemed to go on for miles because we all wanted to call home. I finally got my turn and dialed my mom.

"Mom! Dad's coming home! Dad's coming home, right?"

She calmly told me, "Well, we'll find out soon enough. Probably in another few weeks we will have some kind of answer. But he should be home soon."

Once again, I believed her. Days passed. Then weeks. Then months. I was told my father was still crisscrossing the globe, from Berlin to Russia to places I'd never heard of.

It took another year, but my reality check was about to hit me square in the face like a left hook, right cross combination from Rocky Graziano. My whole entire world would go crashing to the canvas, and not just for the ten-count – it would be for years! I never saw it coming.

6
REALITY

"Kids like you shouldn't be in this school. You aren't good enough to be in a place like this. Your father is a fucking killer…"

In 1954, I was 19 years old, attending the University of Miami trying to live a respectable college life and earn a degree as per my father and mother's wishes. They sent me down south to the "U", away from the mob life of New York City, to be watched over by some of dad's associates and my Uncle Stevie. I was doing well and having a great time. My grades although not great would have been good enough to get me through. I was playing baseball and golfing quite a bit.

For the most part I was staying out of trouble. That is until those vicious words were screamed at me nose to nose by a University of Miami campus police officer.

With those words, a rage that had been festering inside me for seven years exploded like a volcano! As I raised my clenched fist to prepare to take out this this so-called cop, the truth about who my father was and how I found out flashed before my eyes, for it was his past that was causing this.

A few months before dad went away, in early 1940, Uncle Stevie purchased a new house in Queens. It was a lot bigger than our old house. The reason was my mom wanted her family to live with us, so they could help her keep an eye on me. I learned my dad knew from word on the street that at some point, he was going to be arrested.

My mom would need the help. Besides, it was all about family with her. It was the right thing to do. However, it was challenging at times with two full families living under one roof. There was a lot of tension sometimes. These led to misunderstandings, blow-ups, arguments and a few times physical fights with my younger cousin. Seven years of two families living together took its toll, in more ways than one.

I was outside playing with my cousin Michael. We started arguing about god knows what. The next thing I knew fists started flying. We get into a knockdown, drag-out, bloody fist fight. He was stronger than me. But, I never backed down. I managed to get a few shots in. But, I was taking a pounding. I must have been crazy or something, because I just kept going back for more. I guess that sent him over the edge. And in a flash, it turned a different kind of ugly. Everything changed.

"Your father's a killer!" He screamed at me with fury in his voice.

I swung again, hitting nothing but air and fell off balance. Michael's fist came crashing to my face hitting the side of my nose. Blood began to flow.

I had no idea what he was talking about or why he would say such a mean lie; or so I thought.

I jumped at him to avoid his fists and tried to take him down. He pushed me to the ground.

"Your father's a gangster!" He kept at me.

"Shut up!" I screamed back at the top of my lungs. "You're a liar!" My father is in the Navy!"

I started to get up and he shoved me down again. "You don't know shit! Your father's in jail!"

I was dazed and confused. Everything started to spin. I felt sick to my stomach. I thought I was going to vomit. "You're a goddamned liar! Why would you say such things about him?" I started to cry.

Michael just glared at me, breathing heavy. But, his fists slowly began to unclench. I think he began to realize the gravity of what he just said.

Still crying I jumped up and ran inside straight to my mom. She was sitting at the kitchen table with both my uncles. I'm sure they heard everything that went down outside. She was calm as if she knew what was coming.

I yelled. "When's my father coming home?"

My two uncles got up and left the room.

She slowly got up from her chair and came to me with a hug and kiss on the head. Let's wipe off your nose. She took me to the sink, ran cold water on a dish towel and gently wiped away my blood.

Composed and prepared she said. "Let's go upstairs. Let's talk about it."

I loved being at the University of Miami. My Uncle Stevie owned the then famous Thunderbird Motel in Miami Beach. This place was a gangster's haven; a winter get away for them and their families. Naturally, I always felt safe. Not only that, I went there all the time with my buddies. We had a blast. And of course, it was a great place to bring girls!

Needless, to say I dated quite a few. At one point, there was a gal I liked quite a bit, so I started calling her my girlfriend. We went out as often as we could.

The way the University was set up, was the men's dorms were in the main building that was shaped like a U. On the inside of the U, there was a fence separating where the girl's dorm was. If you were going to pick up a girl for a date, you had to go to the House Mother and sign the girl out with the name and the time. Then you had to bring her back to the same place before curfew.

One night I came out of the dorm after dropping her off. I started to walk back to my car. Standing there with his foot on my bumper was a campus cop. He was writing me a ticket. I walked up to him "What did I do?"

"You parked in the wrong zone." He barked in a nasty tone.

I looked around. I didn't see a sign indicating it was a no parking zone. I remained respectful and just said, "Alright. Sorry about that."

He growled at me. "You know you're not supposed to be here." I had no idea what he was talking about. I just took the ticket and went on my way. It was probably $10. I paid it the next day and figured that was the end of that.

A couple of nights later, I went to pick up my girlfriend again. We came out, and there's this cop again, with his foot on my bumper writing up another ticket.

I went up to him. "What's going on?"

He snapped back. "Kids like you shouldn't be in this school. You aren't good enough to be in a place like this. Your father is a fucking killer…" He went into a screaming tirade about my dad and the mob.

My blood began to boil.

He went on. "If you keep going out with these girls, I'm going to tell the House Mother and the administration that these girls are in danger with you."

That was it. I couldn't take it anymore. I blew my top!

As I followed my mom upstairs I heard a voice. It was not my mom's or anyone else's in the house. I had no idea where it was coming from. This voice, who or whatever it was said, "Your father is in jail." It startled me. To this day I can't figure it out. Was it a spirit? An angel? My subconscious? I have no clue. All I know is, I heard it. And, from that point on I was never the same kid again.

We went into mom's bedroom and she closed the door. She patted the white bedspread with pink and orange flowers, prompting me to sit down next to her, which I did. "There is something I need to tell you."

She bent over and opened the bottom drawer of her Mahoney Chest of Drawers. Slowly she pulled out this massive scrapbook. I still have it today. She sat back down next to me and rested it on both our laps. She opened it up and at first did not say a word. She just let me start to take it all in. I was mortified.

Inside were all the clippings and newspaper articles about the Dutch Schultz murder and my father's trial. There were so many. I couldn't believe what I was reading. One had my dad stating that he was going to win the case and beat the electric chair. Another was about his boss Louis "Lepke Buchalter, who did get the chair.

There were a bunch on Thomas Dewey, the Special Prosecutor for Kings County (Brooklyn), and his associates, District Attorney Bill O'Dwyer and Assistant D.A. Burton Turkus. They were the prosecuting team on all the mob cases during that time, including my father's. I picked up quickly that this was Thomas Dewey's real goal: stock pile dead bodies of gangsters to make his way up the political ladder. He didn't want them in jail. He wanted them all dead.

It all added up. That voice I heard was right. My dad had been in prison since 1940 for the murder of Dutch Schultz. In an instant, my entire world turned upside down. I was furious. A rage started to burn inside me that would last for years.

The cop was probably in his 50's – he looked like an old man to me. All I saw was a blazing red, orange and blue fire in my eyes. I tackled him and started beating the living hell out of him, cop or no cop! The torment that had been inside me for so long reared its demon head.

He tried to fight back, but he had no chance. I felt like the strongest man in the world. I just kept pounding on him. His face started to bleed. I didn't care. I just kept slugging him with everything I had. I wanted to kill him!

"You fucking son of a bitch poor excuse for a cop! You know who my dad is huh! Well, now you know who I am!"

I was completely over the edge. He rolled over to try and protect himself exposing his gun. I yanked it out of the holster. I pointed it at his head and pulled the trigger. Thank God, I forgot to take the safety off, or I would have killed him. Right at that moment a bunch of guys came and grabbed me. They cuffed me and drove me to the campus police station.

My head was still buried in the scrapbook. My mind raced with questions and thoughts. My heart pounded. Indescribable anger and hatred rose from the depths of my soul. I couldn't speak.

I started to cry again. I felt my mom's arm wrap around my shoulders. I shrugged her off. I wanted nothing to do with any affection. What I wanted, after seven years of being made a fool of, was answers.

It took me a few minutes, but one after another my questions shot out in rapid succession in a tone that was not nice.

"Why didn't you tell me?"

"Why didn't I know?"

"How and why did I fall for the stuff you all did to convince me my dad was in the Navy?"

At first, I did not receive a reply. So, I just kept at it.

"There were the books, movies, flags, swords, stories, visits! Why would you do this to me? You forced me to believe that my father was a hero in the Secret Service and the Navy. And I fell for it. You made me out to be a fool." I screamed!

"My father is no hero! He is a gangster and a killer sitting in prison! Michael was right!"

I glared at my mother with contempt. "You and everyone have

been lying to me for seven years! How could you do that to me!?

Mentally and emotionally spent, I stopped. Silence filled the room for what seemed like an eternity. I just kept staring at the scrapbook shaking my head.

Finally, my mom spoke up. "I'm sorry Chuck. At the time, we just thought that it would be better if you didn't know."

"You don't know how smart I am and now how stupid I feel. You didn't give me any credit." I was furious at her and instantly hated my father.

I yelled at my mom, which I never did before. "Why did you do this? You made an ass out of me!"

She remained so calm it was disconcerting, like she had been waiting for this day and this reaction for years.

"So, now I know the truth! Happy now? Now what?"

"I know this is hard for you to understand right now." She answered with love in her voice. "But, your father and I did what we thought was best. To protect you."

I changed the subject. "Well. Did he do it? Did he really kill Dutch Schultz?"

"Honestly Chuck, they never proved that your father did what they said he did. There was no hard evidence or eye witnesses. Once he was away we never talked about it." She replied in a somber tone.

I turned silent again. I went back to the scrapbook. I wanted the truth and I wanted it now. I absorbed every page trying to find the whole truth, a truth I had been shielded from for so long.

I asked again. "Did he do it? All of articles say he did."

Mom gave a bit of a shrug. "With no hard evidence, I really don't know. Like I said, your father and I do not talk about it at all. To him it's in the past. I have to respect that."

That concept I could not grasp. But, I had no choice at that moment.

What this cop did and said to me was incomprehensible. He had no right. I was just a student trying to find my way. He knowingly and willingly destroyed that…at least at the U.

After a series of hearings, I was expelled and had to leave the school immediately. The cop wanted me brought up on charges, including attempted murder. Friends of my dad stepped in – the web of the mob had no boundaries. Somebody knew Dean Foster Alter, of the University of Miami, who I didn't know. He knew some friends too, and as a favor he managed to get the case dropped. It was totally expunged. It never happened.

So, I went home, but I couldn't get into any other schools. The word was out about not only me, but who my father was. I was black balled from colleges.

But, mom and dad still wanted me to go. Quite frankly, I wasn't sure if I wanted to. However, I always did what they wanted.

Hofstra University was a big school even back then in Hempstead, New York on Long Island. At my dad's behest, my mother reached out to Tommy Lucchese or Tommy "Three Fingers" Brown as some called him. He was the boss of the Lucchese Crime Family. He just happened to be good friends with a lawyer, who was also on the board at the university. I think his name was Raynes.

I was told to go and visit him at his office on campus, which I did. We talked for a while about my life, good and bad. Two days later, I got accepted into Hofstra all because of Tommy Lucchese. To be blunt, he told someone to let me in and don't ask any questions. He did just that. This once again showed the power and strength my father had with these guys and the loyalties, which came from all directions; Italians, Sicilians, Jews you name it.

After another stretch of silence, mom tried to soothe me. "There is something about your father you need to know." She paused. "His main priority and goal in life was to find the best way he could to take care of his family and his friends who needed help along the way."

"What do you mean take care of?" I asked curiously.

"He took care of the nuns at St. Mary's School for the Deaf in the Bronx. He took care of people down on the east side – all kinds of businesses and old people who lived in the neighborhood and needed help from time to time. He took care of his brothers."

I heard her, but I didn't hear her. The scrapbook told it all. What was in there was as close to the truth as I was going to get at that moment, regardless of what she said. I'm sure at some point I stopped hearing whatever she was saying.

I felt stupid. Betrayed. Confused. I didn't know who my father was anymore, and I began to question who I was. My whole life was based on lies. The combination of rage and hatred consumed me, even after we left that room.

I started to ask a lot of questions to everyone around me. I wanted to know why I was lied to. Everyone's answer was the same, like they were programmed. "It's what your parents wanted. It was to protect you. Just let it go."

Unfortunately, this answer or anything like it, did not help me. My anger would not subside, and my confusion was obvious. I told my mom, often, how pissed off and upset I was about at the whole thing. I give her a lot of credit though. No matter how many times I complained about it, she never got mad at me.

I was a mental and emotional wreck; a speed train gone off the tracks. No matter what the situation or decision that had to be made I felt nothing but anger and torment.

Around this time, I was due to have my bar mitzvah. Your father is the one who is supposed to stand up for you during this sacred ceremony. Well, my father was not around – however, he was not dead either. I kept wondering who my parents had in mind to replace my dad. In my mind, if it's not my dad, it's nobody.

I asked my mom. "Who is going to walk me down the aisle for my bar mitzvah?"

"I was told it's going to be your Uncle Abie." He was one of my father's three brothers.

I started yelling. "Why? My father's not dead! Why should anyone else stand up for me?" I shook my head over and over. "Nope, I'm not going to do it."

The bizarre thing was, no one argued with me. I was waiting for a battle – to further fuel my fire. But, it never came. In the end, my mother did not force me. She understood. I never had my bar mitzvah. My mother was Catholic, but my father was Jewish. Indifference to the situation, they say you are supposed to be what your mother is, but I was what my father was – Jewish.

As a matter of fact, I wear a Jewish star on one side and a St.

Christopher's medal on the other side. The medal was given to me when I was about 16, by a man named Willie Catone, who was with the Gambino Family, and a very dear friend of my father's. Like everything else in my life, I felt like a walking contradiction.

Now that I was back home and attending Hofstra University, I of course began to hear more positive things about my father. However, I just couldn't get my brain wrapped around the hypocrisy of his chosen profession and who he was as a man. To conceptualize that these two parts of his life were completely different was a difficult thing for me. How can a feared man be so loved?

There were so many mixed messages and so much anger still inside of me. The battle of who I was supposed to be still seethed. The torment at times would push me to my mental and emotional limits.

I had no idea who my dad was or who I was supposed to be. I was surrounded by gangsters, but was supposed to be legitimate. I started doing things for people that no one else could. It made me feel powerful. I fed off it. It made me feel strong and indestructible. I was a straight kid with mob powers.

While at Hofstra, I met a man who was a professor of psychology. His name was Matthew Chappelle. I remember him like it was yesterday and it's been over 60 years. Something about me must have struck him. One day after class, out of nowhere he said, "What's the matter kid?"

I got defensive. "What do you mean what's the matter. Nothing is the matter!"

He said. "I can see you have a lot on your mind. Can I help you with anything?"

I was not very nice. "Help me? What are you talking about? I don't need any help. Who the hell are you?"

He stayed very calm and warm. "If you need a friend, I'm here."

I snapped back at him. "I don't have any friends."

A couple of days later after class he approached me. "Chuck. How about staying after class? I would like to talk to you."

Out of respect, I stayed. He talked for a while about my father and the situation. "That's quite a chip you have on your shoulder."

He casually commented.

I knew I had it. I also knew it would take one hell of a sledge hammer to knock it off. "Yeah. It's been with me a long time. So, what?" I quipped.

"I can understand why you are the way you are. I'm just here to help you."

"I don't want any help. I'm fine the way I am." I gave him a glare. "Why are you so interested in me?

"Because I can see right through all of the bullshit you have in front of you. You're really a good kid, but you're afraid of the world."

I snarled back. "I ain't afraid of nobody!"

He just looked at me. "I know better."

He sure did. And he kept at me…day after day. He wouldn't give up. He was on me so bad he called my mother. I had to bring her to school. In my state of mind, I was almost 20 years old, not twelve. I didn't need to bring my mother to school.

My mother went and talked to him about a half hour. Two days later, on a Sunday he went with my mom to visit my dad I jail. My father was very pleased that this man was willing to step out for me and help me.

When, I finally began to listen and accept his wisdom, experience and advice, some clarity seemed to seep in. Things started to fall into place and make some semblance of sense. This compassionate man literally took me under his wing. He got to the core of what was going on inside of me. To this day I am so grateful to have had him in my life, especially at such a crucial time. There is no question he probably saved my life. Without his guidance, I probably would have ended up in the mob in jail or even dead.

Dr. Chappelle became a good friend and mentor, and he came completely out of nowhere. Nobody asked him to intervene or help me. He just did it on his own. He became a big influence on me and wonderful friend to the family for quite a long time.

His message was that I had to stop doing the things that I was doing and stay the course of being legitimate. Through his talks, I slowly began to realize that my parents kept the truth from me for so long because they wanted me to live a normal childhood despite the circumstances.

It took a good six months before I finally agreed to visit my dad in prison. I was 12 and a half years old and still furious. I not only had to muster up the courage to face him I needed time to get my brain wrapped around it. Part of the problem was I didn't know what to expect.

My mom would ask every now and then if I was ready to go. My answer was no, for the longest time. But, I guess my curiosity got the best of me. Deep down inside I really did want to see him. It had been about seven and a half years.

At the time he was in Trenton State Prison. When the day arrived, I became petrified. I had no idea what to expect, either from the prison or from my dad. When we pulled up to this monstrosity the shear vision of it terrified me.

We walked in and I felt weak of the knees. There were guards were everywhere with guns. Huge iron doors that were 10 to 15 feet high that made thundering noises when closed. Nothing but cement walls. The whole thing was incomprehensible. I was literally shaking. I had just walked into a different world. This could not be real.

It came to pass that my mom set the whole thing up ahead of time. She wanted to make sure I was as comfortable as I could be given the circumstances. My dad knew I was coming because special arrangements had to be made. All visitors had to be registered and approved.

The Warden at Trenton State Prison was not crazy about my father. However, the Assistant Warden, a woman named Mrs. Ryan loved my mother and respected my dad. To her my mother was like a princess.

Upon seeing us she took charge and was fantastic to us from the very start. We sat down on what was like a park bench. I became so scared I peed my pants. There was a huge puddle underneath the bench when I got up and I was soaked. Mrs. Ryan and the guards made sure I was taken care of cleaned up and ready to see my father. There was no fuss made about it at all. She acted like it was no big deal. I will never forget that day.

We walked into this huge room with phones and a glass

partition. There were probably 30 phones in there. In a way it looked like a big empty bank. There was no one else in the room. That was something I didn't expect.

It took a few minutes, but finally my dad came in from a door on the far side accompanied by a prison guard. My dad sat down at one of the first phones, but the guard went way down to the other end of the room to give my dad privacy. I later realized that this was special treatment. Guards always stood behind the prisoners while they were on the phone entertaining a visit.

The first thing I noticed was his dark tan. How could a man in prison possibly be that tan I wondered? He was well groomed and well-dressed with creases in his white shirt and his pants. With a stoic expression, he sat down and nodded to my mom.

She sat down first. I stood next to her. My dad picked up his phone and my mom picked up hers. They talked first while. Finally, he looked up at me. My mom handed me the phone. The first thing he said to me was poignant.

"I'm here. You're there. Your job is to replace me in taking care of your mother. You better do it."

He paused for just a few seconds then continued. "You've got a lot to learn." He talked about school and education quite a bit. He demanded that I do well. Most of the conversation was him saying you better do this, and you better do that.

At some point, out of nowhere he said. "Jesus, you are big."

The last time he saw me I was five. I was going on 13. To me I didn't really understand it because I was as big as I was supposed to be at that age. But, I guess when you haven't seen someone for seven years, especially a kid, it's a different.

The last thing he said before I hung up that phone was, "You better take care of your mother." He gave me this order as he pounded his fist on the table.

The message I received was clear. My father expected certain things for me and I better deliver. He expected me to do well in school. He expected me to be respectful. He expected me to become a good straight guy. Above all, he expected me to take care of my mother. That was just the beginning.

During that whole conversation I don't believe I said three words. I just listened.

The standard time for a visit was 45 minutes. We were there for two and a half hours. At the end both mom and I cried. My dad didn't. There would be a few times that my dad cried in front of me, but that wasn't one of them.

As we were leaving, Mrs. Ryan told us, "If I had more inmates like your father I wouldn't even need walls."

7
IT WAS MOSTLY THE ITALIANS

The founding four members of the Mafia Commission in 1931 were the biggest names in the underworld: Frank Costello, Charlie "Lucky" Luciano, Meyer Lansky and Benjamin Siegel.

Each had of them had their own unique set of skills, knowledge, connections and responsibilities pertaining to mob business. Frank's talent was people. He was referred to as "The Prince of the City." His main role was taking care of law enforcement and those in political power. He made sure the right people were on the payroll so that the businesses that the Mafia Commission and Combination Mob were in were left alone.

I can tell you firsthand, he was the epitome of a gentleman. No matter the setting or situation, he carried himself with style, class and dignity. He was always dressed in thousand-dollar suits, hints of gold jewelry and his famous fedoras, always tilted just right. But his most memorable accessory was his huge, infectious smile.

It was hard to say no to Frank. He knew who to approach, how to approach them, when and where. He had a gift, a type of magic that meant smooth sailing for the mob during its heyday. Frank also had his fingers on the pulse of everything and everyone – including my father.

Before my dad went off to Trenton State Prison to start serving his prison term, he requested a meeting with the highest-ranking bosses of the Sicilian Mafia. Frank was there along with Lansky, Albert Anastasia, Joe Bonanno, Vito Genovese and all the family bosses in New York. The entire Commission gathered together, minus Luciano who was in prison.

My dad's main objective was to make certain my mother and I were taken care of, not only financially, but in every way imaginable. He knew it would be the Italians who would pull the strings and ensure his requests were met for as long as they needed to be.

As it was told to me, it was Frank who stepped up and led the way at this meeting. "Charlie, we are sorry about this thing. How it all went wrong and you having to go away for a while."

His usual smile was not there. This was a somber time for all.

"You will be taken care of, as will your lovely wife Katie and Chuckie. However, we want you to tell us exactly what you need. Whatever it is, we will make it happen."

Meyer Lansky, the only Jew at the meeting other than my father, seconded Frank's sentiments. Lansky seconded the sentiment, saying, "We all owe you a great debt of gratitude, not only for our cause, but for others. It is important that we honor you like true friends should and ensure your family and your interests are taken care of. But, to Frank's point, we do not want to make any assumptions. We will worry about the how. You just tell us what."

The room fell quiet. My father did not respond immediately.

"I want to thank you all for coming here today and for offering your assistance while I do my part on the inside." He paused.

"The first thing is making sure my family is taken care of financially until I get out."

For years, my dad was paid on a retainer, possibly more than one, by the bosses of the Combination Mob and the Sicilian Mafia. He was then paid extra for the work he did. However, in most cases, especially for low level ranking mobsters, they and their families were not taken care of financially while they were serving time. The exception were the bosses. Fortunately, my dad was held in a different light. Even though he was not a boss, he was treated like one.

"Of course," Frank chimed in. "Your family will not want for anything."

Not another word was spoken on the subject at this meeting. My father accepted it, never asking for any kind of amount or making any kind of demands regarding money. As far as everyone was concerned, Frank's words were the bond.

It wasn't until 1965 that I realized what Frank Costello's word really meant.

It was my birthday and I was turning 30 years old. By then, Dad had been out of prison for about six months. Back then, I was still married to my first wife, so it was her, my mom, Dad and me out on the town at club called Le Champs. It was a mobster restaurant, but no shenanigans were tolerated. Its reputation was impeccable. All patrons, mobster alike respected the elegant air as well as the amazing food.

Dad never sat with his back to a door. He always wanted to see what or who was coming in. Whenever the door would open his eyes would always go up; nothing else. On this day, it was different. There was to something about his eyes that were different.

The door of the restaurant opened, and he slowly raised an eyebrow to me.

"You expecting someone?" I asked

A knowing grin bloomed on his face. I turned around to look at the front door and almost fell off my chair. Walking towards us, looking like he came straight out of a GQ photo shoot was none other than the "Prince of the City," Frank Costello.

I always knew Frank loved my dad and that the feelings were mutual. He told me once many years before, "If your father was Sicilian, he would be a boss."

Frank breezed past, shot my father a welcoming smirk then kept walking.

I didn't understand. I wondered, why wouldn't he stop and say hello? So, I just waited for my father to do something.

He put his knife and fork down slowly, then wiped his mouth with his crisp linen napkin. "I'm going to the men's room."

I knew what that meant. I had to go with him and block the door, so no one would go in.

I excused myself from the table as well and stood in front of the door with my arms crossed making sure no one would enter. Frank and my dad were in there for about 30 minutes. This was the first time they had seen each other in years.

My dad's concerns when it came to mom and I went far beyond money. "Gentlemen, as you know, my family is everything to me," he told them that day at the big meeting. "I will not run or go on the lam. I do not want my son raised like that."

The mob had presented that as an option and they had it all set up. There was no way anyone would ever find us. But, we would have to move around constantly, no roots, no home, no consistency. I felt bad when I heard this. It was because of me my father did not choose that option. I still feel guilty because if he did, he would have never served 24 years in prison. But, this is another example of why my father was so respected.

"Albert," my father said to the Chairman of Murder Incorporated. "Please protect my family." Albert Anastasia was renowned as one of the most violent and dangerous men in the mob. But to me, he was just Uncle Albert.

Albert nodded. "Always."

That was all my dad needed.

"I need someone reliable to act as a messenger. A go-between for Katie so she can send messages and receive them. Someone with undaunted loyalty and tough as nails. I've already chosen him because he's someone my son knows. I don't want any new faces around for as long as my son is kept from the truth. I would like Frankie Katz to handle this."

Frankie was Jewish, so all eyes went to Meyer. "Of course, Charlie. He fits the bill perfectly."

Everywhere he went, Frankie Katz carried a newspaper under his arm. I found out he couldn't read – not at all. He used the newspaper to hide his trademark ice pick or a knife. He never went anywhere without it.

As requested, he became my father's man on the outside. Every Sunday morning before mom went to visit my dad, he would meet her – later I went too - at Ratner's on Delancey Street. We would eat breakfast together and he would pass on news or questions for my dad that mom would relay to him.

When we came back from the visit, we would stop at Jaymore Hats on Delancey Street owned by boyhood friends of dads. We'd go into the hat store and Frankie would be there. My mom would give him all the answers my dad gave her, and she would tell him what my father said to do. No matter what it was, Frankie would go take care of it. No questions asked. This was their routine for almost the entire 24 years that my dad was away.

One of my mother's famous lines was: "Is that what you want me to tell Charlie when I see him on Sunday?" But it wasn't my father she'd be telling. It was Frankie.

"As we have agreed, the honorable men at this table will handle my family," my father told the Combination Mob that fateful night. "However, there will be lawyer's fees. I will make sure those are taken care of by others. However, I will need your support to ensure that money goes to my wife when it is needed."

When dad said "others," he meant Jewish mobsters. This was a genius play. By spreading the expenses around, he was not taking advantage of anyone. He knew better.

Meyer answered for everyone. "Just tell Katie to let us know who these men are, and I will make sure it is done."

"What else Charlie? How else can we ease your mind?" Frank asked.

"Katie and I have decided that we do not want Chuck to know the truth. That is our wish. When and how that will end, I do not know. But, I need all the influence in this room to help ensure the truth is kept from him until either he figures it out or my wife decides to tell him. It's just what we feel is best right now."

"As far as my son is concerned, I have been sent off to fight in the war. In the Navy. On secret missions. Whatever Katie decides to say, if she needs help with this story to make it believable, she will reach out for help. I hand-picked some other friends who Chuck is familiar with to keep him busy, to take him to baseball games, boxing matches, movies, shows, whatever he wants or whatever anyone can think of. I do not want his mind on me."

He was talking about guys like Frankie Katz, Smitty, Spunky, Red Levine and others. These men, although loyal to the core, played lesser roles. However, to them it was everything because they loved my dad. In whatever way they could help, they wanted to.

Red Levine was a very heavy hitter for the Combination Mob on the east side and a big-time boss in his own right. One day, mom and I were with Red shopping for my father. His job was to supply black hand-balls, black gloves and white on white shirts for my dad to play handball in while in prison. Innocently, he said, "Katie, your husband is the only guy I know who plays in white on white shirts. Why doesn't he just wear a regular shirt like everybody else?"

"Because he's not like anybody else."

Red gave a puzzled look. "What does that mean?"

"Red, do you want me to tell Charlie what you just said?"

"No, no Katie! Let's go buy six shirts!" At that time the price for a white on white shirt was about $45 to $60 per shirt. My mom just kept browsing the shirts.

It was that simple. No comments, no questions, just action.

"What about your legitimate business interests?" Meyer had asked my father as they sat around with the entire Mob gathered to honor him before he left for prison. "Can I help you with that? Would you like your shares to continue to come in?"

My father admired Meyer as much as anyone. Surprisingly, Meyer genuinely respected legitimate business.

Dad shook his head. "That will not be necessary. For all intents and purposes, I have given up ownership stake in my businesses. All I have asked my partners to do is take care of my family."

Meyer expressed some sincere concern. "Are you sure this is what you want?"

"It just keeps things clean and a bit easier for all involved."

When the bathroom door finally swung open at Le Champs, it was as if it had been an eternity. I stepped aside and finally relaxed. Frank walked out first. He gently touched me on the shoulder, nodded then winked. I felt kind of proud, that I just did something important for one of the most powerful Mafia bosses this country has ever known.

My father came out a few steps behind Frank. I headed towards the table after my dad passed me.

Frank went right over to my mother and gave her a kiss on the cheek. "Katie, you're looking as lovely as ever."

Then in a flash, he was gone.

My gut told me that my dad chose this place because he knew Frank was coming by. I have no proof of that, but what were the chances? A lot of dad's old friends frequented the club, but it was no coincidence we were there that night celebrating my birthday. We only went on special occasions. My birthday, I guess, happened to be special enough. It was truly amazing.

Dad and I sat back down and finished dinner. Not a word was spoken about it from anyone. When we got outside, I don't know if I was stupid, brave or what, but I had to test the waters.

I whispered in my dad's ear, "So what was that about?"

He never turned towards me. "What was what about?"

Typical dad. Something happened, but it didn't happen. I don't know why, but I find humor in that.

Many years later, I told this story to our dear friend K.O., Harold Konigsberg. It was Harold who told me the truth about that day.

"Frank used to always carry a $5,000 bill under the lapel of his suit held by a pin." He told me. "On that day, in the bathroom, he gave your dad that $5,000."

I couldn't believe it. Even after he came home, he was still being taken care of by the most renowned Mafia bosses in the country. Now that is the definition of reverence.

"This career path we all chose, knowingly and willingly," my father told all the highest-ranking men of the Combination Mob that evening that they'd gathered on his behalf. "It is what it is. Hopefully, you all will continue to prosper and lead long, happy lives. But this is my final request. It is not negotiable. If anyone tries to pull my son into this life at any time, he will answer to me when I get out."

Every man at that table knew exactly what he was talking about. He did not have to repeat himself.

"I am trusting that you will help me with this whenever I feel something needs to be done. My hope is that will not happen. I am not just talking about while I am gone. I am talking about forever. I realize many of you will step forward after Chuck finds out the truth. To him, you are his uncles, his protectors. You have my permission to set him straight whenever you feel it is necessary. You can make sure he has a clear understanding that these are my wishes and that they will be followed."

This request was abided by dutifully by every man in the room. The word was passed down through the ranks and carried over for decades. That was a door that would never be opened for me – no matter what I said or did. And believe me, there were many times during my life I wanted to bust that door down. But, I never did. I was always stopped – usually by my protector and godfather.

At over 80 years old, it is still that way.

I could have become a gangster with the snap of a finger. Except I didn't. Because I knew my father did not want me to be, and I learned down the road that I was no mobster. I did not have the stomach for it. If I would have gone in that direction, I could very well be dead today.

The story of the night where my father addressed the most powerful men in the Mob taught me how important I was to him.

Throughout my childhood I was taught that the most important thing that I had was family. But unlike most people, I had two families like that. The first was my blood. The second were mobsters.

When my dad went away, my godfather, Charlie "Lucky" Luciano, had already been in prison for four years. That did not stop him from keeping tabs on what was happening with all of us. He made sure we were looked after, even from behind bars.

Charlie had been sent to prison in 1936 then was eventually deported to Sicily in 1946. In October of 1947, he made his way to Cuba to be with Meyer Lansky, who was building an empire of hotels and casinos there. In February of 1947, he was extradited back to Sicily once again.

Charlie had a carrier named Sammy "The Handkerchief" who I often played golf with. Tall and muscular with deep olive skin, he was Sicilian himself and would fly back and forth from Sicily with messages, deliveries, whatever Charlie needed.

We played at a club called Cedar Brook Golf & Tennis Club in Glen Head, New York. We would set up a date and time and meet at the first tee.

On this day, at Cedar Brook Golf Club in Glen Head, New York, Sammy called me over to his golf cart. "I have something for you. It's actually for your mom." He reached down in to his golf bag and pulled out a brown paper bag. "Tell her it came from a special friend of your father's. It's to take care of that thing in the house."

By this time, I was smart enough to know that this was not only a huge sum of money, but it came directly from my godfather. I graciously accepted the gift and tucked it into my golf bag. "Please tell him thank you on mom's behalf."

"I will."

That was when it finally dawned on me that our golfing was set up by Charlie Lucky to send gifts whenever we needed something. I can only imagine that my mom told my dad that something needed to be done with the house then Dad would get word out.

Simple. Efficient. Effective.

All the way from Sicily, Lucky was still taking care of us. The Boss of all Bosses never forgot about my dad, my mom or me.

About two years before my father was released, I went on a road trip with my Gyp DeCarlo and his partner, Jack Pannels. My Uncle Itch, one of my father's brothers, tagged along too, even though my dad did not care for him.

We drove to Pennsylvania in Gyp's yellow two-door Cadillac. I was in my late 20s at the time.

The trip took hours, mostly in silence. Eventually we pulled up to a stately brick house. There wasn't a bush or tree around from the front of the roadway to the door. The driveway was completely lit up with lights. I had no idea whose house it was and was never told. It was not my place to ask either.

Gyp led the way, and all got out of the car. We entered single file, walked in through a short hallway and went right down to the basement. The mode was calm yet alert. I knew better than to speak. To my amazement, there were bocce ball courts set up down there, rolls of them perfectly manicured. However, the basement was flanked by armed bodyguards.

In the middle of the room and on the right side of the bocce court sat a long table with a white table cloth. There were four men seated there, all watching us.

Gyp turned to my uncle and pointed. "Go stand over there".

My uncle didn't have a choice and he knew it. So, he did what he was told.

Gyp led me to the table and I held my breath.

A heavy-set man in suspenders with a cigarette hanging from the corner of his mouth pulled a fat envelope filled with money out of his lapel pocket then placed it on the table. He tapped it. "That's for you when Charlie hits the street," he told me, then he pointed to a modestly dressed man on the other side of the table, he had bags under his eyes but the kind of stare that could strike fear into the heart of a guy twice his size.

"When he does, you come back," the second man said. "We'll be here."

I didn't know what to say. This had nothing to do with any arrangements my father made before he went away. This was extra. Some Italian crew who felt it was important to help my father out.

Once my father was finally released, I told him about the meeting. He and I drove back to the same house. The same envelope was given to him by the same guys I had met two years earlier.

That was how it worked. Though there were many powerful Jewish mobsters, like Abner "Longy" Zwillman and Milty Tillinger, the real protection and extra money for my dad came from the Italians.

Other than my mom, nobody else had more of a positive influence on me than the most notorious Italian gangsters this country has ever known. They did it out of honor, respect and most of all, love. And they did it during a time where I was a very angry, confused young man, yet they never failed me. The question I was left with was: what can I do so that I don't fail them or my father's legacy? Despite everything these powerful men had done for me, that was what I had to figure out on my own.

8
THE KID WHO PLAYS GOLF

Lee Trevino put his arm around me. "We're gonna have the biggest gallery of the day, buddy. Get ready. The other guys aren't going to have anybody. Everyone is here to watch us!"

I laughed. "You're probably right. Let's give 'em a show then, huh?"

The warm spring air seemed to carry the murmur of the crowd on the breeze. In the distance, a sea of eager faces, golf fans of all ages. Lee smoothed the collar of his polo shirt as the host of the Northville Long Island Classic, Sr. PGA Tour event announced our names as we prepared to tee-off. As always, the ovation for Lee was thunderous. He had one of the most loyal and huge followings of anyone who has ever played the game.

Then they announced my name. To my amazement, the reception for me was just as crazy. Lee beamed. "They love you, Chuck."

I waved to the crowd and smiled big. I was on my home turf – Long Island. Chants of my name started. I couldn't believe it.

Though I had been on tour for a few years, it was moments like this that I had to pinch myself to remind me it was real. My dream of playing on the PGA Tour with the greatest golfers in the world had become a reality.

I took in the picturesque par four first hole, a vista of lolling green sea. This is what brought me to life. Both Lee and I smacked good drives and headed down the fairway. Most players walk with just their caddies. Not Lee. He walked with me and as always was already chatting up a storm, talking to people as they yelled for him. There had to be two to three thousand people following us. It was awe-inspiring.

What most people didn't know was that my first true love in sports was baseball. I played from age seven all through college. During those years, it was my passion and I had big dreams to maybe make it to the major leagues.

One day, when I was 15 years old, me and some friends were playing stick ball in the street outside of our house in Queens on

181st Street. A big black Lincoln sedan pulled up the street. The car slowed down then stopped right by me. A tough looking guy in a weather-beaten fedora leaned out the car window. "Where's the Workman house?"

I pointed. "Over there." I paid no attention.

He asked again. "Which house?"

I pointed again. "Right over there!"

The car pulled away and stopped in front of my house. I watched curiously, even though this was a common occurrence when friends came to visit mom while dad was away.

The right passenger door opened, and another guy got out. He was much smaller, dressed in an impeccably tailored suit and silk tie. He walked up to the front door and rang the doorbell. When my mom opened the door, they exchanged hugs and kisses.

She yelled out to me. "Chuck, come over here now please."

I knew better than to ever disrespect my mother, so I went over. She proudly introduced the man. "I'd like you to meet your Uncle Joe."

"Hi Uncle Joe." I extended my hand and he shook it.

"Hello, Chuck. Pleasure to make your acquaintance."

I turned to head back to my friends. "Where are you going?" Mom asked.

"I'm going back to finish–"

She gave me a look. "No, you're not. Uncle Joe is here to take you for golf lessons."

I took a step back and gave a crazy look. I couldn't believe what I was hearing. "What? Golf lessons? Golf is for fags! I don't play golf."

"Well, you are going to learn how to play starting today."

"Can't it wait until the game is over?" I begged. Usually when I showed resistance to certain things I got my way. Not this time.

"You are going with your Uncle Joe right now."

I did as I was told, said good-bye to my friends and got in the car. We drove in silence. I wanted nothing to do with it. We arrived at the Kassina Golf Course, which is still there today. The club pro was sitting in a chair waiting for me. In those days, the price for a lesson was five or ten bucks.

The instructor set me up and I couldn't hit the ball to save my life. The lesson was 30 minutes, but it couldn't end fast enough for me. I hated every second. It was like punishment. The lesson ended, then me and Uncle Joe got back in the car and drove home again without a word spoken.

Once we arrived back home, Uncle Joe said, in an unforgettable thick Sicilian accent, "I see you next week."

I was rude. I didn't even say goodbye. Under my breath I said, "Yeah right."

I ran into the house. I wanted an explanation. "Mom, what is this with golf stuff?"

"Your father wants you to play golf and meet nice people. That is all I can tell you."

"I play baseball. Dad knows that! Who the hell plays golf and who is this guy?"

"He's a friend of your father's."

That was the first day of my career. Only I had no clue.

Lee Trevino and I initially crossed paths at a tournament in Columbus, Ohio in 1986. I was anxious to meet him because he was a golfer who I truly admired. As he approached, I extended my hand to introduce myself. "I'm Chuck Workman. I'm the new guy on the tour."

"I've seen you," he stated with a warm smile. "You hit 'em pretty good."

"Yeah, I hang in there." I said returning the smile.

"Well, you keep doing what you're doing. You belong here," he encouraged.

"Thank you. I will do my best," I replied graciously. It was such an honor to hear him say that that I was surprised I had the presence of mind to reply.

We were not paired up in that tournament, but he'd made a great impression on me as he was certainly the same man in person off-camera as he was on. I must have made an impression on him as well. I think part of it was because of all the trial and error I went through to finally get on tour. When I got there, I not only talked the talk, I walked the walk. I'd competed with the best, respected the game, my fellow pros and acted accordingly.

Lee and I didn't see each other much until the Northville Invitational on Long Island. I played a few practice rounds with him and we got to know each other quickly. We got along marvelously then wound up in the same pairing during the tournament a few times. Those were the most memorable and exciting rounds I ever played.

Herman, his famous African American caddy was also one hell of a guy and we got a long great. At times, Herman seemed more popular than Lee, which Lee got a big kick out of. They were both characters, real charmers with big hearts. They fed off each other. It was magic. Lee loved to share the spotlight. He wanted everyone to be a hero.

In the northeast, my home turf, fans would gravitate to me the way they did to Lee. Ironically, in my mind, I was a nobody despite my last name. But to true golf fans and aficionados, I was somebody. That made me feel incredible.

The week after my first golf lesson with Uncle Joe, I rode my bike to Cunningham Park at 220th Street on Union Turnpike to play in a baseball game. In the middle of the game, out of nowhere, the same big black Lincoln from the week before pulled up. The guy drove it right on to the middle of the fields like he owned the park. There must have been nine games going on and they all came to a screeching halt. The driver was the same guy, this time in a brown suit and the same weather fedora. He got out, opened the trunk and shouted, "Chuck! Come on! Bring your bike."

Stunned and embarrassed, I grabbed my stuff, hopped on my bike then peddled to the car. He put my bike in the trunk. "Let's go. We're going to the golf course."

Uncle Joe was waiting for me in the back with Uncle Joe. I was furious. "Who are you?" I demanded.

"I'm a Joe Bonanno. A friend of your father's. Your father wantsa you play golf. So, I'm a gonna take you."

That name I knew. I was old enough by then to realize who was who throughout the Mafia and Combination Mob. The broken English he spoke was unforgettable. "I'm a gonna picka you up every week."

The reality of the influence and respect my father had with these guys was beginning to set in. From behind prison bars, he had gotten one the most powerful mob bosses in the world and a storied member on The Commission to take me for golf lessons. It was almost incomprehensible.

The method to his madness was if I played golf at classy country clubs, I would meet good, straight, legitimate people. I guess you can say he was half right. What he did not know was that most of the prestigious golf courses were run by mobsters.

After a few more lessons, I started to get hooked. I got a little bit better each time, just enough to intrigue me. Now, I wanted to play. I needed to play. I had to become the best. That was my personality. It didn't take long for me to become obsessed.

During one of my practice rounds with Lee at Meadowbrook Country Clue, he made a comment about being hungry or needing something.

"Don't worry about it." I told him. "Watch what happens when we turn the corner on the next hole. There will be hamburgers and hot dogs waiting for us and anything you want to drink. They are going to bring it to us."

"Ah! Go on! You're full of shit." Lee was looking at me like I was nuts.

We made the turn and sure enough there were my people. They walked over with some hamburgers, hot dogs and sodas. We sat in the cart with our feet up and ate lunch. Herman loved it. He must have eaten three hamburgers. The look on their faces were priceless.

Lee shook his head in awe. "If I didn't actually see it, I would have never believed it."

After we ate, we pulled up to the tenth tee. Most good caddies put a towel over their golfer's bag, so the golfer he is playing with does not have the luxury of seeing what club he chose to use on any given shot. When I played with Lee, Herman would always take the towel off the bag, so I could see what club Lee chose. Not only that, he would lean the bag in my direction, so I could see what club was missing. This was unheard of especially in competitive play. This was a testament to how Lee felt about me. The feeling was mutual. Whatever I could possibly do for him, I would.

After about a month of taking golf lessons with Uncle Joe, I couldn't get enough. But I didn't have my own equipment. "Mom, I need golf clubs. I can't keep playing golf with this borrowed stuff. I need a good set of clubs."

"Alright. Let me make some calls and we'll take care of it."

That Sunday morning at around 10 o'clock a car pulled up to the house. The horn was going off like crazy. I opened the front door. A guy got out of the car with a gigantic cigar in his mouth, a huge hat, dark glasses and his sleeves rolled up. I recognized him on sight.

"Uncle Albert!"

It was Albert Anastasia, the CEO of Murder Incorporated and dear friend of my mom and dad's. He drove up with Marty Stone, the head of the latherer's union.

"Come on! Get in. We're going to get you some golf clubs!"

In those days, they had "Blue Laws," meaning retail stores had to be closed on Sundays. That is, unless your name is Albert Anastasia. The President of Abercrombie and Finch was waiting for us at the front door with Jimmy Thompson, the great PGA Tour Player. I was flabbergasted, eyes wide with shock.

They opened the big brass doors to the store. Jimmy introduced himself. Albert did nothing but grunt. They knew what he wanted.

Marty said to Jimmy. "This is the young man we talked about?"

"Great. Come on in." Jimmy replied with a smile.

They took me to a net in the back of the store and I started hitting golf balls. Jimmy moved me this way, then that way. He adjusted my hands, my feet, and my hips. He was fitting me for personalized golf clubs. I was in heaven, hanging on his every word and suggestion. By the time we were done, I had a new set of shiny Spalding / Bobby Jones irons, a Burton golf bag, two-tone golf shoes and a Ben Hogan hat. Honestly, that's the only thing I really wanted.

Then they gave me about two dozen golf balls.

Jim and Marty packed everything into the car then we headed back home as I stared happily at my hat, my trophy of the day. Mom was waiting on the front steps outside.

"Katie, good to see you." Albert said politely. "He's got everything he needs. Make sure he continues. If you need anything, let me know. We'll speak to you soon." He gave my mother a hug and a kiss.

"Thank you, Albert." My mom said graciously then shot me a glance.

I got the hint. "Thanks Uncle Albert," I shouted.

He turned around as he was getting into the car. "You're welcome, kid. Make us proud."

So, the beginning of my golf journey started with Joe Bonanno and Albert Anastasia, two of the most notorious mobsters in American history. Uncle Joe took me to all the great courses to take lessons and play. Uncle Albert always made sure I was fully equipped with the best and most modern golf equipment and clothes. How many people can say that?

I practiced almost every day. The harder I worked, the better I became. I began to feel a sense of accomplishment.

When I was around 17, things began to click. I found my swing and my confidence rose. One thing I liked the most was the solitude of it. I felt like I was in my own world. I was in control. I loved it.

Soon you couldn't keep me off the golf course. Every day after school and all weekend long, that's where you'd find me. I even skipped school sometimes to play. I could tell I was learning how to strike the ball. Not great yet, but I was getting there.

During my years at Jamaica High School, I would take my clubs to school and hide them someplace – the gym, a locker, a closet, even in the bushes, anywhere I could find. I would cut the last two or three periods, run across Grand Central Parkway, jump over the fence and be on the 14th hole at Hillcrest Country Club before my teachers could miss me. I'd play from 14 to 17, not 18 because I'd end up at the club house. Then I'd go back and play those holes again. These holes were giving me the repetitions I needed to turn into something special.

I can't tell you how many times I got caught and thrown off the course. But I kept going back. One time I teed off on the 14th hole and I hit it down the hill in the fairway. As I started to make my way off the tee, this giant burly guy came walking up the hill towards me. He was a hulk of a human, towering at over six and a half feet. His massive size was hard to miss, but harder still was the fact that he was holding his head with a towel and bleeding like a stuck pig, his face, head and shirt were soaked red. He looked around, then focused on me.

"Did you hit that ball?" he bellowed.

I looked around hoping to see somebody else. Except I was the only one there.

Sheepishly, I said, "I guess so."

He charged at me like a raging bull then beat the living hell out of me with the golf ball!

I covered up for dear life, but he nailed me so many times, I lost count. I didn't think it would ever end. He must have been afraid to kill me because he finally stopped. But, not after throwing the ball at my head for good measure. I was wrecked and now covered in as much blood as he was. How I got up, I can't recall. Miraculously, I managed to climb back over the fence with my clubs and walk home. As I limped through the door, my mother gasped. "Chuckie! What the hell happened? Did you get hit by a car?"

I told her the whole story. She was enraged. She called all three of her brothers, my uncles, Johnny, Red and Stevie. Within a half hour, they were all at the house. One had a baseball bat. The other a two by four with a nail through it. The third had a gun.

"Let's go!" my Uncle Red hollered as I held an ice pack to my face.

"Where we going?" I asked.

"Back to that golf course and you're going to show us who did it."

I may have been beaten up, but I wasn't about to miss this for the world. We jumped in my Johnny's car and high-tailed it to the course. Shoulder to shoulder my uncles strode straight in the front door of the country club and headed for the lounge.

"Where is the son of a bitch?" my Uncle Stevie demanded.

I pointed him out. "Over there."

The hulk of a man had posted up in a comfy chair and was nursing a cocktail, a white bandage standing out starkly on his huge head. One of my uncles went right to him. "You know who this kid is? Do you have any idea what you've done? We oughta lay you out right here!"

The guy started to stumble over his words. He didn't know what to think, say or do.

"You ever hear of Charlie Workman?" Uncle Red asked menacingly.

The giant turned ghost white. "Yeah. I know who he is."

"That is his son you just beat up!"

He had the fear of death in his eyes. "Oh no! I'm sorry! I didn't know! I would have never! What can we do! I gotta make this right!"

This giant was literally near tears.

My uncles traded glances, then Red said, "Get him a membership! That's how you make this right!"

"A membership? Yeah, Yeah! I can do that. No problem. I'll personally take care of it myself."

I'd never seen such a big guy look so small.

The next day, I was a member. From that point on, I walked in the front door. No more jumping over the fence. Technically, I wasn't in the right. However, I sure didn't deserve that beat down, so he was even more in the wrong. But just by mentioning my dad's name, that wrong was righted.

That was not the first, nor the last time this type of thing happened.

Later, we found out that the giant was a bookmaker. Of course, he knew my dad and who was who in mob circles. He also understood that from that day forward, his ass was on the line.

Word began to spread about my talent for golf among my father's associates. In mob circles, nicknames are often used just in case rooms were bugged or someone was listening. When talking about me they began to refer to me as "the kid who plays golf." And they still do to this day.

9
RESPECT THE GAME

"I can hit this one through the trees," Lee Trevino once said to me during a practice round for a tournament.

"Ah, you're full of shit," I replied. So, we'd bet... or I'd come back with. "I can hit right around those traps." We'd bet again.

Besides that, he never stopped talking. He played to the crowd. He was a showman. Other guys, if you drop a pin or make a noise, forget about it. They'd go crazy. Not Lee. The louder the crowd, the better he played.

He flat out loved the game. He took in every second, every shot, every fan. Every opportunity he had to share his passion he took it. He played every tournament like it could be his last. I never saw anyone have such a blast and play so well under so much pressure. That attitude rubbed off on me. I looked at the game differently and always tried to enjoy the moment.

Without a doubt, he was the best ball striker I ever saw. He could make the ball do whatever he wanted. He talked to the people, but his ball did the talking for him on the course.

What made playing with him even more fun was that we were both action guys. We'd make little side wagers every time we played. It could be in a practice round or right during the tournament. No matter what the challenge or bet, we were both always up for it. It was just a great way to play and helped take the pressure off the fact that we were playing a pro tournament.

Lee would find the most innocent of situations and turn it into something hysterical. During one round, there was a guy walking across the fairway, just as we were ready to tee off. Lee shook his head and laughed as he placed his ball on the tee. "Look at that guy! Watch me hit this shot right over his head!"

"Jesus! What if you hit him! You'll kill the guy!" I replied laughing.

Lee shrugged with a wink. "That's what I've got you for! To protect me!"

I shook my head and we had a hell of a laugh. Of course, he waited until the guy crossed the fairway before teeing off. He would never do something like that. It was just his way of finding levity whenever he could.

We sat with dad at a park bench in the rotunda of Rahway State Prison. The benches in front of us and behind us were both empty. No one sat there out of respect for dad. I was probably in my late teens or early 20's. When dad talked he never took his eyes off mine, because they said more than his words. And I knew better than to look away. He was always larger than life to me and I feared him in a way that most children should fear their parents, even though he was behind prison walls.

There was a message coming. I could always tell. He took his time with his words. Every conversation started with my responsibility of taking care of mom. This was no different. I didn't have to say much other than to recommit my promises. Mom came first and that was it.

He paused. His eyes seemed to turn shape or something. This meant the conversation was taking a turn. That turn was towards me.

His facial expression did not change. "You're doing good on the golf course?"

I knew he knew the answer but, that was irrelevant. "I'm playing well." I offered with a half-smile.

He squinted. I got the message. Wrong answer.

The Cobblestone Country Club in Palm City, Florida was a very upscale club that was extremely difficult to get into. It was owned by some Italian friends of mine from Long Island. It was mostly an exclusive Italian club.

One time they were hosting a charity Pro-Am event for Larry Loretti, a dear friend of mine and full time Sr. Tour Player. Lee played in it. I decided to bring a camera crew down from New York to make a television commercial. I was opening a driving range and golf school up in Long Island, so I needed some publicity. The place was to be a top-notch joint with all modern equipment like pop-up tees, weather covers, turf instead of matts, etc. Way ahead of its time.

I wanted Lee and few other guys for about 30 seconds to help make up the commercial. Lee said, "Absolutely."

He started out by saying, "You know, I've played golf with Chuck several times. Every guy gets caught in a mud hole at one point or another. When Chuck gets caught, he goes into the mud hole and comes out looking the exact same way. Now you figure out how that happens. Are they afraid to get him dirty? Or what?"

Once he did his bit, a bunch of other pros, did a 10 to 20 second spot. We put together a nice commercial – all because Lee got the ball rolling.

When we were done I asked Lee. "Do you ever go out to eat?"

"No, not usually. We get some fried chicken or something, go back to the hotel and eat."

"Why do you do that?"

"Honestly, Chuck it's because I never get a chance to eat. I get mobbed wherever I go for autographs, pictures, stories. People think I belong to them. It gets a bit crazy. I don't mind it on the course or around the clubhouse, but sometimes I need a break. So, we just stay in at night and relax away from everyone else."

"Would you like to go out and eat some Italian food?"

"I would love that!" He said with wide eyes and a huge smile.

It was a Saturday I believe. "I will have a car pick you up at around four and we'll get there at around four-thirty. How's that?"

He said. "The place is going to be mobbed. I don't want to go there. I will have to deal with the same thing I always do when I try to go out to eat."

"Don't worry about it." I assured him. "I will take care of everything. That won't happen."

A dear friend of mine owned a restaurant nearby. It was one of the top drawing Italian restaurants in the area. I had a small piece of it. I called Joe, the guy who owned it and told him the situation. "I know we usually open up at four-thirty, but let's hold up until around six or six-thirty."

"Jesus! Chuck, are you kidding me? The people will be breaking the door down. We can't do that." He yelled.

I set him straight. "Listen. This is a favor for me. With everything I do for you, you can do me this solid."

"Okay Chuck. Okay. Get here before four-thirty. I will personally get you all set up."

We got there and walked in the back door. We sat at a small table near the kitchen, all white linen, candles. He came out with antipasto, lobsters, shrimp, clams and several pasta dishes. I didn't think it would end. Lee was in heaven. We ate like kings. Herman was there too. I really got a kick out of just watching them eat and having a great time without being bothered.

By five o'clock, people were lined up outside waiting to get in. They were banging on the doors and the windows. They started screaming. "Why aren't you open?" "What's going on?"

Joe told us. "They will all wait until you guys are completely finished."

We didn't leave until a little before six o'clock. We went out the back door as hordes of people plowed in through the front door. Neither Lee nor Herman could get over it. Lee asked with wide eyes. "How could you do that? That guy must have lost a couple of thousand dollars in business."

"Well, Joe's a friend of mine. He's with us."

Lee shook his head. "He doesn't even know me! You've got that kind of stroke? That's unbelievable. So, when are we going again?"

I winked. "I don't know. I have to think about it." I said kiddingly.

Giving a wrong answer to dad always made me feel stupid. I know that was not his intent, but I felt that way. I also felt like I let him down for not catching on to his meaning. I began to rack my brain. I only had seconds. "I'm making good money."

"You making a name for yourself?" Dad asked quietly.

"I just love playing dad." Shit! I said to myself. Wrong answer again.

"That's not what I'm talking about."

I began to get warm under my collar. "I'm gaining a reputation as a money player."

"That's it?"

I began to catch on, or so I thought. He had me dead to rights.

"I hustle."

"You do what you have to do." His eyes were steel.

"If I don't gain the edge, my opponent will. That's how you really win – before the match starts."

"Smoke and mirrors bullshit." He shot back.

I didn't know what to say. "We find a weakness or play to our strengths."

"We?"

It felt like someone slapped me in the back of the head with a three iron. He was talking about my guys. "My guys help me out."

He nodded slowly with a deadly stare. "You think you have some power?"

I swallowed hard. "It can get dangerous playing some of these guys. They're not all straight up."

Again, not a single word. A knot formed in my stomach. I couldn't wait to get the hell out of there. He was referring to me using my crew and my last name as intimidation, which everyone knew I was doing, including him.

My mind began to race back to the beginning. One time, Joe Bonanno took me to the world-famous Concord Hotel and Country Club. It was there I met the famous pro golfer Jimmie Demeret. Jimmie was not only the club pro, he was a three-time Masters champion. He was old-school and lived by the code of respecting the game. While giving me some lessons, he tossed in some unforgettable advice that stuck with me forever.

"When you play this game look good. Dress-up. Play the part. Be different. Most importantly, never play or act scared. This way, you will always have a leg up on your opponents."

I was mesmerized by his words. "You earn your reputation along the way. Always pay when you lose and collect when you win. Never walk away slumped over if you lose. Never play for more than you can afford to lose. Let your game speak for you. It will tell the story."

He wasn't done yet. "While playing at another place always purchase something, a shirt, golf balls, towels, anything. Show appreciation. Express your gratitude in being allowed to play there.

This immediately puts their guard down. It's all part of the set up."

These were my first mental golf lessons I was ever taught along with the first messages of how to set up a hustle. I started to take his advice right away.

With dad sitting right in front of me, I began to question whether I was crossing the line with hustling. But, I knew there was no line. There were no rules. I knew dad realized this, but again, I was missing something. We were in a stare down, with me scared to death.

Golf became my refuge and the course my sanctuary. My entire existence began to evolve around it. I cannot tell you how good I felt playing. I was good at it, getting better and I knew it. I loved that it was an individual sport, because it was all up to me and me alone. It gave me a way to get even with the world. I started to travel and play with the best. I became accepted by my peers because of my golf and nothing else. I got to be known as a top dollar player with a lot of brass and no fear. I loved it I used it. And it was all because dad said "Play golf. You will meet nice people."

The better I became the more my self-esteem grew. I could stand tall, be proud and stand-up for myself with my head held high. I didn't care what the rest of the world thought or said. I let my playing do my talking for me. They could never take that away from me.

Forcing me to take golf lessons, was without question one of the most influential and life changing parental decisions my parents ever made for me. At the time, golfing was the last thing on my mind. However, when it was all said and done, it was golf that helped define me. I get an incredible feeling of accomplishment every day through the sport of golf.

For the first time, dad shifted his eyes subtly up to my mom. I did not look back. Then he settled back on me. "Respect." That's all he said.

Bang! The one thing my father had from just about everyone. The one attribute that rose above all else…so much so that it buried his dark past. It was one single magical thing: respect."

I nodded. "I understand."

"When you show and give respect you get it back ten-fold."

I began to breathe again.

"Respect the game." He firmly stated.

End of conversation.

Although, it would not be the last time I heard it, that one word stuck with me as I got older and set my sights on the tour. I let my playing speak for me, but I showed ultimate respect to the game, my opponents, officials and everyone involved with the industry. My actions spoke louder than my words. I acted like a true professional and gentleman. I truly believe this is one of the things that drew Lee and me together.

On the 18th hole of an unforgettable round at the Northville, Lee and I made our way up to the green. The gallery that had been following us all day was still with us. It was the most overwhelming thunder of cheers and applause I have ever heard.

People were screaming our names, but this time, mine were louder. It was crazy. Lee backed off a bit and let me have my moment. We were both beaming.

It was an incredibly proud and humbling moment. I was speechless. Somehow, I managed to maintain my composure. We got up to the green and the crowd quieted down allowing us to line up and hit our putts.

When we were done, we gave each other a huge hug. We walked off the green and Lee kept his arm around me. The cheers for me became even louder. As we walked up the pathway Lee said. "Geez. I thought everybody knew me. Man! I can't believe it."

The crowd was all over me. It was my home town after all. Lee decided to step aside and just watch. He was genuinely happy for me. That's the way he was.

After a few minutes, I yelled over. "Hey Lee! Come on over here. Join the crowd. They're all with me!"

Now I was reveling in it. Just watching Lee's expression was priceless.

"This is crazy. You're famous over here." He was genuinely proud of me.

"No. I think the word would be more like infamous!" We had one hell of a laugh and more importantly, one hell of a day.

All through the years he was always gracious to me. No matter where we were playing, even if we were on opposite schedules, he always went out of his way to say hello. That is worth more than any sum of money I could ever win. To this day, even though we don't speak often, I still feel he is the type of golfer people should emulate.

In the mid 1950's, I played the famous Bayside Golf Course in Long Island for the first of what would be many times. I have some unforgettable memories at that place. But, nothing beats that first round. I played it with Frank Costello, Luciano's right-hand man. He heard all about my golf success and wanted to play with me. Imagine that.

Uncle Frank was the epitome of a gentleman. He always carried himself with dignity and honor. He was gracious and generous. Even on the golf course, he was dressed like he walked out of a golf fashion photo shoot. He'd watch me intently with that famous smile. It felt like he was learning from me. Yet, he was decent player in his own right.

He was surrounded by his crew. Most of what we talked about was golf, mom, dad and how proud I was making everyone. To me, that was all I needed. It was an honor to play with him, which I did a few times. He was the epitome of honor and respect.

While at Bayside, if I wasn't playing I would practice for hours on end. This is where I met another great under the radar golfer, Mike LoBosco. He was one of the greatest hustlers I ever met and only played for big money.

He won just about all his bets on the first hole. He made games other guys couldn't win. He made it his business to be one step ahead and have the edge. But, he would win by just enough to make the guy come back for more. Hustlers never tell you their secrets. But, he told me all his.

One thing was for sure. By the mid 1950's, "The kid who plays golf", was well on his way.

10
HOW DID I GET AWAY WITH THAT?

When your godfather sends for you, out of respect you go.

When your godfather is Charlie "Lucky" Luciano, the most powerful mobster in the world, you not only go, you go quickly, no matter where he is.

In 1936, Lucky was arrested and prosecuted by Thomas Dewey for facilitating prostitution. He was convicted then sent to the Clinton Correctional Facility in Dannemore, New York – nicknamed "Siberia".

Like most high-ranking mobsters, he ran the prison. The prison did not run him. It was the same with my father. Lucky was easily able to conduct business while incarcerated. Meyer Lansky, Frank Costello and Vito Genovese were his eyes, ears and voice on the street, following his orders.

During World War II, Lucky offered to help our military and government with his influences in Italy. What exactly he did, the world will probably never know. The point is, most people think the sole purpose of his offer was to get out of prison. I am not saying that wasn't his plan. But I can tell you first-hand, these guys loved this county. There are many well documented stories of mob leaders offering to assist with the war effort.

Thomas Dewey led Lucky to believe that as a reward for his assistance he would be paroled to the United States. In 1946, Dewey pulled a fast one. He used and manipulated Luciano to get what he needed. Then instead of paroling him to the U.S as promised, he had him extradited to Italy.

Luciano returned to Italy as ordered, where he continued to run his empire. Meanwhile, Meyer Lansky and Ben Siegel were cutting deals with the Cuban government to build hotels and casinos where the potential to make millions was limitless.

Lucky made his way to Cuba in October of 1946 to begin working with his partners. He held a commission meeting there to discuss the "Cuba Plan." By February of 1947, Dewey caught wind of it. Once again, he went on the offensive, spun his wicked web and worked with the governments of Italy and Cuba to have Lucky deported back to Italy permanently.

This was my world, my godfather, my family. I didn't know any different.

For a long time, nobody I knew gave me enough credit or thought I was smart enough to understand the vast scope of what my father was involved with. From the moment, I found out the truth about my father, I turned into an angry young man. I felt like a complete fool and in my mind my family caused it. That and trying to come to grips with who my father really was and what he did.

As time went by that anger evolved into a raging fury burning like a candle that wouldn't go out no matter how hard the winds of change or turmoil at home blew. I was without question a psychiatrist's dream.

To say I struggled with moral development would be an understatement. Under normal circumstances during teenage years, children begin to learn from their parents about actions and reactions, decisions and repercussions. The hope being, the things you do are acceptable to society.

For me, that development was not a smooth one. It was an emotional meat grinder that haunted me for over 25 years. I didn't know who I was, what I was or what I was supposed to be. I didn't know if I was a good kid or a bad kid.

Furious. Confused. Spoiled. Arrogant. Hate-filled. Heart-broken. Conniving. The war that raged inside me is difficult to put into words. I was tormented. What I did not realize was that my awful behavior was expected, prepared for and well handled by my immediate and extended family. Of course, it started with my mother and father. Their patience with me staggers my imagination to this day. I was never punished or even threatened. Even though my father could not see me on a daily basis, he knew everything I did and said. There were times where he let me have it verbally during visits, but that was it.

Once I got used to visiting him, things changed a little. His authority and demands on me to take care of my mom, do well in school and stay legitimate were constant. He began to speak to me more like a man than a boy. His tone towards me was hardly ever angry, unless I really did something wrong.

"How are you doing in school?" he'd ask regularly.

"I'm doing fine, Pop."

"Chuck, I want you to do well. It's important you get a college education."

"I know, I know."

I attended PS 163 grade school. I had a rough time and got into more fights than I should have. Sometimes I didn't even know why or what caused it. Other times I did, but I could not comprehend why these kids were so cruel. I didn't do anything to them.

They threw things at me, even rocks. They did anything they could to scare me and keep me down. I heard their words, but I was just too young to understand the hatred and cruelty. No one ever offered up an explanation as to why this was happening.

Many times, parents of kids would tell my mom they didn't want their sons playing with me. Back then I was never told why. I found out later it was because they regarded my father as a hoodlum, a killer, a mobster and whatever else they called him. They didn't want their sons associated with me or my family.

Many kids at school thought they were better than me. And they told me so. I was teased about being Jewish. I was antagonized time after time by kids saying mean things about my father. More than anything else, it was these episodes that set me off like a ticking time bomb. The slightest harsh word about dad would set off a physical fury that resulted in a fight. When it happened, I usually threw the first punch.

They'd yell things like: Your father's a bum; or You don't have a father; or Why is it when your mother comes to school on parent's night your father never shows up? It got so bad at times, that if a kid would just look at me funny, I'd start a fight. As sad as it is to say, I felt good when it was over. It was a release of my emotions. Even if I got the worst of it, I still felt better.

I spent more time in the principal's office than most people sit in their favorite chair. He would always glare at me from behind his big mahogany desk and ask, "Why do you keep doing this Chuck?"

"He was making fun of me." I'd reply.

"That's no reason to start a fight. You need to learn to control this anger of yours."

"They are calling my father names." I'd say in my defense.

"Chuck, if you keep fighting, you are going to get suspended or expelled."

How do you explain to someone that you are fighting because you are furious at your dad and the situation you are living with? It got to the point where I really didn't know what to say or how to answer. I just kept quiet.

My mom got called in to school numerous times about my behavior. Somehow, she managed to keep me in school. This added to the chip on my shoulder. I learned I could do or get anything I wanted.

Sometime after I started playing golf, around age 15, some guys my mom knew came to the house to talk to me. One was from New Jersey and the other was from New York. That's all I was told. One of the men, who looked like your typical gangster all dressed up in dark suit, white shirt, tie and fedora spoke up. He glanced at my mom, who nodded in acknowledgment.

"Chuck, we need to fly you down to down to Miami by your Uncle Stevie to visit a dear friend of your father's."

"Who is it?" I asked politely.

"He is someone special who wants to talk to you face to face. It is important that you go. Your dad and mom know about it. So, it's okay."

"Why?" I asked again.

"Things are changing. This is a message you need to hear man to man. You will be safe. There is nothing to worry about." He assured me.

I looked at mom, who just smiled, conveying that she'd

approved the trip.

I thought it was kind of cool, that someone important in that world wanted to see me. I was going to see my Uncle Stevie, who was going to take me to see someone special. I was excited and couldn't wait to go.

Many years later I learned that the man who did the talking was Longy Zwillman, a high-ranking member of the Combination Mob and dear friend of my dad's. I also learned that he set up the meeting because he was concerned about the way I was acting. He felt I needed some guidance from a powerful man, who just happened to be my godfather.

They did not have to do this. It was done out of love and respect for my dad, mom and me. Little did I know that with the turmoil I was going through, the timing was perfect, and that trip would have a profound effect on me and how I viewed my dad as well as the world.

"When am I leaving for Florida?" I asked to anyone who would answer.

"Tomorrow." The guy from New Jersey answered.

"How long will I be there?"

"Not long. You will be back home in two days." The other guy replied.

I couldn't believe this was happening. In a way, I felt like a gangster. My chest must have pumped out about six inches during that conversation. I couldn't wait to go. This was going to be great. The ironic thing was, I didn't realize the indelible significance of it all. There was a method to the madness. I just didn't see it. All I could picture was being in the warm sun of Florida and visiting with a very important friend of the family. I didn't care about anything else.

The next morning, I got up early. I dressed sharp with gray slacks, a nice new white shirt and shiny black loafers. I packed an expensive black-pinstriped suit that my mom had purchased for me. I had another white shirt, with a purple silk tie and handkerchief that went in outside lapel pocket.

Before I realized it, we were there. Thick Miami heat, the sun sparkling between the palm trees, and me on pins and needles waiting to see who I was about to meet.

As I walked down the stairs of the plane to the tarmac I could see Uncle Steve waving at me.

"Come on kid. Let's get back to the hotel. You can go for a swim, rest up and we'll have a nice dinner before you head out in the morning."

I was on cloud nine.

We got back to the motel and it was packed with wise guys. All of them came over to me to say hello, smothering me with hugs, kisses and peppering me with questions: "How's your mom?" "How's your dad?" "What brings you down here?"

I went for a swim in the kidney shaped pool that was surrounded by several floors of rooms. My uncle has set me up in one of his high-end suites. I tried to enjoy it and take a nap, but there was no way I could sleep. All I could think about was who was this mystery man I was going to see?

While eating dinner, Uncle Stevie spoke up. "Tomorrow, you are going on a short plane ride to Cuba to see some friends of your dad's. We just want you to understand the way things are going. What's happening in the future. Okay, kid?"

"Okay." I echoed rather flippantly. I was smart enough to know that Meyer Lansky was in Cuba at the time. I figured maybe I was going to see him.

The whole school thing became very confusing. It seemed liked even teachers, either liked me or hated me. Some would constantly pick on me whenever I did the slightest thing wrong. They would say the meanest things. "You want to end up like your father?" "You're acting like a hoodlum, just like your father and his friends." "Your father is a bad man. Is that what you want to be too?" Back in the day, teachers could say and do just about anything.

Yet, on the other hand, I had teachers and mothers, who stuck up for me if they heard other kids starting something, like my sixth-grade teacher Mrs. Priebe. If anyone gave me a hard time in front of her, she would not stand for it. In a stern voice she would call the kid out and reprimand him in front of the whole class. She was my personal protector. It didn't hurt that she was a pretty woman. I had quite a crush on her. She was like my guardian angel.

A few times after being given a hard time at school by boys who lived in the neighborhood, my uncles would go to their houses and talk to their parents. The teasing would stop. These were good neighborhood people who knew respected my mother and father. These families were so great that when Feds or cops would go to see them, and ask about my dad, they would not answer. They would say, "They are my neighbors. If you have any questions, ask them."

I did manage to make some good friends like the Orlandie boys who lived three houses away. Their father knew my dad and was a bartender in Jackson Heights, New York. A lot of New York Rangers players lived in that area and hung out at this bar, like: Bryan Hextall and Neal Coville. So, they were always at their house. When I went over to see them they always took their teeth out to scare me. I became a big New York Rangers fan.

You would think people like this would help balance out my life. But, my resentment and anger far outweighed the good. The only place I could channel it into something positive was on the golf course. Even there I felt like I had to be better than anybody else, because I considered myself to be different. In my mind, if I gave someone an opening to prove they were better than me they would bury me. So, I worked harder than anyone. This work ethic stayed with me most of my life.

Throughout my teenage years and beyond, I learned how to manipulate situations to get anything I wanted. My family needed me happy. For instance, there was a time when Roll Fast Bikes were popular. They were expensive. But, if you had one, you were considered cool.

"Mom, have you seen those new Roll Fast bikes?"

"I have heard of them, but I don't think I have ever seen one."

"I really want one of those. All the kids think they are cool."

"Okay." She answered with a wink.

A few days later I had the bike. Talk about a spoiled brat.

As time went on, I learned how to use my last name to scare people or ward them off. I used my mobster leverage to my advantage. I openly admit that. I carried a lot of weight and power because of my name. I'm not condoning it or saying it was the right thing to do. Because, in all honesty it wasn't.

Back in the winter of 1947, there was a major blizzard. Whenever it snowed, guys would go around with shovels and shoveled out people's driveways, walkways and dig out cars for money. So, I got three friends and started a little shoveling business. I made it known that our territory was 69th Avenue to 73rd Avenue. We'd shovel out every house and every car. We made a lot of money. It got to the point where no outsider would even approach that neighborhood. They knew who I was and what kind of power I had behind me. I fed off it.

In the back of my mind, I was getting revenge for being fooled for so many years. Now it was my turn to fool with people. The reality was however, I wasn't fooling anyone. Every time I took advantage of someone or a situation, my family and protectors knew exactly what I was doing. I should have had my ass handed to me on many occasions. But, I didn't.

Every attempt was being made to steer me away from a mobster's life, as per my father's wishes. But, with powerful gangsters at my disposal and Charlie "The Bug" as my father I felt strong and invincible. I wasn't a member of the mob, but I acted and felt like it. I threatened people with the wrath of not only my mob friends, but my dad to get what I wanted. I tested the boundaries left and right, doing things most young-men would have been put away for.

Willie Catone, one of the most powerful, yet unknown Mafioso in the country took me to a gathering at the infamous Ravenite Social Club that was thrown by the Combination Mob. Man, did I feel like hot shit that night. Willie walked in ahead of me and did some glad handing; hugs and kisses everywhere. He looked back at me. "Chuck! Come on over. There's some friends of ours I'd like you to say hello to"

As made my way over, Aniello Dellacroce, the underboss to

Carlo Gambino of the Gambino family walked towards me. I'd met Aniello a few times before, but I had not seen him in a few years. "Hello Aniello." I said and stuck out my hand to greet him.

He tossed me a mean glare and shoved by me. He completely ignored me. "What the fuck was that?" I asked myself. I was respectful to everyone in that world. If I wasn't my dad would have my ass.

I walked over to Willie and he introduced me to some guys. Everyone greeted me warmly. When they walked away I pulled Willie aside. "Willie. What's wrong with Aniello?" I asked in a perturbed voice.

"Nothing as far as I know kid. What's the beef?"

I told him exactly what happened.

Willie's eyes turned cold and his face stoic. "I have no fucking idea kid, but I'm sure as shit going to find out."

He went to Aniello, pulled him aside and gave him an earful. In seconds, Della Croce made his way over to me with a huge smile. He threw his arms open. "Chuck! I am so sorry! I didn't recognize you. My sincerest apologies. I meant no offense." He gave me a huge bear hug and kissed both my cheeks. Honestly, Chuck I thought you were your Uncle Itch's kid. The kid is okay, but your father's brother I really don't care for."

I nodded. "I understand. Simple mistake."

If I didn't feel strong before I sure did now. It became more apparent than ever whose blood coursed through my veins. It was a powerful and intoxicating feeling.

Honestly, all through my teenage years, I was not a good kid. My brain was so messed up, in a constant state of confusion and disarray. But, the need to lash out seemed to be never ending. I gave everybody a hard time, including my mom, who did not deserve that. What exacerbated my situation was the guys I hung around with. They were wise guys after all. They took advantage of every situation they could to make a buck. And they loved hanging around me because I could win them money playing golf.

I started hustling and robbing guys on the course at a young age.

I was literally playing with the devil. There was a huge fork in the road that led to Hoodlum Street and Legitimate Boulevard. Sometimes I'd walk down one side and then jump a fence to go back to the other.

I got into the University of Miami on a music scholarship. Can you believe that? Not baseball or golf – music. Well, when you have the connections I had, you get what you want. I wanted the "U" and I got it.

When I first got down there I needed a car. So, I called mom. "Mom I need a car. I can't take a bus. There's no public transportation down here."

"Alright. Someone will call you in the next couple of days."

I was living on campus, as a freshman.

Sure enough, a few days later some guy called me. "I'm gonna come down there. I'm gonna pick you up on Monday afternoon."

"What for?"

"We're going to go buy you a new car."

On that Monday, this guy showed up. I didn't know him from a hole in the wall. He took me to the Used Car Market on 36th Street in Miami.

He picked out a green 1951- four door Buick. But, I drove out of the lot in a white, Pontiac, with a convertible top. Once again, whatever I wanted, I got. In retrospect, it was wrong.

I was a "C" student at best. But, I managed to get a lot of B's by manipulating the professors. They knew who I was. I took them out to the golf course and we'd play for free. I took them to my uncle's motel on the beach, the famous Thunderbird. There they met a lot of wise guys, who took care of them, even got some of them laid. They were taken care of to say the least.

I even took some legit friends there. I acted like the boss of the place. We'd take up five rooms. We were treated like movie stars. Some guys would go up to the second floor and jump off the balcony into the pool. My uncle would go crazy. "You can't do that!"

I was no more than 20 years old, with a real f-you attitude; Little did I know, the guys at this place were with Meyer Lansky. More eyes on me that I did not know about.

Unfortunately, that dream life ended when I beat the hell out of that campus cop.

Back in New York, while going to Hofstra, I was driving one time with my girlfriend and another car cut me off. Instead of just letting it go, I started chasing the other car. I was acting like a hot-head maniac.

Out of nowhere, two guys in the care started shooting at me! They were undercover cops in an unmarked car. I hauled ass out of there. Somehow, I made it home unscathed and hid my car.

My mother again, bless her heart, called the cops. She told me. "We're going to the Police Station to find out why those people were shooting at you."

"They were cops mom, I saw the guys......"

"You didn't see nothing kid!" She yelled at me.

"There was a flashing light...."

She cut me off. "There was no flashing light kid. You got it?"

Finally, I understood where she was going with this thing.

She went to the police station with a few friends of ours. A court date was set for at the end of my school session during holiday break. During the hearing the cops were testifying and had to account for every bullet they fired. They shot at me about six times. I don't remember the whole story, but it seemed like I was in big time trouble.

Out of nowhere, some guy walked into the courtroom. He saw my mother and threw his arms around her with a big hug. He stood about five feet two inches tall, had a big nose with a cigar in his mouth that was about a foot long. He wore this big tall hat. His name was Yiddell "the Fixer".

Yiddell asked, "Where are the cops?"

My mother pointed. "That's them over there."

He turned to me. "Don't worry kid. Things will be fine."

During the lunch break, after these guys crucified me all morning, Yiddell took the cops into the men's room.

The afternoon session was called to order. The cops one after another began to testify again. Their whole story changed.

"We made a mistake."

"It was the wrong car."

"We shot in the air just to scare them."

"One time the gun went off by mistake"

This went on for a while. Finally, the judge banged his gavel hard. "Case dismissed!"

Yiddell said. "See ya Katie" That was the first and last time I ever saw him.

I got up early again, showered and put my suit on. I was about to walk out the door when my uncle came pounding on the door. "Chuckie! Come on! Get up! We have to get you some breakfast and to the airport."

As I opened the door, his eyes bulged. "Holy shit, kid. What the hell time did you get up?"

"I just wanted to be ready."

"Well, that you are."

I looked back at my suitcase, but before I could even ask. "You won't need any of that stuff. You're coming right back in a few hours."

Uncle Stevie drove his car right on to the tarmac. There was a small twin-engine plane with eight or nine mob guys surrounding it.

"Go ahead, Chuck. You're in good hands. Those guys will take care of you."

I respectfully nodded to each bodyguard and climbed into the plane. In less than 30 minutes, we landed. The air sizzled off the airstrip in ripples that blurred the deep green scenery. We got out of the plane where four other guys were waiting for me in a long black Chrysler Imperial. I climbed into the back seat, which was cooled by air conditioning. There were two jump seats. One guy sat facing me, the other sat next to me. There was another guy next to the driver and then the driver.

Within minutes we pulled up to what had to be the most dazzling structure I had ever seen in my life. A humongous, luxurious white stucco building about eight stories high stood right before me. The main hotel was crowned by two magnificent bell towers while man-made rock waterfall flowed continuously out front. I was in complete awe. It was the Hotel de Nacionale, owned by Meyer Lansky.

The inside was even more glamorous and regal with leather seats and couches with gold trim. The walls and counters were Italian marble. Large throw rugs with gold lace covered the marble floors. There were incredible paintings and statues decorating the hallways. I couldn't take everything in fast enough.

The four men I was with formed a diamond around me, walking in perfect rhythm. It was like I was the President being led by Secret Service agents. We took an elevator up to the top floor. I was so mesmerized by what was around me that I wasn't thinking about where I was headed.

We exited the elevator in the same formation. The man in front put his hand out instructing me to stop. He knocked on the door. Someone opened it slightly. I couldn't see in. The door closed and then quickly opened again, revealing a luxurious private suite with a vaulted ceiling and opulent furnishings. There were two long gray marble bars flanking each side of the room with bartenders. Dozens of tables filled the room covered with virgin white linens. All the chairs were black leather with gold trim.

There were probably 30-40 men in the room, decked out in hand-tailored, summer-weight suits. For the first time, my nerves caught up to me. I was not expecting a room full of mobsters. Sweat trickled down the small of my back.

I looked around and instantly recognized the man I was sent to see – my Godfather, Charles "Lucky" Luciano. He was wearing a light-colored silk shirt, khaki slacks and light brown Italian loafers. He slowly made his way over to me. I couldn't believe it. I was holding my breath.

He smiled. "Chuck, please come and sit down." He warmly gestured to two chairs that were on the veranda.

I followed him outside and took a seat. A balmy breeze blew by, rich with the smell of tropical flowers. He was drinking orange juice.

"Chuck, would you like something to drink? Orange juice?"

"Yes, thank you." I answered politely.

Before I knew it, some guy was handing me a glass of orange juice.

Suddenly it hit me. I was sitting in the Hotel de Nacionale in Cuba with the guy who ran everything. Whatever was going to happen, he was the guy to say yes or no. A chill shot up my spine. Here he was sitting right in front of me, larger than life. It was surreal and incredibly humbling.

I felt honored that he still called me Chuck even though my real name was Solomon. That meant a lot to me. It showed me how much I meant to him, because I was named after him in his honor.

According to the history books, Luciano was in Cuba from October of 1946 until February of 1947. Except I met him there in 1950. According to the law, he was never to be allowed back in Cuba again. So much for the law.

We exchanged some pleasantries then he asked how I was doing in school and how golf was coming along. Soon though, he got down to the heart of the matter.

"Your dad's away. It is what it is. You have to do what you have to do." He paused but kept his eyes on me.

"There were a lot of choices that needed to be made and sometimes choices are dictated by other things that aren't controllable. Nobody planned it. We need to make the best of it." He glanced away for a second, as if the beauty of the cloudless skyline caught his eye, like he'd never seen this paradise before or was seeing it through my father's eyes for the first time. After an exhale, he continued.

"Your dad is making the best he can out of a bad situation too. All the things that are taking place are his choices. His."

He was referring to the fact that my father did not go on the run. That was something I always felt guilty about. If it wasn't for me, Dad would have never gone to prison. Hearing Lucky's words really hit home.

He leaned in closer to me. A hint of his cologne wafted towards me. It smelled more like money and prestige than the entire hotel did. "Chuck, whatever you do, make us proud. No matter what it is. We are looking for different things from you. We are really looking for you to make us proud."

The message was clear, the timing uncanny. I was at a real crossroads in my life. He helped me look at things in a slightly different light. However, I was nowhere near smart enough or open minded enough to completely grasp the meaning. At least not yet.

What was truly remarkable was after all this time, they never forgot about my family and they never changed their mind about taking care of us. It was forever. Loyalty, love and respect beyond comprehension. Everything they said from day one was still the same and stayed that way right up until mom passed. Although it does not continue monetarily, it carries on in the same vein even today.

After I got home from the trip, even after that talk, the battle of who I was supposed to be still raged. Dad remained in prison because he was a gangster and a killer. Yet I kept being fed these wonderful stories about his kindness and generosity, which everyone admired him for. It just did not make any sense to me. How could a supposed stone-cold killer – gun for hire – held in high esteem in the Combination Mob be such a genuine, caring, generous and giving man? If that was my father, who was I supposed to be?

Eventually, these stories began to resonate with me and seep into my subconscious. My dad was different, special in his own way.

As I grew into my 20's, the guys I hung around with began to treat me more as an adult. Their relationship and perception of me started to change. It was no longer, "Let's take care of the kid." It was more like, "The kid can take care of himself."

Not only that, I took care of others. People asked me for help or to do things they wouldn't normally do, so I used my connections. I enjoyed it. I never took money for it – just did it for the power feeling. I got off on it. My need for it grew. When I think back about it, this was probably the first time in my life I began to portray the same kindness my father gave his whole life.

I migrated to the only thing that made me feel free: golf. It was my safe-haven. Thankfully, I was becoming a hell of a player along the way. I knew it made my father happy. From what I heard, he bragged to people about it all the time. I started to make incredible money at it and I was barely 20 years old.

It was one thing to have my godfather, Lucky Luciano, the most famous mobster in history, ask me to make him as well as a large part of the Mafia outfit proud. It was another to truly make my father proud. It still had a lot to learn about the difference between being prideful and doing something to be proud of. But, that message did not totally sink in. At least not right away.

But, a lot of these gangsters who I hung with, played golf too. These friends and golf became my world. I was already a student at "the art of the hustle". These men played a key role in an education I could not learn in a legitimate world. I was fast becoming a well-known golf hustler.

11
GANGSTERS AND GOLF

They say the best golfers have the determination to stick with the game but the patience to wait for the breaks. What I had to learn was patience.

During my summers while in college, I worked at the Concord Hotel Country Club making $35 a week and up to $75 with tips but I was spending $100 a week for golf lessons from Jimmy Demeret, a PGA Masters Champion. To cover the difference, I stole golf balls out of the pro shop and sold them to members. I thought I was getting over on Jimmy.

Just before Labor Day, at the end of my last lesson with Jimmy, before I headed back to school, he took out a wad of bills, gave me a hug and handed it to me. "That's for you. And I won't tell your dad about all the golf balls you took."

I swallowed hard. "What?"

He laughed. "You think I was born yesterday kid?"

My first real golf job after I graduated college was handed to me by the crew I hung out with. Engineers was a very prestigious, high-end course in Roslyn, New York and I was named the Assistant to Head Pro Jack Oliver, a well-known golf pro. It came to pass that quite a few of my father's best friends played there too, like: Bob Feldman, Abe Margolis – the owner of Zales Jewelry, Eddie Condon, a fight promoter, and Bill Fabricant, another jeweler, who is still in business today. All these guys were on the fringe – they had connections with the mob but were not "made" guys.

I did my job and practiced obsessively. I made good money there hustling. I loved the club and loved going to work every day. However, I carried myself like I was untouchable, because I was the "Bug's" Kid.

How wrong I was.

A few months after I started, I saw a pair of black and white shoes that were sitting around in the pro shop not selling, so I took them. Jack Oliver put in a beef on me, so I got fired. Nobody could go to bat for me because I did it. I fucked up and got what I deserved. To this day I am not proud of it. I learned a hell of a lesson. If I did wrong, I was on my own – words I would here many times.

I was left without a golf job and I needed to work. My mom offered to get me a truck driving job for Yellow Freight and I could make $600 per week. Back in '50s, that was a hell of a lot of money.

"But mom, I'm a golf pro. I'm not going to drive a truck."

She said no more on the subject but the Sunday after I got fired from Engineers, Mom came home after visiting dad and told me: "You have to be at the Weak Wake Diner in Newark, at seven o'clock tomorrow morning. Somebody is going to meet you there and take you for a job."

"How am I going to recognize him?"

"He's going to where a red flower in his lapel. He's also huge." She left it at that.

Both of my parents were cryptic in their ways, less talk, more action. You'd have thought I would get accustomed to it after all the years of uncertainty, but they had their ways. It was their world. I was just born into it.

I arrived at the diner five a.m. The chrome tables and Naugahyde seats were dotted with commuters and long-haul truckers. I must have had two dozen eggs and as many cups of coffee. I waited for what seemed like forever. Finally, this mountain of a man walked in. He was so big he almost couldn't make it through the door. His long flat face showed zero emotion. In a booming voice, he yelled. "Where's Chuck?"

I waved. "That's me."

"Come on." He ordered.

"Where we going?" I asked.

"I'm taking you for a job. We'll go in my car." It was a huge black Oldsmobile.

He was smoking a long Italian cigar with a powerful aroma. I stuck my head out the window just to get some fresh air. I could barely breathe and started getting nauseous. We drove in silence for what seemed like an hour. I started to get scared because it felt like one of those mob-hit, one-way rides.

We drove to Scotch Plains, New Jersey and pulled up to this gorgeous Country Club called Shackamaxon. It had a circle driveway, a palatial clubhouse and a rolling sea of rainbow flowerbeds surrounded by perfectly clipped grass. It was a golfer's paradise.

The guy parked and lumbered out of the car, so I followed. Even though clubs were closed Mondays, we walked in the front door. A pretty, red-headed girl was sitting at the switchboard.

Again, in this bellowing voice. "Is Frank here?"

"Who shall I say is calling please," she asked trying not to cower.

"Tell him Harry is here."

I would soon learn that he was Harry Serio, an ex- boxer and a dear friend of my dad's. He fought some of the toughest middleweight fighters of his time and retired in 1943 with a record of 38-5. After that he started his own amusement company and opened two taverns in Newark, New Jersey.

He eventually became part of the Teamsters Local 478 where he worked his way up from Trustee to Business Agent to Secretary Treasurer. By this time, he was owned by the mob. Somewhere along the way, he got into a beef with the wrong guys. A contract was put out on him. Except he was so close to my dad, no one would touch him. If they did, they knew they would feel my father's wrath.

So, they waited. Eleven years after dad passed, he was killed on October 23rd, 1989. I was devastated. I tried to find out what his murder was all about. But, it was to no avail. All I was ever told was: "It didn't concern you, Chuck. You have to let it go. It was a decision made from high up. Let it go."

An older man with a big belly jogged out to the front desk, flushed and completely out of breath. "Hey Harry! How ya doin?

"Frank. This is the kid we were talking about." He gestured to me.

Frank sized me up. "When can you start?"

"Start what?"

"You're the new club pro."

I took a step back. "What?"

"Yeah. Can you start tomorrow?" he asked with a huge smile that was more for Harry's benefit than mine.

With dad pulling some strings, just like that, I had a new golf job. Frank took me around and introduced me to everyone. I may have been a naïve kid, but I knew heavy hitters when I saw them. It turned out the mob owned the club.

Regardless, I went to work every day excited. I did everything I could to impress my bosses and earn an extra buck or two. I was very social to everyone. I got introduced to hundreds of guys. But the ones that migrated to me were all knock-around or connected guys. How did I know? Every time I met someone new, I ran their name by Mom. Her response was always the same: "Oh, he's friend of your fathers."

One afternoon, I was playing for $10 a hole for nine holes with the infamous Gyp DeCarlo, Anthony "Tony Boy" Boiardo and a buddy of theirs who I didn't recognize and who nobody deigned to introduce me to.

Gyp was not only a very close buddy and associate of my father's, he was one of the most powerful mob bosses in the entire country. According historians, he was part of the Genovese Family and with Sam DeCavalcante of New Jersey. However, contrary to what these so-called experts believed, he was an independent boss, who controlled certain mob businesses in New Jersey. He earned his unique status because he was a huge earner and always did the right thing when it came to paying homage to the big-name family bosses in New York. He was regarded as a man of honor, respect and feared by many. Little did I know this exceptional man would play a major role in my life, and would be the catalyst behind getting my dad out of prison in 1964.

We were taking the tee-offs in stride on that overcast day, making small-talk, Gyp and Tony both utterly inconspicuous in plain khakis and collared shirts, looking the picture of average businessmen. On the first hole, the guy I did not know went up to the green, which was up about 20 feet higher than the fairway, to attempt about a 40-foot putt. In seconds, he was back down.

I was shocked. "What the hell just happened? Did he make that putt?"

Tony chuckled. He was a capo in the Genovese Family. However, he was following in Gyp's footsteps and everyone knew who he really was with. "Dunno. Why don't you ask him?"

We went to the second hole, which was next to the road. I whacked my drive down the fairway and headed back to the cart. The other guys were already driving down the fairway. I never saw them hit their drives. Either they were fast, or I was going blind. Next thing, three of them are on the green putting. I caught up to Tony. "Did anybody hit drives or second shots?"

"You know kid, you're not too bright."

"What do you mean?" I snapped back.

He threw up his hands and shrugged. "It's the road hole."

Puzzled, I said, "So?"

Again, he said. "It's the road hole." With the emphasis on road.

"You're right. I'm not too smart, because I don't understand you."

He made a funny noise with his mouth and shook his head with no response. Then it hit me like a golf ball in the back of the head. "They don't play the road hole!" I blurted out.

Tony started laughing so hard, I thought he was going to crash the cart.

By the third hole, I was incensed. "Gyp just moved his ball in the rough. He's setting it up, so he could hit a wood."

Tony looked the other way. "So, what do you want me to do?"

I yelled to Gyp. "You can't do that!'

Without even looking at me, he replied "You play your way. We play our way."

I couldn't hit another shot straight. I was done. They set me up. I couldn't believe it. I lost $90 to all three guys, $270. I had $20 in my pocket.

"Where's the money?" Tony asked.

"Let's go, kid. Time to settle up" Gyp demanded.

Embarrassed, I admitted, "I don't have that kind of money on me."

"Well you better go fucking get it," the guy I didn't know insisted.

Gyp gave me a scary glare when I told him I didn't have the money. I went over to Fred, the bartender and pleaded for the cash from the till, offering to pay him back tomorrow.

"Geez, I just sent all the money to the bank."

"Frank, you don't have any money around?" I yelled in a panic.

"No kid, I'm sorry."

I went around asking every guy I knew to help me out. Finally, it hit me. The whole club was in on it and there was nothing I could do. With no other choice, I jumped in my car and drove 90 minutes back to Queens to get the $270 from my mother. Then I drove all the way back.

Gyp was sitting at the bar, his eyes an icy glare. I walked up and sheepishly handed him the money. "Don't ever play for something you do not have unless you are bigger than the guy you are playing."

Everyone who was in on it came over and busted out laughing. I felt so stupid. Even though I was the pro, I had to be taught a thing or two. I had a college diploma but clearly what I needed was my "Gangster Golf Education."

That was not only a golf lesson, it was a life lesson.

I had a life of privilege. A powerful father, clout, connections money and a network of America's most dangerous men to back me up if I needed it. But nobody would let me forget the rules of the game.

12
THE ART OF THE HUSTLE

"Golf is a mind game, whether you are playing in a tournament or hustling. You do the opposite of what your opponent does. If he's slow, you're fast. He plods, you run. He talks, you don't. You do anything and everything to gain a mental edge and get inside his head." This was what the great Doug Ford, a PGA Masters and PGA Championship winner told me, the very first day we met at Shackamaxon, while talking at the practice tee. Doug was considered a big man in stature back in the day at five feet eleven inches tall and about 180 pounds. And he sure did play big, winning a total of 19 PGA events. He was the first of many big names in the game to give me advice that I never forgot.

Jack Mahoney was a handsome, charismatic man with an infectious smile. Everyone wanted to be around him because of his charming personality, love for people and incredible sense of humor. At one time he owned the famous Page Two Night Club in Oceanside, New York. He made that place so famous it was as big as the Copacabana at one time. He was a pure joy to be around and one hell of an inspiration for me. Besides that, he was an incredible golfer and unbelievable hustler.

"When a guy makes a bet with you, he usually starts at his maximum then he goes down. If he says $100, you say, no let's play for $200. Just like that, he's already out of his comfort zone and on the defensive. Find out as much about your opponent as you can. Find his weaknesses and play to them."

Jack was the first golfer to ever share with me a piece of advice that truly encompasses a hustler: "Sometimes you have to lose in order to win."

I had been all about winning every match so that approach threw me, but once I understood it, I must've won at least 100 times with that piece of advice in my mind.

Jack also taught me how to set up a golf course. "If you are playing a low-ball hitter, wet the front of the greens and the green itself so the ball won't roll. If your shot is a draw, put the pins back left on the greens. If you are playing on your home course, cut the greens across so they can't see the differential color of green on the green. On par three holes, put the tee markers to go against his best shot. If you are not on a home course, pay a guy a few bucks to take care of things for you. You need to know all the angles and how to create your edge. Always try to take away your opponent's strengths."

His advice set me up for success. From then on, I always made sure I had the edge going off the tee. It is unusual for world-renowned golfers, to share their secrets, thoughts and approaches to the game of golf, especially when big money is involved. So, why would such great golfers such as these, go out of their way to help me?

I'd like to think they liked me, and they liked the way I played the game. I'm sure that was part of it, but the truth of the matter is, the one common thread that led these men to share with me was my father. They all respected him and thought highly of him. It's that simple.

Deceptively simple. Endlessly simple. That's how Arnold Palmer described golf. The fact that my father's influential web stretched so far and influenced my life at every turn, although hard to comprehend, was quite simple. He was always with me. And he still is today. The stories I could tell about people who helped me because of my father's web could fill a book.

One day, I looked out the pro shop window at Shackamaxon and watched a big powder blue Lincoln four-door convertible pull up. The trunk opened and the top closed at the same time. I said out loud to no one in particular. "Jesus! What a car. I've never seen anything like it! What does that guy do?"

Some guy replied, "He's a TV repairman."

"A TV repairman? What a job that must be! What's his name?"

"Shtuppie Ensburg."

"What the hell kind of name is that?"

"You don't know what Shtuppie is?"

The guy put his fingers up in the form of a gun. "He's a hit man for the mob just like your dad was."

Shtuppie entered the club and caught a glance of me in shop then walked straight up to me. "You're Charlie's kid, right?"

"Yeah. I am."

"Your dad's a good guy. I'd like you to give me lessons." I immediately became his golf instructor. Eventually, we became good friends.

Bernie Yasseen was another well-known hustler and connected guy, who came from the same Jewish neighborhood as my dad. They were good friends from childhood. When he heard I was at Shackamaxon, he made it a point to bring his game. He treated me like his own and took good care of me. Bernie was on the bigger side, with a bit of a belly, large beak nose and balding head. I guess you could say he looked Jewish.

One day he came up to me. "Chuck, we're flying out some guys from Vegas next Sunday afternoon. We'd like you to open the shop on Monday. We'll give you $500."

Even though the club was closed on Mondays, I agreed. "Oh, sure, Bernie, absolutely."

"Be here before seven in the morning," he instructed me.

"Bernie, what time are you going to play? About nine?"

"Just be there at seven, Chuck."

As he asked, I was there at seven. This was the first of many solids that I would do for Bernie. I was happy to do it even though I had no idea what to expect. To help a powerful guy like this was fun to me.

Within minutes a monstrous guy, with slicked back black hair and crocked nose, wearing a white polo shirt and khaki slacks walked in. They called him Tiny. He was part of Bernie's crew. "Give me a dozen balls for Bernie," he ordered.

I grabbed a dozen of our best golf balls off the shelf. He took them all out of the wrappers and put them in his pockets. I got in a golf cart with him and he began to strategically place balls all over the course. That's what's called "salting the course." I started laughing. There was no way Bernie could lose a golf ball, no matter what. He didn't often anyway. He was good.

Just before he left, Tiny told me. "Don't clean Mr. Yasseen's golf clubs. I'm going to take care of them."

I gave him a curious look.

He grinned. "I put a little Vaseline on them."

Bernie cleaned these guys for $15,000. I got my $500 plus another grand for being quiet.

This became a regular thing with Bernie. I watched all his scams and set-ups. I played my role doing whatever I was told. He'd say jump. I'd ask how high. I was paid well for it.

What an imagination these guys had. One guy had a wedge with a concave face. He'd hit the ball 150 yards, then while driving by pick it up with the fixed club and carry it another 150 yards. No one had a clue what happened. The shit he taught me was priceless.

I took full advantage of my new knowledge and started playing for big money. The mob guys loved it. They'd set matches up to give me an advantage and my skills did the rest. I felt powerful. I was good, had an edge and felt safe. Don't get me wrong, I took my lumps with some shady set-ups. But I'd always get my revenge with my powerful combination. Look, there are no rules when it comes to this type of competition – other than gain whatever advantage you can.

In the summer of 1959, my guys set up a match for me at the South Shore Country Club on Staten Island. They told me I was playing three other guys for $1,000 each. This was one of the only times I showed up at a non-home course by myself. I was expecting the guys to arrive soon after. The reason was, we had the first tee time of six in the morning.

When I arrived, the sun was just coming up and a thick morning mist covered the course. There was no one there, so I headed up to the pro shop to check in with the starter, who I assumed was inside. While walking up, I heard a few cars pull up. I stopped and turned around to see if I possibly knew them.

One of the guys got out of his car. He was so big it seemed like forever for his whole body to get out of the car. He wore black slacks with a maroon polo shirt and straw Ben Hogan type golf hat.

He walked around to the back of the car and opened the trunk. I watched him intently.

He reached into the trunk pulled out what looked like a Beretta a gun and put it in his bag. Then he pulled out a small revolver and put it in his waistband. I panicked. I knew this was not going to end well for me. Another guy, dressed in beige khakis, powder blue shirt and dark fedora headed toward me. I waved "I'll be right back. I'm just gonna head to the john!" Instead I made a bee line to the pay phone behind the pro shop.

"Where are you?" She asked furiously.

"Staten Island." I answered in a panic.

"Stall these guys. I'll get somebody over there in 10 or 15 minutes."

Within then minutes, a car came roaring into the parking lot, pebbles and gravel flying everywhere. It stopped right behind the guy's car who pulled out the guns. A tall guy with wavy black hair, dark eyes and bulb nose jumped out of the car yelling. "Where's Chuck?"

Two more guys got out of the back seat with dark overcoats and black fedoras. All three stormed over to the pro shop. Once they arrived I came out from behind the pro shop. The tall guy, who must have been the boss, pointed to me. "You see this kid? He's with us. We're going to ride around with him. If he catches cold, you're dead. If his hair gets mussed, I'm going to kill you."

The two players were shaken to their core. They couldn't hit a shot. I won $2,000. Their idea at the beginning was they would never pay, and they'd drop me if they had to. Even though I won, I needed to show them who I was.

I went nose to nose with guy who had the guns. "Okay, now let's go see your man." I ordered.

They were with Joe Ricabone, the boss of Staten Island – this just happened to be the guy my mom called. Yet another friend of my dad's. We drove over to Victory Boulevard to a gin mill where Joe was. The place was dark, dungy, empty and stank of stale beer. A long mahogany bar ran along the right side of the wall. There were no light fixtures over the bar, just light bulbs maybe half were lit. Under one of them sat Joe facing the door waiting for us.

I approached him and put $1,200 in cash on the bar where he sat nursing a tumbler of scotch. "I appreciate the fact that you sent a couple of guys to help me out of a tight spot."

He pointed to the rest of the money in my hand. "What are you doing with that?"

"I'm going to give my mother a couple of dollars and keep some for myself."

He nodded. "Go ahead, take it all."

Through my teachers, I learned the ropes of not only the game of golf, but the art of the hustle. The ladder was different as there were no real rules. So, you needed protection, which I had. However, at the same time I had to prove I was my own man and stand up for myself when the situation called for it.

For a long period of time, I made an incredible living as a golf hustler. My guys and me were a match made in heaven – or hell – depending on how you look at it. I just wanted to play. They wanted big money. I found out I was playing for $10,000 to $20,000 sometimes. I was told: "Win Lose or draw your money is 10% guaranteed, just for playing."

At first, I was fine with it because I made a mint no matter what, doing what I loved. However, I was doing all the work. I wanted a bigger share.

One cool, windy spring morning, in tough playing conditions I beat a guy for $10,000. The wind wreaked havoc on long shots and I had to play under it at times. It was probably 55 degrees, way too cold for my liking. But, I did my job anyway.

Fluffy, a short guy around five feet five, with grey curly hair that looked like it was fluffed up, hence the name fluffy, who handled the money, gave me my $1,000. He was a small-timer but connected nonetheless.

I was exhausted from fighting the elements during the match and my patience when it came to the money was gone. I kept thinking about it the whole game. I looked Fluffy square in the eyes.

"From now on, my end is 20 percent." I said in a stern voice with wide eyes.

He did not expect this and took a step back. "You got no downside. What are you complaining about?"

"Yeah, I get that, but I'm the one playing. I deserve the 20 percent. I'm making you guys a shit load of money. The ten percent doesn't work for me anymore."

This request turned into a big deal. So, they decided to have it adjudicated through Gyp. We had to attend a meeting at his place in Jersey in a small secret room that had four folding tables and a few chairs.

I knew I wouldn't lose a sit down if he was at the table. At the meeting, everyone fessed up and told him what was going on. Gyp listened and didn't move an inch. Without hesitation, he calmly said, "Give the kid the money." And that was that. From that point on, my take was 20 percent. These low-level gangsters began to understand the power I had behind me.

Yes, I had Gyp behind me, but if I wasn't such a good golfer making these guys so much money, there is no way the ruling would have gone in my favor. They were taking advantage and it had to stop, simply because I deserved it. My performance on the course was helping me step out from behind my father's shadow.

I played with and against so many famous hustlers, pros, athletes and entertainers, if I made a list it would be ten pages long. One was Bobby Riggs, the famous tennis player who played Billie Jean King. He was also a golf hustler. I played him at Bayshore Country Club in Miami on a sweltering morning. The temperature was pushing 100 degrees. I beat him for $400. As we headed to the club house both soaked in sweat, I asked for my money.

He angrily snarled, "Go fuck yourself."

I stepped in front of him. "How about Fuck You! Now, you'll see who I really am."

Back at the clubhouse, I found "Trigger Mike" Coppola, a capo in the Genovese Family, another close friend of dad's and by then, mine as well. Mike was paroled for murder from Rayford Prison to

Bay Shore Country Club with a bizarre twist. He had to stay on the veranda. He couldn't go in the clubhouse or even on the course. So, he'd sit there with is crew and take care of business.

Mike was one mean looking son of a bitch, with a constant nasty snarl, wide nose and beady eyes. People would just look at him and get scared. Mike was sitting in a white wicker at a glass table playing cards.

"Mike," I said, "Sorry to interrupt, but I'm in a spot here. I just beat Bobby Riggs and he's stiffing me."

"Is that right?" He nodded to a few of his guys and they followed me.

Riggs was not a big man, maybe five-foot-three. Two of Mike's guys grabbed him and lifted him off the ground with his feet dangling about four feet in the air. He started moving his legs as if trying to run away. They hauled him right up to the veranda and put him down right next to Mikey.

Mike had a fierce look in his eyes. "Did you just play Chuck?"

"Yeah," Riggs admitted.

"You beat him?"

"No, he beat me."

"You pay him?" Mike asked.

A typical smart-ass, Bobby asked. "What for?"

"Because I said so, you little fucker!"

Bobby got the picture right quick. "I don't have it on me."

"Then go to the fucking bank and get it. Now! Guys go with him," Mike growled.

Twenty minutes later they came back and put the money on the table. I offered some to Mike for his help. With a wave, he said, "Take it all."

As I was leaving he yelled. "You make sure you tell your mother you saw me."

"I definitely will."

"We'll be here if you need anything."

There were a lot of assholes out there like Riggs, who thought just because they had a name, or they had a gun they could get away with anything. When you are in a game with no rules you sometimes needed help. I was fortunate enough to have that. If I didn't I would have thousands upon thousands of dollars stolen from me and I could have ended up dead.

One of the great things about Shackamaxon, it was right around the corner from Rahway State Prison, where dad was. Every Sunday at 11 o'clock in the morning, I would leave the club and go to Rahway to meet my mom, so we could visit him together. While I was away from the course, nobody would ever ask where I was. Everybody understood how important that time was.

If I had a rough time with someone, I always told him. He never reacted emotionally. He would just ask in a calm voice "Is it over?"

By then, it usually was so I would say yes. But, I had to make sure I told him who go involved. Whether it was Gyp, Trigger Mike or anyone else he knew, he'd say. "He's a good man. Stay close to him."

This may not seem like much, but I know it was important to him. He wanted to make sure I was safe. He also wanted to make sure the guys, who were supposed to be protecting me were keeping their promise. Even though they all did, I could only imagine what would have happened to them if they didn't.

Everybody wanted in on the golf hustle. But not everyone had what it took to stay in the game. One of those people was Milton Berle. He hung out at Shackamaxon and golfed a little, usually for big money. Unfortunately, he had his weaknesses. He was a compulsive gambler. He ran up big debts on the course as well as in Vegas. However, for the most part everyone liked him. But, not enough to give his debts a pass. At one point he owed $50,000. He had to pay up. Somehow, someway.

Milton had a famous television show called The Texaco Hour. At the end of the half hour the curtains would close with Milton standing in front of the curtain. He'd yell "Makeup!" Then this rotund guy would come running out and hit Milton in the face with a humongous powder puff.

That guy's name was Fatso Marco, who was part of Gyp DeCarlo's crew. Fatso was given that role and paid $2,000 a week, which went right to Gyp to pay off Milton's gambling debts. Only someone with Gyp's imagination could come up with something like that.

I used to see Fatso every now and then and once I asked: "What kind of guy is Milton Berle?

"He's a fucking pain in the ass. Let that guy gamble with somebody else's fucking money. That's why I'm doing what I'm doing."

"How hard do you hit him?" I asked curiously.

"Hard enough so that he will remember us." Ha!

George Raft, a handsome, famous actor known for playing gangster roles in movies would also pop in to Shackamaxon to play occasionally. The real reason he hung out was to study mobsters to help him in his movies. He modeled himself after a banger named Whitey Krackower and Benny Siegel. He'd imitate and emulate them at every turn.

George knew the score though. He was a class act and a gentleman. He'd always ask. "How's your father doing?"

I'd tell him, "Why don't you just go and see him?"

He replied sadly. "I can't. My reputation…"

I understood, but I didn't. No one would have known.

I played with everyone from entertainers to athletes like: Frank Sinatra, Dean Martin, Groucho Marx, Buddy Hackett, Jackie Gleason, Joe Louis, Evil Knievel, Rocky Graziano, Jake LaMotta, Joe DiMaggio, Yogi Berra, Mike Schmidt, Bill Kenny, and Ted Rhodes. They would call me to fill in the group. I could putt and chip like a burglar. Most of the time I won my individual bets and wound up winning the team's as well. I would go home with $500 to $1,000 every time I played. I loved it.

I can't tell you how many times Gyp DeCarlo would call me and say, "Don't make any plans for the next couple of days."

I would ask, "Should I bring my golf clubs?"

They would fly me everywhere from Vegas to Miami to Palm Springs to play. I won a ton of money, not only for me, but for the guys, with Gyp at the top of the list. I had so much fun and met lots of America's best-known characters like: Titanic Thompson, Dave "the Fireman," Leo "the Mover," Amarillo Slim, George Lowe, Hampton Auld, Ed Furgol, The Fat Man, Mysterious Sam Montaghou, Dick DeMane, Bob Feldman, Jules Gatsey, Tony Pacifico, Chester Sanok, Paulie "The Falcon," Lenny Marinello, "Smiley" Quick and Mike LoBosco. Every one of these guys was featured in a Life Magazine article. I played them all and I'm proud to say I won my fair share of matches.

Besides these course legends, I played with, against and hustled more gangsters than I can remember and almost every one of them had ties to my dad, including mobsters such as Lefty Mafrese, Tony Boy, Richie "The Boot," Harry "The Blade," Paul Vario, Joe Scotto, Sonny Franzese, Tony Ducks Corello, Sam Tattlebaum and Lou and Bill Fugazie, all powerful men with fierce reputations. No matter who won or lost on the golf course, they treated me with respect and always asked about Dad. I always made sure I gave him the message

There is no question, I was having the time of my life. Yet something was off. I had an identity, but I didn't. To the outside world, I was now a top-notch golf hustler. I guess it was not such a bad thing. Still something was gnawing at me. I was still The Bug's son

I hung out almost strictly with mobbed up guys. I was doing some things I probably shouldn't have. I was setting up games to gain an advantage. I was using mob muscle to intimidate guys. I had a huge boulder on my shoulder with an inscription that said, "You cannot touch me."

The deeper I got into this world. The more dangerous it became. Even though I was no mobster, I was acting like one.

With that came not only power, but constantly knowing "the score", knowing what was going on in that world. Things started to change. Changes that caused great concern both inside that world and outside.

13

RADICAL CHANGES

On a sunny morning in May of 1957, I unfolded the New York Daily News to the front page. The headline read: "Frank Costello Is Shot: Ambushed at Apartment Door "

It was like someone cracked me over the head with a baseball bat. That warm spring day suddenly turned dark. I quickly skimmed through the article to see if Uncle Frank was alive. Thank God he was. The gunman fired from close range in the foyer of the Majestic Manhattan apartment building. What I didn't understand was how this professional gun for hire, missed. Either Costello was the luckiest guy in the world, the trigger man was a horrible short, or it was just a message.

I'd been hearing rumblings that the landscape of the Mafia and Combination Mob were changing. But trying to take out one of the original four architects of the Commission was more like an earthquake than a tremor.

There was no way proper mafia protocol was followed. This decision was not approved by Luciano or Lansky. They would have never sanctioned this. It turned out it was greedy, power hungry factions of families joining forces. Their message was clear. They wanted the old-school bosses gone.

That Sunday, mom and I went to see Dad. Not a word was mentioned about it. This was typical dad. What was going on inside of him, I can only imagine. Frank was one of his favorites.

It didn't take long after the attempt on Frank's life for word to leak out that Vincent "The Chin" Gigante got the contract. As a made-man, he had to follow orders. It was that simple. Those orders came from Vito Genovese, who had been at odds with Frank for years over control of what was originally Charlie Luciano's family. Vito did what he wanted to do. He deliberately defied the rules of the Commission and sadly got away with it.

However, what most people do not know, is that Gigante never really wanted to do it. He liked Frank and respected him. I heard this from more than one source. I had also seen with my own eyes Gigante with Frank on many occasions. They were not enemies.

They were anything but. In my opinion, because of how he felt about Frank, he didn't try too hard. Do you really think a known banger like Gigante would miss from that close?

I don't.

After it happened, Frank was called in by the cops for questioning. He was asked the usual questions. "What did you see?" "Did you see anyone?" "Did you recognize anyone?"

His reply time after time was, "I didn't see anything or anyone."

Did he see Gigante? I'm sure he did. However, he steadfastly adhered to the code of Omerta.

I was told that shortly after the police interviewed him, The Chin sent word to Frank to thank him for honoring the old ways. The message was specifically, "I knew you were stand-up guy."

Frank got the message and retired. He was never bothered after that. I am sure Luciano and Lansky made sure of that. Very few top bosses from the original era were allowed to live out their lives to die of natural causes. Three of them were originals: Luciano, Costello and Lansky. Another was my father. The writing was on the wall.

Little did I know what was yet to come.

1957 should have been a good year. At 21 years old, I had just gotten married to a woman I loved dearly less than a year before. Our wedding reception was like the wedding scene from the movie The Godfather. An elaborate and beautiful set up – every bride's dream. All white linens, beautiful floral settings at every table in a magnificent, over-sized banquet room highlighted gold trim and magnificent chandeliers.

A large contingent of the guest list consisted of mobsters, led by: Albert Anastasia, Joe Bonanno and Frank Costello. Out of respect for them, very few pictures were taken, for obvious reasons. There were a few with mom, my bride, my in-laws, uncles, but that was it. The Feds and cops, who were all over the place outside took more pictures than we did.

When it came time for the guests to give their gifts, instead of handing them to my bride and me, my mother took charge. They all went directly to her. As always there was a method to her madness. She wanted everyone to know that whatever the gift was she and my dad would be judging it.

After the wedding we sat at the kitchen table at mom's house and watched her open every envelope. She recorded every gift and who give it in her little black book with comments.

"Joe gave $400. That's not enough." So, she jotted it down.

"Mary and Albert gave $500. That's fine." Again, a note went into the book.

During her next visit with my dad, she gave the list to him. What he did with it I do not know, but I am sure they used it for future reference when other couples got married. That's an Italian thing. It was humorous to me.

I was working at Shackamaxon, a club I loved, making good money as the pro, giving lessons and hustling. It seemed like I met someone new every day; legitimate and nice people. To this day, it is one of my favorite golf jobs. I couldn't have asked for more at that time.

Unfortunately, it wound up being one of the most tumultuous years of my life. Besides all the chaos going on in the mob world, I hit my first major bump in the road on my golf journey. It was due to my association with the knockaround guys.

My mom received a certified letter from a man named Harold Zink. Mr. Zink was the head of the New Jersey Parole Board. The letter stated that my mother and I needed to attend a meeting with him on a specified day and time at the Parole Board Office in Trenton, New Jersey.

I had a sick feeling in my stomach. I could not fathom how this could be a positive thing.

On the appointed day, we made the three-hour drive to Trenton from Queens and arrived as ordered. Zink was a small man barely over five feet tall. His desk was set up on a pedestal, so he could look down at people. The room was not well lit, so it seemed like you were in a hole looking up. His desk lamp was pointed at us as if we were under interrogation.

Zink picked up a huge black book and slammed it on the desk. He opened it to a bunch of photos, leaned over his desk and pointed to two pictures. "Is this you?"

I had to climb on to the pedestal to see. The first was a picture of me teeing off at the first tee at Schackamaxon. The other was me sitting at a table on the veranda with some friends of mine; mob associates. "Yeah, that's me."

He pointed to another picture. It was of me sitting with Ray at a table in the clubhouse eating lunch. "And who's that?"

"That's Ray DeCarlo."

"Who is that?" It was a shot of me standing outside the pro shop talking it up with a guy named Tony Boy.

"That's Tony Boy." I looked at my mom. Her expression was resigned.

He slammed his finger on another face. "Who's that?" Another shot of me no the practice tee with a friend.

"That's Jimmy Blue Eyes." My blood began to boil.

"What do these guys do for a living?" He snarled.

I shrugged my shoulders. "I don't know."

"Do they give you money?" Every question came with a more vicious tone.

"Yeah, all the time."

"What's the juice?'

"What are you talking about juice? I play them for money on the golf course. If I win, they pay me." I shot back angrily. It was as if the gray cinder block walls were closing in around me. I could sense my mom in my peripheral vision, her hands folded in her lap, stock still, listening hard.

"They've never loaned you money or anything like that?' He asked in a sinister voice.

I shook my head. "Absolutely not."

"Do they talk about your father?" Zink continued with his barrage of questions.

"Sure, every once in a while they ask how he's doing." I started to get smart with the guy.

"Where do they hang out?"

"I see that at the golf course. Other than that, I don't know." I yelled back.

He took the book and slammed it shut so hard that his desk shuttered. He gave one of the evilest glares I have ever seen. "Know this! As long as you are at that club, your father is never coming home!"

My mother was visibly upset. I was devastated knowing I had to leave that job. I could not put my dad's parole in jeopardy.

We left the meeting distraught. Mom gathered herself like she always did, then ordered: "Forget the golf course. Bring me to Gyp." We drove straight to Gyp's club in Mountainside, New Jersey.

Mom was out of the car before I had it in park. She stormed toward the door of Gyp's private hideaway tucked in the back of the woods behind a restaurant. Mom made a beeline for the backroom, cutting past empty tables with red and white checkered table cloths and green leather chairs, the smell of stale beer hanging in the air. She breezed past the guard at the office door. The look on her face told the beefy guy to stand aside. She flew through the door without knocking. Gyp was sitting behind his dark oak desk, in is swivel black chair as if he was expecting us.

Trailing, I saw Gyp's face as he a saw my mom's. He raised a wary brow then deferred to me with a blink, so I told him everything that Zink had said.

I ended the story by saying, "I gotta quit and get out of there. I'll give my notice right away. I'll work another week then that's it. I'm done."

"You do what you have to do." He stood patted me on the cheek. "See you on Sunday."

He knew I was going to see dad and that I always stopped at Shackamaxon after we were done finishing our visit with dad. "Bring your mom this time," he added.

The following Sunday, we told my father about the meeting with Harold Zink. He became visibly upset.

Holding the phone to his hear, his face drew sullen. "I'm sorry I put you in that position son," he said in a soft voice.

I could tell how bad he felt. I just stepped aside and gave the phone to my mom.

Right after, we went back to the golf club to put in my resignation. My heart was heavy as I took in the last magical aromas and images of that wonderful place. Mom and I walked into the club house banquet room where Gyp, Toke, Jack Pannels, Sy and a cast of others sat a long table with a pristine white table cloth and red linens. We took spots next to Gyp and told everyone what had happened with Zink. You could hear a pin drop. They were all stunned.

Out of nowhere, without saying a word, Gyp slid over an envelope. "That's for being a good kid."

I gave the envelope to my mom. She took it gently and held my hand for a second. In it was $10,000.

When it was time to go, everyone stood up and gave me a kiss and a hug. They said, "You can always come back and ask us for anything as long as you don't cause the problem."

That was the last time I was at Shackamaxon.

And it was the last time the Mafia and Combination Mob were held in the same light they were when they were originally created. The tumultuous times continued with a revolution that would soon descend into total chaos.

On a crisp October morning a few months later, the headlines of the New York Daily News once again sent me reeling. This time it was more like someone had ripped my heart out of my chest with their bare hands. Al Anastasia Feared Murder: Hunt "Black Glove".

Now Uncle Albert was dead. I jumped up and turned on the television. The story was on every channel. From every angle they showed the pictures of Albert lying on the barber shop floor of the Park Sheraton Hotel on 7th Avenue. I became sick to my stomach.

There was no way this was sanctioned, just like the attempt on Costello. Luciano was in Italy. Meyer was spending lots of time in Cuba. The new family bosses were carrying out their plan: all old school mobsters were to be eliminated.

I called mom. "Do you know anything about this?"

"No." The frailty in her voice told me she was shaken.

"Are you okay?" I asked, concerned.

"I don't want to talk about it."

That was that.

No one came to tell me when it happened. No one called. I suppose because they knew how close my father, mother and I were to him. So, I paid a visit to some friends of or ours. I wanted answers. I deserved them.

Or so I thought.

Yes, Albert was everything the papers said he was: CEO of Murder Inc.; a feared, vicious, stone-cold killer and a self-serving boss. However, he always had Luciano and Meyer Lansky's backing, so he must have been doing something right. To me, he was Uncle Albert. He loved my dad, my mom and me. He always took care of and protected us. He was one of my original golf handlers. I unabashedly loved the guy.

It was obvious no one was safe. The bosses in the states were doing whatever they wanted to do, using any means possible, including paying off men to turn on their bosses. In my opinion, that is what happened with Albert. His bodyguards left him in the barbershop alone – that would never happen under normal circumstances.

When Dad got the news, he seemed to silently buckle under the weight of it. All I remember him saying was, "Things never do stay the same. But radical change is never any good."

From that day on his demeanor was more solemn. He was never quite the same. If he had not been in prison, he would have been involved with that kind of decision and he for sure would have not approved it. I believe he felt guilty about that; just like the attempt on Frank and me being forced out of a job I loved. Him being locked up was having profound effects on people's lives; and he was more and more powerless to protect the people he loved.

I'm sure both of my parents were wondering if anything was going to change for us since Albert was one of our biggest benefactors and supporters. Fortunately, they didn't.

What did change were the mob families. The Luciano family was now the Genovese family. The Gagliano Family became the Lucchese Family. The Mangano family turned into the Gambino Family. The Profaci Family was taken over by the Colombo's. Although the Bonanno family name remained the same, Joe – my Uncle Joe – was phased out and retired to Arizona.

The lure of big money in the drug business was changing the game and changing the rules. Fast. Worse yet, the gangsters themselves started using it and getting hooked, making them even more violent and untrustworthy than ever. Honor disappeared. Protocol was ignored.

Gyp was the exception. He was much younger than my dad and his associates. He was left alone, simply because he was too strong.

It seemed like every single day for months on end there was another story in the newspapers about the Mob. This made it very difficult for Dad during the last seven years of his incarceration. Every time something mafia related came up, his parole was denied. They were waiting for him to talk. Except he never did.

He was asked about a million questions about the changes going on. His standard reply was: "You figure it out."

By this time, there were only two old school bosses left to run things. Gyp DeCarlo and Abner Zwillman. By the end of February 1959, they got to Abner as well. He was found hanging from a ceiling rafter in his basement of his West Orange, New Jersey home. They called it suicide. Everyone knew better. The word was he died at the behest of Vito Genovese.

Abner was the last of the old-school Jewish Mob Bosses, who wanted things to stay the same and he'd made that known on several occasions. That was his death sentence.

Almost all the original bosses were dead. Those that were alive were out of the picture. Luciano was exiled to Italy. Meyer was trying to create legitimate businesses and was left alone. Joe Bonanno was banished to Arizona. My dad was in prison still.

Don't get me wrong, we were still taken care of and none of this craziness affected us, but it was sad to see. Right before our very eyes a horrible metamorphose was taking place.

I needed something I could rely on to take me away from the madness going on in that world. Golf – it was always golf. It's all I had to keep me somewhat sane. On the course or on the lesson tee, I was Chuck Workman the golfer. The sport was the only place I could find peace and carry my own identity despite watching a world I'd come to love crash down around me.

After leaving Shackamaxon, I started giving lessons at The

Cedar Hurst Golf Range. I don't really remember how I got the job, but the place was owned by some legitimate people and a guy named Chapman, who liked me. So, things worked out well.

It was at Cedar Hurst where I first met Jack Mahoney. He came to me for lessons and that is how our relationship started. I worked on his physical game and he worked on my mental game. It was a match made in heaven. I loved Jack from the start. Giving lessons with him was like not even working. I was getting just as much from him as he was getting from me.

One summer starlit night after a long lesson we sat down on the benches together and Jack said, "I opened up a driving range at the Inwood Golf Course, which is like right around the corner from here. How about you come over and be the golf pro?" He asked with that charming, toothy smile of his.

"You're kidding?" There was no way I could say no to Jack. Plus, I knew my business would probably skyrocket.

"Chuck there isn't anyone I would want but you. Your customers will follow you. You're that good."

Jack stuck his hand out to shake mine. That's how deals were sealed back then. A month later, I was at Inwood. The place was gorgeous. The clubhouse looked like the White House with big white pillars in front except the building was made of red brick. The course was a combination of what is called "links" and "parkland" styles. It was a straightforward yet very challenging course. The driving range was meticulously set up. Everything was brand new even the driving range balls.

In no time, my clientele doubled. Jack and I were having a blast, sharing knowledge and hanging out. I even began working part time as a bouncer at his night club, the Page Two Nightclub in Oceanside, New York. This was one of the most popular clubs in the area.

"If you're going to be a bear, be a grizzly," Jack Mahoney told me during another one of his famous speeches to me about golf and hustling.

My problem was that I wasn't satisfied to be a grizzly. I kept taking things to the next level. That wasn't exactly what Jack had in mind. I knew it, but I kept doing it anyway.

When I was giving lessons or playing for fun, I was a

gentlemanly pro golfer. When I was hustling on the course for the mob, I was a dangerous animal, the kind a grizzly would back off from. I was a walking contraction. Gentleman golfer. Mob golfer. Straight guy. Mobbed up guy. Who the hell was I?

I didn't know. And I was starting to worry that I didn't want to find out.

14
AM I A GOOD GUY OR A BAD GUY?

"I hear your father's coming up for parole. He's a murderer!" Tony Marco blurted out in a smart-ass tone at Middle Bay Country Club.

With those words, the fury that continued to burn inside me exploded into a violent inferno. Like gas thrown on a campfire, I could literally see blue, white, yellow and orange flames. With a golf ball in my hand, I curled up a fist and smashed his left cheek. Blood began to ooze out of a cut caused by the blow. I hovered over him just to see what he would do. He rolled around and tried to get up. I kicked him square in the ribs with everything I had. Rage seethed through my pores as he somehow made it to one knee. Bang! I hit him again with a right. He dropped down again with a groan.

Onlookers passing by the first tee their slacks and golf shirts froze. My pulse pounded in my ears.

"Stay the fuck down you piece of shit!" I growled.

He was out like a light. No one came near me, not even my crew. The looks in their eyes said it all: "Yeah, he had it coming, but bad move Chuck."

I started to walk away. One of my guys whispered in my ear, "You should have let us take care of that."

"Someone insults my family, they pay the price. I don't need anyone to fight by battles anymore."

My adrenaline slowly began to ebb. Then the realization of what I did began to set in. I was in big trouble. But I must admit, it felt good. Then that feeling of satisfaction quickly turned into, "Oh shit. I'm done."

Abe Traub, the owner of the club, saw the whole thing from across the clubhouse. He followed me to the pro shop, approached me calmly and put a hand on my shoulder.

"Chuckie, I love you. But, I can't save you this time. You've got to go."

While working with Jack Mahoney at Inwood, it came to pass

that a large majority of my clients belonged to another club called Middle Bay Country Club in Oceanside, New York. They would come to Inwood for lessons then go over to Middle Bay to play.

Several clients said, "What's the sense of us coming over here to take lessons with you when we are at Middle Bay all day long. Why don't you come and work there?"

I was very flattered, and a move there made a lot of sense. However, I did not have an "in" there – or at least I thought I didn't - and they already had a well-known golf pro who had been there for years. Tony Marco.

My guys made it happen. I could have stopped them from throwing their weight around to get me the job by sheer force of intimidation. I didn't. I let my mob influence and my father's reputation go to work for me yet again.

Abe Traub, another dear friend of my dad's, took the reins on this one. Abe was a lawyer, a partner at Doral Country Club in Florida and the President of Middle Bay. He was the guy who made all the major decisions. I have no doubt Tony wasn't thrilled. However, he didn't have a choice. If I was in his shoes, I wouldn't have liked it either. Thinking back, that whole situation was wrong, and I probably should have seen a showdown with Tony coming. My problem was I still wasn't looking at my future. I was too gripped by the past and confused by the present.

After I'd muscled my way in, the members were stuck trying to decide what they wanted to do with Tony because I was taking over all the lessons. He was a good instructor and nice guy. But I was better. The PGA decided to make him PGA President of the Metropolitan Section, a big-time job to help him keep his job at Middle Bay Country Club. He gained a lot of power, respect and notoriety in the golf profession in the Metropolitan region. Regardless of the highly respected job he'd received, he never let go of that fact that he was forced out.

After the fight, I didn't blame Abe Traub for firing me. I took my punishment like man.

So once again, I was out of golf, due to my own stupidity and uncontrollable temper. Slowly but surely, I began to migrate away from golf as a full-time profession. I stayed in the game, playing and hustling, but nothing like before. I lost the spark as well as the drive.

I didn't have a steady job. I was acting like a gangster and being just plain stupid. I was in dangerous territory with a chip on my shoulder and surrounded by gangsters. This was not fair to my family, especially my children.

The timing of this whirl wind couldn't have been worse. Our third son, Kenny, was born at Mt. Sinai hospital in 1962 with a collapsed lung. He needed immediate surgery and we couldn't get anybody to operate on him. I was going out of my mind with worry, so I reached out to the only person I knew could make something happen – Dad and his associates.

He was still in Rahway. My mother had rolls of nickels and we stood in the phone booth at the hospital making calls. We called Rahway and the warden was a man named Pinto, who we later found out was related to friends of friends of ours, which was our in.

They managed to get Dad out of the cellblock and into the Warden's office, where he spoke to my mother – not once but about 15 or 20 times. Every time she hung up she had to call another number then call my dad back. He was telling her who to call and what to say.

Every second was precious. Kenny's life expectancy was less than 48 hours. The folks at Mt. Sinai told us about a specialist in New York, who was the best in the area at this type of surgery. We went crazy trying to find this guy but couldn't reach him. Mom was finally told to call a certain mob acquaintance of ours who could find him.

My mom was picked up by some of my father's associates, who promptly found the doctor and brought him straight to the hospital in a tuxedo. They got him there at around 4 o'clock in the morning. It turned out that Carlo Gambino, the leader of the Gambino Crime Family, was the one who searched this doctor and told him what the situation was. It was his guys who took mom for the ride and who escorted the doctor into the hospital where he immediately performed the surgery, no questions asked.

I am happy to say, Kenny is still alive and well at 56 years old. If it weren't for Carlo and his crew, God only knows what would have happened. I owe my son's life to him. This was another example of the kind of esteem my father was held in.

Even this near-death incident of my son didn't set me straight. Instead of appreciating the magnitude of my family connections, I continued to question my role and play fast and loose with my life. What little golf I was playing, I was losing. It felt like I was dying inside.

Unfortunately, my marriage was faring just as poorly. It takes two for a marriage to work and two for a marriage to fail. I did my damage. I was no saint, that's for sure. It was ugly. I was totally lost. I felt like my world was crumbling around me.

"You have to do the right thing for you and your children," my mom would council calmly.

"That's easier said than done, especially when you don't know what that is."

My dad was out of prison by then and said simply: "You know exactly what needs to be done. Just do it."

"I honestly don't know what kind of man I am supposed to be, which is hard enough. Now, this whole thing with trying to be a good husband is confusing me even more."

I'd never been so candid with my parents. I felt like a little boy lost in the woods. I'm not sure who was more stunned by my admission – my parents or me.

Out of nowhere, Dad said, "Go to Florida and when you come home everything will be fine."

"Your father is right Chuck. Take a break. Go down to Miami and visit Uncle Stevie for a few days," Mom added.

I thought they were simply telling me to take a vacation, to think about things, that being away would help clear my head. As always, I heeded their advice. I was driving through the Holland Tunnel headed to Newark Airport in New Jersey when it hit me.

My father was going to have my wife whacked.

I slammed on the breaks, turned the car around and headed

back to the house at Mach speed.

Blasting through the door, I hollered. "Dad! You can't do that! Please don't!"

He was sitting at the kitchen table reading the paper and calmly replied, "I had the hole dug already and now you're changing your mind?"

Thank God it never happened, but that was for sure the plan. That's how terrible the whole situation between my first wife and I had become. I loved my children and I loved her for being their mother. More importantly, I was no killer.

After brutal and contentious divorce proceedings, I grew even angrier. My brain was ready to explode. I had no direction. For the first time since I started at age 15, I gave up golf. I took crazy jobs and became even more entangled with mobsters.

This identity limbo I lived with was riskier than being a made-guy. I was playing both ends against the middle. When I needed to be legit, I was. When I needed to act like a mobbed-up guy, I did. That's a death wish. That's when wannabe's make mistakes and end up missing. However, no one could touch me. They knew if they did, it would be the end of them.

My last name was still Workman.

Using this approach on the golf course was all about making money. Using it in the legitimate world was just plain stupid. It certainly was not what my father had in mind.

I started working with Harry Serio, who was heavily involved with Local Teamsters Union 478. I used to go to Newark during the labor strikes and do whatever he asked. Every time something bad was about to happen, he'd tell me, "Go wash the car."

That car became the cleanest car in the state of New Jersey.

One time, trucks were set on fire. Another time someone blew up a building. Then some guy got his legs broken. On each of those occasions, I was sitting in the car at the car wash. They purposely kept me away from the bedlam that went down. I wasn't even allowed on the fringe of anything. I was just there on the payroll but barely doing much that mattered, which added to my sense that I didn't matter, that I didn't really have a place in the mob world or the straight world, an outsider.

The problem was I kept behaving like I was a mobster.

Frankie Fask, who my dad gave Montrose Motors to, had a son named Lenny who was just like his dad – always finding some business scam to make a buck. I needed to make more money myself and he mentioned that he'd started a new business leasing out Port-o-Potties. Since they were used at nearly every construction site around, most of which were run by the unions, customers would be easy for me to come by.

I told him, "Let me see what I can do."

Thrilled, Lenny said, "We just started so I could probably pay you about $100 a week. I'll also pay you commission on everyone you lease, like $50 each."

I put in a quick call to my mom. "Don't we know somebody at the construction site at Idlewild airport?" It was being turned into JFK. All the runways were being redone, among other major construction projects.

"Yes," she told me. "There's a guy there named 'Little Gangy' Harry Davidoff. He's with the Teamsters."

I saw Gangy first then met the head of the Teamsters Local 10, who was from the East Side and knew Dad very well. I told him what I was selling. Not only was he interested, he took me around to various other job sites. Within a few hours, I must have sold 150 of Port-o-Potties.

I called Lenny right away. "How many of these portable outhouses do you have?" I asked excitedly.

"We've got 10."

"You need 140 more, Lenny. I just placed 150 for delivery next week at Idlewild Airport."

"Holy shit! How am I going to get them?" I thought he was going to have a heart attack.

"Let's get a truck with a winch and steal them from competitors."

Lenny had no way to buy more but he couldn't turn down the opportunity, so he followed my lead. We spent the night swiping them from job site and within short order placed 90 of the 140 that were needed. Once they were out there, it was a steady stream of income until the jobs were done.

I must've made $7,000-$8,000 in a matter of a few hours.

I understood the law, but I did not respect it. I could think fast on my feet, but I wasn't walking the straight and narrow path, not by a longshot. Except I didn't see any harm in what I was doing. All I saw was profit. It wasn't a matter of ego. It was simply the way my mind worked. You make a call. You make a plan. You make money.

I was really walking a dangerous, razor-thin line. I put myself in numerous volatile situations that could have easily gotten me whacked. I couldn't shake this extraordinary power I had inherited. Nor could I shake the confusion about my identity. There was still so much anger in me.

It was around then that I got a call from one of Willie Catone's men. Willie wanted a sit-down with me. That did not bode well.

Catone was one of those rare gangsters who managed to stay insulated and out of the public eye. If you search for him, only the most accurate mob history books bear his name. Google him and you'll be hard pressed to find a word about him. He was not only a powerhouse and a major player, he was my godfather at one time.

I racked my brain to figure if I had done something specifically that would upset him. I knew I was safe. But I had a feeling I was going to get an earful.

We met up at a little coffee shop and mob hangout. Catone had a thick build and the steady gaze of someone who seemed like he could read your thoughts just as easily as he could have your brains blown out. This was not a man to be trifled with. He swirled a spoonful of sugar into his coffee methodically as he said, "Listen to me, kid. You can come to us for anything. I mean anything. That is as long as you're right. If you aren't or you caused the problem, you are on your own. We can't help you. If you create the problem, we don't want to know you."

I felt like a little kid at the adult table, small and weak under the weight of his words.

"Chuck, you are no fucking gangster. You are going to get called out if this does not stop. If you do, we cannot help you. Capisce?"

I was doing stuff and involved with things I shouldn't have been near. My reputation was growing. My status was so exaggerated that on several occasions young wise guys wanted to ride the coattails of my family name to get ahead. Things were taking a darker, heavier turn.

Not long after my sit down with Willie Catone, I was with Aniello Dellacroce at a gathering of wise guys, a big dinner at a known mob restaurant. Long tables were flanked with made-men who could take their custom-tailored jackets off and relax because they were surrounded by dozens of their own kind. Course after course came out, a meal that would last for hours in the safety of that sort of company. Between courses, Aniello pulled me aside. "Chuck, you came to us because of your father. You stayed here because of yourself."

That was my second warning.

Milty Tillinger, was a dear friend of my dad's and a high-ranking Jewish Mob boss, told me so many times: "You're a golfer kid. Stick with that."

Consider that warning number three.

Number four came from the famous Gyp DeCarlo.

I would often meet up with Ray for lunch or dinner at various places. One restaurant in particular was called La Martenique a well-known, high-end Italian restaurant on Route 22 in Hillside, New Jersey. People would travel many miles to eat there and be seen. Even entertainers like: Frank Sinatra, Dean Martin, Jimmy Durante, Tony Bennett etc. This is where many politicians and mobsters rubbed elbows.

Behind it, in the backyard of was a building called "The Barn". This is where Ray DeCarlo, his crew and numerous other mobsters hung out. It was their clubhouse, just like the Ravenite Social Club, but bigger and classier. His crew and special invited guests hung out there. If you did not receive a special invitation you were not allowed in.

The Barn had their own chef – a guy named Stud – who would cook anything for them. He also played housemaid, caretaker, and watchdog – constantly cleaning, and picking up after the guys. He got paid well, so he was happy. He was a sweet guy, and boy could he cook.

I met so many people there and not just once – on several occasions: Tony Bennett, Frank Sinatra, Milton Berle, Roger Mark, Sterling Hayden, Richard Arlen, and Jimmy Roselli; I can't even remember them all. But, all big-time entertainers, who knew some of our guys would wind up there at one time or another. Many of these guys knew my dad. Some of them were from Brooklyn or the Eastside area we came from.

They all came to either pay their respects, have a bite to eat or do some business. Mobbed up guys had pieces of so many of these entertainers. One guy's job was to make the phone calls to the right people whenever he knew someone big was coming in.

This is where I got called in for a sit down with Gyp.

"You're running around trying to be something that you're not. Your father is your father. There is only one Charlie Workman. You better stop doing what you're doing or you're going to find yourself in trouble and alone."

Right then and there I knew I was destined to be a good guy; wearing the white hat not the black hat. This was that crossroads moment when golf not only became very important again, it became my whole life and reason for being. As had been the case for so many years it was a powerful mafia boss that set me straight.

This is something that just does not happen today. You don't read stories about powerful mob bosses taking someone under than their wing and leading them to a straight, successful and prosperous life. Back then it was a different era. Today's wise guy life is completely different.

I'd had more than my fair share of lucky breaks and people looking the other way on my behalf. Meyer Lansky's son got whacked in 1944 for doing far less than I pulled. Milty Tillinger's son was also killed for not following the rules. Technically, I should not have been treated any different. Somehow, I was.

After all the years of feeling caught between worlds, I finally realized that I wasn't different. I was special. Why else had these men treated me this way? My father's word carried a vast amount of weight, but it dawned on me that they saw something in me beyond the threat of his wishes. They saw promise. They saw potential. They saw a future they wouldn't have.

I finally saw it too and that changed everything.

15
THAT'S NOT ALL YOUR DAD WAS

"Cab Calloway, I would like you to meet a dear friend of ours and our golf pro here at Charter Oaks, Chuck Workman."

I was having dinner one night at the Charter Oaks Dinner Club with some friends, when a guest brought over the one and only Cab Calloway. He was slickly dressed in a white suit and black shirt with a black silk handkerchief in his lapel pocket, sporting his famous thin mustache.

"Cab, Chuck is Charlie "The Bug" Workman's son."

Calloway's eyes lit up like high beams of a Cadillac. "I am so happy to meet you." he beamed.

Unassumingly, Cab pulled out the extra chair at our table and sat down. I had no idea where this was going or what he had on his mind. A waiter brought over a drink for Cab and me another coke. Cab thanked the waiter and turned to me. "Your father was a very special man."

Starting as a teenager, I began to hear stories about him that confused me. I heard them from his closest friends and associates in the mob life and from legitimate, straight people, including entertainers, athletes and businessmen. These were all incredible tales that allowed me to see my father in a whole different light.

From what I was told, he took care of a lot of neighborhood people during the Great Depression. To these people, he was a generous and caring man. They saw beyond his career choice.

"There is something you need to know about your dad that I will never forget," Cab continued. "This is something I have held very near and dear to my heart for many years. If it weren't for your father, there would never have been a Cab Calloway. Your father gave me my start at the Cotton Club while he was part owner. He could have chosen dozens of other entertainers, but he chose me."

My heart swelled with pride as Cab went on. "I came to New York from Chicago in 1928. No one would hire me on a steady basis. That was until I auditioned with my band for your father in 1930. He hired me on the spot and put me on the map. The Cotton Club was the place to be back in the day. Everyone went there. This where many major acts were discovered by the top managers in the business. Being on stage there is how I was discovered."

I sat there mesmerized. The only word that came out of my mouth was. "Wow!"

"I'll tell you something else too. Your dad protected me and looked out for me in every way possible. He made sure I was always safe."

What he meant was, because everyone knew he was with my dad, no one could get their hooks into Cab. He was a free make his own decisions and deals. If anyone tried to lean on him, they would have to answer to my father.

Back then, if an entertainer was managed by a gangster, he would lose a large percentage of his earnings in return for protection and couldn't get out of it unless the guy managing him sold his rights.

Cab took a sip of his scotch. "You know my hit 'Minnie the Moocher?' The one with the chorus that goes hi-de-hi-de-hi-de-ho? The funny thing is I improvised and made that up on stage at The Cotton Club because I forgot the words to the song." He started laughing. "But it became my calling card. From that moment on, my career took off."

Cab explained that he'd heard about my rising star on the golf circuit and said, "Your father played a major role in both of our careers. He always protected us."

Protection is a loaded word in the mob world. It's true that my mom and I were protected while my father served his time. However, a better way of saying it would have been that we were safe.

What people often forget is that both my mother and I often worried about how safe my father was. On the outside, he was both reviled and revered. Being in prison isn't at all like life on the streets, though.

In March of 1952, my dad was transferred from Trenton to the Rahway State Prison Farm. A month later, riots broke out in the prison. The cons took over – setting fires, taking guards hostage, destroying parts of the prison and much more.

All visitors were kept outside across the street. Families of prisoners wanted to see their loved ones. They were screaming for help. Crying. Yelling. Praying. It was hysteria, pure madness. All we could do was watch and wait with smoke and flames coming out of some windows.

The inmates wanted media representation and asked for Walter Winchell. My father hated Walter Winchell. Walter worked with Thomas Dewey, Burton Turkus and Bill O'Dwyer to set up Louis "Lepke" Buchalter's arrest. Lepke was in hiding. Through his close associates, they got word to him that they needed his help. They made up a bullshit story about mob infighting and lots of money being missing. They needed him to calm things down. In return, he would do a very short stint in prison then he would be free. They used Winchell as the bait. Buchalter agreed and met with Winchell, who said all the magic words. Buchalter turned himself in. As soon as he did, they arrested him for first degree murder, among other things. He eventually got the electric chair. Lepke was my father's boss for many years and they were extremely close, which is why he hated Winchell.

The day of the riot, dad took over. Even though he held nothing but contempt for Winchell, he put it aside. He convinced the cons to state their grievances and not lay a hand on Walter. They agreed.

I looked up at a prison window and saw dad stick his head out with a bullhorn in hand. "Send him in! I guarantee nobody will touch him. He can come at his leisure and he'll be as safe as if he was in his mother's arms."

First Winchell's men went in to make sure everything was okay. Then Walter entered the prison. A few hours later he walked back out, unscathed as promised.

Whatever the inmates had to say about the abuse they were suffering at the guards' hands must have had some merit. Soon after, things changed. The atmosphere had less tension and there didn't seem to be as much friction.

There is a book called Inside Out: Fifty Years Behind the Walls of New Jersey's Trenton State Prison by Harry Camisa and Jim Franklin. Harry was a corrections officer at the prison. He states in the book how every time he saw my father, he was clean and neatly dressed in either his prison blues or khakis. He wrote that my dad kept mostly to himself, only mingling with guys who were close to him.

I was told by more than one prison official: "The warden administrates the prison. Charlie runs it."

When my grandfather passed away, the funeral was supposed to be in Brooklyn, where he resided. However, the powers that be would not let my father go to Brooklyn. He was in a New Jersey prison and that was outside of their jurisdiction. As a result, the family decided to move the funeral to Jersey City.

My dad arrived at the wake in an unmarked police car with several cops dressed in suits and ties. He got out of the car wearing his prison blues and shackles on his hands and feet. A raincoat hung over cuffs. He maneuvered his way to my mother and me, gave us a hug and a kiss.

He turned to one of the cops. "Take this coat off me. Everybody knows who I am and where I am. What am I hiding here?" The cop took the overcoat off his cuffed hands but stood by his side the whole time. Dad shuffled over to some of the people who were there to say hello.

After the service, everyone got into their cars for the precession to the cemetery. I opened the backseat door to get into the car to be with mom and dad and quickly noticed my dad was unshackled. Before I could get in, someone grabbed my arm. "You get into the next car, son."

I did as I was told and left my mom and dad in the car with the driver. When we got to the cemetery, the driver drove the car slowly around the entire cemetery like a hundred times. By now, everyone knew what was going on. That was the first time my mother and father were physically together for in well over fifteen years. My grandfather was supposed to be buried at two o'clock. Instead he was buried at four.

A friend of my father's, Georgie Schwartz, who was the head of the Stevador's Dock Hands union, made the arrangements with the cops. Rest assured, that is not something they would have done for anyone else. They knew he wouldn't pull anything, and he didn't.

When I met Cab Calloway, I probably should have realized that dad did help entertainers. It just didn't cross my mind until one evening when mom and I were eating dinner at a restaurant on the East Side on Delancey Street. An unusual looking man with the biggest nose I've ever seen sauntered over to our table with a giant smile. "Katie! How are you? How's Charlie doing?" He gave her a big hug and a kiss. They started to chat.

I interrupted, saying, "I know you. Where do I know you from?

He gave a chuckle. "Your little TV box."

My eyes went bug wide. "You're Jimmy Durante!

"That's right Chuck."

With that, he grabbed a chair, sat down next to me and put his arm around me. He immediately started talking about dad. "Your father gave me a lot of help during my career. He took care of me back in the day."

Jimmy performed frequently at a placed called the Elegante in Brooklyn, New York, which was owned by Joe Profaci. It was famous back in the day. Jimmy was a true gentleman, known for being kind and generous. He did a lot of good things for a lot of people. I think that's one of the reasons he and my dad got along so well. They were cut from the same cloth.

Jimmy gave jobs to guys who came out of the joint or reform school. He'd put them to work in some capacity whether it be driving his car, shining his shoes or running errands. He would often sign for some of these guys when they came out, which meant he took responsibility for them.

It wasn't only celebrities that remembered my parents fondly. Old women would run down from their apartments if my mom and I were walking on Delancey. "Katie! Katie!" They'd come down with this bowls of soup, bread, all kinds of wonderful homemade delicacies. Sometimes line would form of people from all walks of life, who wanted to send regards to my father. It was surreal.

Years later when I'd walk those same streets by myself, I would get the same treatment. People came up to me I didn't even know. I'd get free meals at restaurants so often, I began to feel guilty. I had to stop going to these places. There was Sammy's in the Bowery and Rothman's Restaurant. I would beg them for a check. Their response was the same. "Sorry, Chuck. I can't give you one."

It all came down to the same thing. My dad helped them or someone close to them. I found out that the Rothman's ran into a hassle over condiments, table cloths and other things that were not only made by mobbed-up manufacturers but were delivered by trucking companies owned by the mob.

While visiting my dad one time, my mom mentioned this to my father. This is the message he told my mother to give someone. "These are neighborhood people. They have been good to us. We should be good to them. Leave them alone. They deserve to make a living."

The Rothman's never had a problem of any kind ever again.

I was giving a golf lesson to a long-term client one day when he finally broke down and admitted to me that he'd known my father.

"My friends and I used to play ball. We had a team and your dad would walk by and watch. One day the ball went into a window of the candy store. The guy who owned it took the ball. He was pissed off and told us he wasn't giving the ball back. Your father happened to be coming down the street. He came up to me and asked, what's the matter? I stood up and said to him that guy took our ball and he won't give it back. Your dad walked into the candy store. Not only did he get the ball back, we got a new one and the owner of the store bought us uniforms. We became a baseball team sponsored by the candy store."

"When was this?" I asked.

"About 35 years ago. I never forgot your dad. Why do you think I come all the way from Rockaway just to get lessons from you?"

Once again, I was stunned. "Here I was thinking you were coming to me because I was good."

They say no good deed goes unpunished. For my dad, his good deeds were never forgotten.

He had an affinity for helping anyone that came from his neighborhood. He made it his business to protect anyone who could get hurt or who needed help. Jack Parker grew up on the east side with my dad and was from the Henry Street Settlement House. He was a legitimate self-made guy, who built and owned the Concord Hotel and Resort in the Borscht Belt part of the Catskills on Kiamesha Lake, New York. Jack was a true visionary. On a piece of land that he was told could never hold a golf course, he hired famous golf architect Joe Finger. He told him, "Build me the best and toughest golf course in the world."

That is exactly what Joe did. It became one of the most impressive golf facilities in the country. The list of great PGA professionals who would go there just to play is endless: Ed Furgo, US Open Champion; Jimmy Demeret, the first ever three-time Masters Champion; Cary Middlecoff, who had 40 tour wins including three major championships; Doug Ford a two-time major winner; Jackie Burke a Masters Champion.

The Concord hosted many Metropolitan Regional Tournaments and held the Metropolitan PGA Sr. Championship. The tournament they were best known for was the Metropolitan PGA Pro-Pro Championship, where players would pick their own teammates. A hundred teams entered every event. I won it six times with Roger Ginsburg. Then I won it again with Joe Moresco. I played in eight and won seven.

When I first met Jack, he echoed a refrain I'd gotten accustomed to hearing. "Chuck, if it weren't for your father, I wouldn't be where I am today. There would never have been a Concord Hotel and Resort. When I opened, your dad made it known. Hands off. So, no one tried to muscle in on me. On top of that, it was your dad's idea to send famous boxers up here to train. When that happened, my rentals increased by the hundreds. Every time a big match was coming up, one or both fighters would come here to train. I wound up building a fully equipped gym and boxing rings. It was a huge hit! All the big-name boxers trained there: Muhammad Ali, Rocky Marciano, Rocky Graziano, - you name it. Most boxers back in the day were owned by the mob. In a sense your dad was helping them and me. He gave the boxers a great place to train to help his associates and he increased The Concord's business."

Then there was Paul Grossinger. He and dad not only grew up together, they were best friends. Paul was another legitimate successful man. He built and owned the famous Grossinger's Catskill Resort.

When Paul started building the resort, he told my dad. He wasn't looking for help. He just wanted to let him know what he was doing. My dad told him: "Build it. I will make sure there is no interference."

That was when strikes were running rampant due to nonunion workers working on job sites. My father made sure Paul never had a single labor problem and the only time he was approached by a mobster was for a room or a tee time.

If my father was merely a notorious hitman, a thug, would any of this have happened?

I doubt it.

What these people did for my family because of my father. Nothing was done out of fear or due to a debt. They did it because they wanted to. There's a big difference.

Little did I know that this goodness – which truly defined him as a man - would eventually become a trademark of mine. Once I was established and became my own man I unknowingly began to inherit my father's affinity for the underdog. After I'd resolved my confusion and anger, I focused on the community, kindness and mentorship.

If there was ever a dichotomy, it was my father. To be honest, it drove me nuts. It made me feel like I knew him the way you know a movie star, from a far rather than in person. I still had many questions. I needed details. I set out to find the truth. Little did I know, I would get more than I bargained for.

Cab reached out and touched my hand. "I want to say thank you to your dad. Please tell him that. And tell him how much I love him."

"I will do that."

He continued. "His driver...I forget his name, would drive me everywhere. He brought me to the club. He brought me home. He took me wherever I needed to go. I never felt safer. He was a good man too.

"You're talking about Benzo." I reminded him.

"Yes! That's his name. He was a great guy."

Ben Orlinsky, otherwise known as Benzo, was dad's driver and bodyguard for many years. They knew each other since they were eight years old. He was loyal to the core, a great guy, but a real bad ass when he had to be. He was the perfect fit for my dad. Like dad, he always dressed to the nines. Their personalities were the same;

quiet but dominant.

I met him for the first time with my mom in the Garment Center, when I was around 18 years old. I think my mother and father set it up, because it was a bit too convenient.

"Chuck, this is Benzo. He and your father grew up together. He was your dad's best friend and driver for many years." My mom told me.

Benzo was a handsome man, with striking features, dark eyes and slicked back black hair. In my mind, Benzo was an extension of my father and my heart swelled. He smiled at me and extended his hand. We shook hands hard and he gave me a big hug. "I am so happy to finally meet you Chuck. I always wondered if I would ever get the chance."

I immediately liked him and could see why he was so special to my dad. "Nice to finally meet you too." I said smiling big.

"Your father is a special man. I loved him then and always will."

I was elated to hear words like this. "He loves you too Benzo." My mom replied for me.

"You need to know some things about your dad." He stated poignantly.

I gave curious look. "Like what?"

"First and foremost, when your father was arrested and eventually went away, I could have easily gone with him. But, he never so much as mentioned my name. No one knew who I was, never mind my association with him. In other words, your dad made sure I was kept out of prison."

I thought about that for second. It resonated with me.

"We grew up together. But, when I was down and out, your father took me in and put me to work immediately. He stepped out for me and I'm not the only one."

"What do you mean?" I asked.

He pointed in general around the entire block. "I can easily name 15 to 20 guys on this street who wouldn't be here if it weren't for your father."

"Why what did he do?"

"What did he do? He set them up in business."

"And what was his end?" I thought I was so smart.

"His end? His end was nothing. He did it out of the goodness of his heart. That's who your father really is."

"So, he didn't get a cent?"

"Not one! He not only set guys up in business, he got countless guys jobs, when times were bad and not only for hoodlums, but straight people. When he made a call to a guy and said, "When I send you a guy who needs help or a job make sure he gets it. Lots of guys did this with ulterior motives. Your dad didn't. That's how you need to remember him."

16
ABOVE THE LAW

There is nothing like the crisp scent of a golf course early in the morning – the slightly metallic aroma of fertilizer combined with freshly cut grass and morning dew. That smell can bring me right back to the day right before Dad came home in the summer of 1963.

I was around 28 years old and playing a friendly round with a retired police officer named Eddie Egan at Commack Golf Course in Commack, New York, who I had played with several times before. He was of Irish descent; but a man's man for sure. Tall in stature he commanded respect. He was a straight shooter, a good golfer and fun to be around.

I liked him a lot. He was extraordinarily nice to me and always went out of his way to say hello. Honestly, I could never figure out why.

"Chuck, I have never told you this before, but I feel it's time," Eddie said as we were about to tee off on the seventh hole. "I was one of the police officers assigned to your dad's case from the moment he turned himself in."

My jaw dropped. "You're kidding me?"

Eddie shook his head slowly. "I was in the middle of a lot of things that went down"

My heart started racing. I couldn't believe what I was hearing. I looked down the long fairway, wind rustling in the distant trees and tried to regain my composure.

"How much do you know Eddie?" I asked with burning curiosity.

"Enough to set the record straight on a lot of things."

I was stunned. "So, what was your role in all of this?" I asked, looking up into the sunny sky trying to pick one of the millions of questions that were firing through my brain

Eddie took a deep breath, as if to fuel the story to come. "My main assignment was guarding Tannenbaum and Reles"

It was if I was hearing him under water. The words seemed muffled through time and history.

"Chuck, there are two types of men in this world. Stand up guys, like your dad, and cowards like those two. Tough guys when they had a gun in their hand. When the tables were turned, they cried and sang."

"I don't get it. They were supposed to be his friends."

Eddie picked up his tee after his shot. "There are no friends when you're facing the electric chair."

"My dad was too, but he was smart enough to not only work around it but do his time."

"They could have done the same thing. Just did the time, but they were afraid of that too. I don't care what side of the law you are on. No one has respect for chickenshits like that."

I fell silent as I teed up my shot, a long dog leg left. Somehow, I put the ball in the fairway not really thinking about what I was doing. When we got to my ball, I spoke up again. "I heard Tannenbaum was left alone."

Eddie nodded slowly. "Unfortunately, yes. From what I understand that order came from up high up amongst your father's associates."

"Why? He should have been killed!" I yelled with fire in my eyes. Other players glanced in our direction then averted their gazes.

Eddie squared his shoulders with mine. "He should have. They just wanted it all to stop, to take the heat off." He paused then cleaned off his five-iron. "However, one person got the best of him."

I took a step back. "Who?"

"Your mom." Eddie approached his ball for a shot to the green and chuckled. "You don't remember do you? Coney Island?" He started to laugh.

The memory came hurtling back to me. "That day we went to Coney Island and my mom beat the shit out of some guy with her shoe?"

"That's right."

"That was Tannenbaum?"

Eddie flashed a smirk. "It sure was. And after that he disappeared, supposedly ended up in Atlanta or something. Nothing got by your mom. She was as tough as your dad. A true Workman through and through."

"Well, it's probably better that I wasn't old enough. Because I would have killed that son of a bitch!"

"Your mom almost did."

Eddie and I stopped at the tenth hole to grab a bite and talk more. We ate hot dogs. Eddie had a beer and I had a coke.

He went on to explain that Abe had been working with Thomas Dewey for months, helping to build cases against his fellow gangsters, including my dad, Lepke Buchalter, Charlie Gurrah and others. When the time was right, Reles finally turned state's witness. Because of him, my father received life in prison, Lepke got the electric chair and Gurrah went to prison, where he was killed when someone shot him up with air bubbles while in the infirmary.

I know for a fact, that Abe made up the story about my father to save his own ass. He was not there. He was not a witness, nor did he have firsthand knowledge of it.

As Eddie finished his beer, I asked, "Were you at the hotel that Reles was staying at when he fell out the window?"

"Yeah, I was there." He leaned in close to me and whispered. "Chuck, that was no fall. That rat got exactly what he had coming to him."

My jaw dropped. A feeling of justice and satisfaction washed through me. The cops on that detail gave him a little help out that window. Finally, someone paid for what they did to my father.

Eddie put his hand on my shoulder. "I'm sorry. I wish it would have happened to him sooner."

This is how Abe "Kid Twist" Reles got the name and a book written about him called "The canary who sang but couldn't fly".

Did the cops do this for my father the hit man? I honestly don't think so. They did it for Charlie Workman, the man.

I didn't know what to say, but I was truly grateful. Not only for what these guys did, but for him telling me to truth. This was the beginning of me gaining some closure.

This also spoke volumes of how members of law enforcement, especially local cops, felt about my father. They had a great amount of respect for him despite his Mob ties. He may have been a killer, but he was much more than that. He had to be, for them to feel this way and step in like they did with Reles.

The entire fiasco that surrounded my father's trial is something you would see in a movie. In the end, it was a severe blow to him as well as the entire mob syndicate. The code of silence, which the Sicilian Mafia calls "Omerta," was broken by two high ranking Jewish gangsters, Tannenbaum and Reles.

The Combo and the Mafia were shaken to their cores. No one saw it coming. Not only did these men turn, they turned on a friend. If dad could be hung out to dry, no one was safe.

The breaking of Omerta – considered a cowardly and incomprehensible act – was an automatic death sentence. Tannenbaum and Reles had to go. But, with so much heat being put on the mob, acts of vengeance had to be methodical, well planned and possibly even avoided.

I learned even more about these stool pigeons through things I read and from some close associates of my father's. However, those that I talked to were so disgusted with Tannenbaum and Reles that they didn't even want to talk about them. I was never told the gory details. All that was clear was that they wanted to save their own asses. Weren't they all supposed to live by the same rules of the road?

I was only five when my dad was taken away. Those first seven years of what my parents went through were blurry other than what I had read and heard. The contradiction of it all was almost incomprehensible. Eventually, I learned that what they endured was not only a travesty of justice, but extreme abuse of power at the highest levels of law enforcement and government.

It all started with the prosecution team assigned to my father's case. Thomas Dewey, Burton Turkus and Bill O'Dwyer, truly believed they were above the law. And I guess, in the end, they were.

The Schultz murder happened in New Jersey. Their prosecution team was supposed to be, in charge of the investigation. Thomas Dewey, who as a special prosecutor in New York, hired to specifically destroy the mob, changed all of that. Somehow, he managed to swindle his way across state lines and take over the case. This was unheard of. How he pulled it off, I can only imagine. I read and was told that when he approached the State Attorney of New Jersey, they had no idea who my dad was, never mind his involvement. Their investigation was on-going, and my dad was not part of it. That all ended when Dewey and his crew flipped Tannenbaum and Reles.

The trial was held in New Jersey with Dewey and his team blazing the way. My dad was confident he would beat the case. The record shows he'd had an ironclad alibi. A dear friend of his, Louie Cohen, testified under oath that my dad was working for him that night.

This did not sit well with the prosecution team. As the story goes, Bill O'Dwyer dragged Cohen into the police station and had a closed-door meeting. He threatened to charge him with all kinds of crimes and throw him in prison for a long time. He bullied him into going back into court to recant his testimony. This is how desperate Thomas Dewey and Bill O'Dwyer were to put my father away. Between the two stool pigeons and Cohen, the odds were stacking against my dad.

Finally, there was the straw the broke camel's back.

One morning as my mother entered the courtroom, she said hello to my father. This was before Cohen even had a chance to go back on his word.

Dewey jumped out of his chair. "Judge! I want her locked up as a material witness!"

My dad went crazy! If the guards had not held him back, he probably would have killed Dewey right then and there.

This was quite a play of intimidation and Dewey knew it. He hit my father where it really hurt: my mom. For the record, you cannot force one spouse to testify against another. However, with all the power Dewey was wielding, he would have for sure thrown my mom in jail, even if it was for a day.

Now that was being held over my father's head. Then my dad's attorney, Harold Kessler, informed him that Louie Cohen was going to take the stand and recant his testimony. They all knew he was going to lose.

Their strategy had to change. The choices were clear. Continue with the trial, probably lose and get the chair, or change his plea to non-vault. In New Jersey in the 40's, that was not an admission of guilt. It was just no defense. The sentence for this plea on a murder charge was life in prison with the possibility of parole after 12 ½ years.

The decision was to immediately switch his plea to non-vault. This took the electric chair off the table, ended the trial immediately and prevented my mom from being thrown into jail.

Everyone truly believed he would serve his sentence and be sent home. As they took my father out of the court room, he told my mom, but more so, to the reporters, because they were badgering him: "See you in about 15 years." He figured it would take a few rounds with the parole board before he was set free.

For one of the only times in his life, he was wrong.

As expected, the first few times dad came in front of the parole board, he was rejected. What did not make sense was the amount of time they kept adding to his sentence. Usually its six months, a year, maybe two. They were adding three, four even five years.

*****

Circa early 1930's: Charlie "The Bug" Workman in his prime in Murder Incorporated

Dad and me Miami, Florida 1935

Dad and mom having fun in Miami, 1935

October 24th, 1935: Dutch Schultz slumped over a table after a mortal gunshot wound at the Palace Chop House, Newark New Jersey. He expired 20 hours later. A bad man was taken off the streets: one who wanted to kill law enforcement.
Daily Record Headline of the Shooting.

Dad and me Miami Florida 1937

Dad 1938: Brooklyn, New York.

Dad 1938, Hot Springs, Arkansas.

Mom and Dad, Miami FL 1938

The family. Rockaway Beach 1939

Me and Dad. Brooklyn 1940

Dad on the horse he saved: Chief, 1940.

Dad just a few days before his arrest March 1940

Charles (The Bug) Workman (right), got life as Schultz's murderer, but mystery remains unsolved to so-called "insiders."

Dad, the day he turned himself in, after the police officer, seen here handcuffed to dad, gave him 48 hours to get his affairs in order.

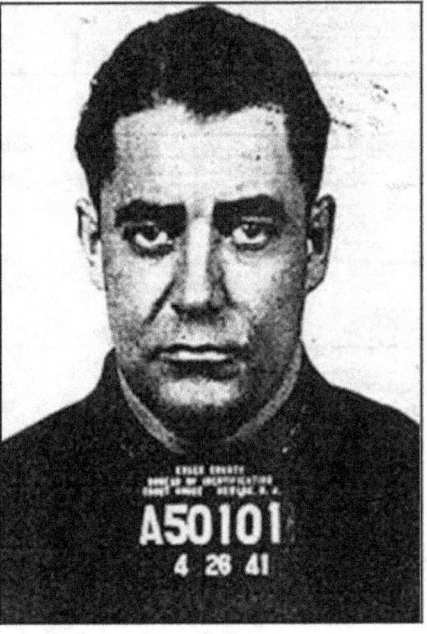

Dad's official front mug shot. March 1940.

One of the first golf pictures of me taken at Oak Hills Country Club
in 1950. I was only 15 years old
the first golf pictures of me taken at Oak Hills

One of the only photos my dad ever allowed taken of him
while in prison. Wearing one of his famous
white-on-white shirts, 1961.

After 24 years, Dad walks out the front door of Trenton State Prison. March 11, 1964.

Page one of dad's New Jersey Certificate of Parole.

Dad at my cousin's wedding in 1966.
When he walked into the reception hall,
the band stopped. Everyone stood up and gave
him a five-minute standing ovation

The Champ – Rocky Graziano in 1968 with my three sons

One of my favorite pictures.
Me with Ken Venturi at the 1974 U.S. Open Championship

Dad, my son Scot and mom in 1975.
This is when dad's health began to decline.
It is one of the last pictures ever taken of him
before he passed.

Teeing off at the Long Island
Open 1977.

Elyse and my wedding at
Charter Oaks 1977.

Charter Oaks 1977   Fox Run, formerly Charter Oaks, 1986

Getting ready to start at the 1986 Sr. PGA U.S. Open
Scioto Country Club, Columbus, Ohio.
I went into the final round in 2nd place.

Bethpage Pro Shop 1987, right after I took over.

Front cover of the Met Golfer
Magazine May 1987

Bethpage 1988

Bethpage Skins Game 1988

My dear friend and PGA Travel Partner: Quinton Grey

Jerry Pate, Elyse and Me, Bethpage 1990

Official PGA Tour Picture: 1990

Me and my caddy. Portugal Spain 1990

My official PGA Sr. Tour Autographed Photo 1990

Golf Digest Photo 1991

Walking up the 18th Fairway to a heartfelt standing ovation at the 1991 Nynex Tournament, Sleepy Hollow, New York

Elyse and I at the Azores in 1991

Unforgettable photo of Me and Lee Trevino (See back cover)

Chi Chi Rodriguez putting on a trick shot show At Bethpage 1992.

PGA Stop, Cerington, Kentucky 1992

Receiving the prestigious Jewish Man of the Award, in 1992. One of my proudest moments, as a man, to this very day.

Elyse and I traveling the PGA globe. Japan 1992

Charity Event at Lido Country Club 1993. We raised over $75,000 for Make A Wish Foundation

Me putting on a little show at Marina Lakes Country Club, Florida

PGA Photo: 2002   Giving lessons to PGA Player
Jesse Smith 2004

2015

*****

At first, it just seemed like he was unlucky. Soon though, everyone figured out what they were trying to do. They were trying to break him – get him to talk about anything concerning his mafia life or his associates. What they didn't count on was the fact that he was unbreakable.

It seemed like every time my dad was up for parole a mobster made the front page of the newspaper. Then it would start all over again. For instance, in October of 1957, Albert Anastasia got killed. Dad just happened to be up for parole for the 14th time, three weeks after the hit. The parole board started hammering him with questions all over again.

"You guys are the law. You go find out. I don't know anything," he told them defiantly. With that, he got up and walked out.

In total, he was rejected 15 times. He never bent or broke.

It was like one big game to them. Yet the Warden at Rahway during those later years said to us. "Geez, if I had a couple of guys like Charlie Workman, I wouldn't need any guards and I wouldn't need guns either. There would be no problems at all."

That was the kind of impression my dad made, no matter where he was.

Years later, a tell-all book was released by Burton Turkus, one of Thomas Dewey's Assistants in my father's case. He played a prominent role not only in my father's ordeal, but in making sure he was rejected parole, especially in the early years. The book he wrote was called "Murder Inc."

In it, he penned something to the effect of: "Charlie Workman was one of the most unusual guys I ever met. If I ever had to have a partner in something, he would be the guy." He also wrote that he enjoyed talking with my dad and liked him. "He would have been a great friend but a mortal enemy."

He admitted that my dad, while he was still in prison, volunteered through the Secretary of the Navy, Harold Simpson, to go with a death squad of other "lifers" and kill Hitler. My father's plan was to take five other "lifers" with him and get the job done by dropping behind enemy lines. He was turned down, but of course

Turkus left that part out of the book.

That's another thing that was never acknowledged about my dad and his associates. They were all extremely patriotic. They would do anything for the country they loved. And believe me, they had the means to do it. Their network and influenced reached all over the globe.

After reading mountains of books and articles and watching hundreds of movies, I can say with certainty that it is very rare anyone gets anything right, never mind a whole story. The information and the facts are convoluted, false or made up. I guess you can call that literary license. Most people don't know the difference.

But, when you've lived it and know the details it's an insult as well as a heartbreak. I don't know who these people talk to, but it certainly was not the men that I knew and who helped me during those years. Today especially, it boggles my mind how new information comes to light when all these men are dead.

There was an old movie about the killing of Dutch Schultz, called "Murder Inc." which starred Peter Faulk, Richard Widmark and Henry Morgan. In it, they rewrote history and had my dad being killed, which was a million miles from the truth. We retained a lawyer, who wrote a letter to the producers and director of the movie. We forced them to change the ending, unless they were willing to pay the rights to use my father's name and image. They changed the shooter to a black man, who the mob shot when he got into the get-away car, which is absurd.

Even well-known authors who are supposedly regarded as top-notch Mafia aficionados get it wrong. In almost all cases, their information is off-base or downright lies. They never talked directly to the men involved. They talk to third fourth or fifth generation people who knew nothing about what happened or offer hand-me-down tales that have been twisted out of proportion with each retelling.

No matter what any other book said or implied, my father talked to nobody. That's how I know most of these books, especially Tough Jews, is full of crap. The book reads as if my father talked to the guys that were mentioned in the book. That was an outright lie.

The bottom line is the stories are simply not correct. They use their literary license to sell a lot of books, so people believe them. Not one of these big-time mob authors ever got a word out of me. Not one. Most of them never even approached me. And Dad would never give an interview to anyone.

If they would've done their homework, they would've found out that I'm still here.

The only time my father made any comments about anyone that was involved with that life was when I told him someone had died, or someone went to prison. His response was usually brief and centered on what he thought of that guy. For instance, if he didn't like the guy, he'd say, "He was a rat bastard. He's now where he supposed to be."

If he liked the guy he would say something like, "Oh, that's too bad. He was a good guy." That was the extent of any conversation that had to do with the mob or his associates. It was as close to small talk as the weather. That was just my father's way. He did not speak of himself, his work or his Mob affiliates. To do so would have disrespected them, but more so, him.

When I told my dad that Albert was gone in 1957, all he offered up was: "That's a mistake. They ganged up on a good guy. Things are going to change. That was an inside struggle. It should have never happened."

All the truths I learned about dad – from who he was as a man to how Dewey steamrolled him using any means necessary – helped me gain clarity and perspective as to what really happened. Slowly but surely, I came to grips with all the mass confusion and chaos that was my own family history. When my father was finally released from prison after the sixteenth parole hearing, it made it easier for me to accept him with open arms.

17
TRUTH AND ACCEPTANCE

Ben Siegel was very close to my dad. They had known each other since childhood and grew closer as they worked the streets of New York's east side, eventually taking the same turn in the road that led to the life of a mobster.

My mom absolutely loved Ben. He was one of her favorites. She typically didn't let on to that type of thing, but Ben was the exception.

To me, he was Uncle Ben. He played a prominent role in my childhood up until dad went away. I was so young, that I don't really have any memories of doing things with him. I just remember him, like a warm, constant presence watching over me.

On June 21st, 1947, only a few months after I found out the truth about my dad and just before I finally decided to go see him, I was sitting at the kitchen table with my mother eating breakfast. She was reading the New York Daily News then suddenly, her entire expression changed. She let out a slight gasp, something I never saw her do, and put her hand to her mouth.

"What's wrong mom?" I asked concerned.

She slid the newspaper over to me, so I could read the headlines. "Bugsy Siegel Murdered."

"This could certainly change things." That was all she said.

She was referring to the landscape of the mob, my dad's standing and us being taken care of. Benny played a major role in many decisions. Because of this senseless murder, my father lost his friendship and some respect for Meyer. He had only been in prison for six years at the time and was convinced Lansky could have avoided it through a sit-down. There was a lack of a reasonable voice when this decision was made.

Dejected, he told my mom during one of her visits: "It should have never happened."

Dad was the type of guy who felt like he could do anything. I know he felt like he could have helped, even stopped it, if he were not in prison. Just like he did for countless others.

With Ben gone, I leaned on Gyp DeCarlo even more. He was a second father to me and

I learned more about being a man during those years than any other period in my life.

One day before dad came home, we were having lunch as we often did, and I asked, "Gyp, why are you doing all of this for me?"

"I wouldn't be here if it weren't for your father." He sipped his coffee and spoke as if he was taking about somebody else's past, rather than his own, an estranged memory.

"We all went a certain way and became very good at what we did. We came from the same place and cared about one another. My reputation in that world took longer. Your dad had more responsibilities than me. Because he became so good at what he did, his reputation in that life became one of honor and respect."

Gyp went on, a heavy evenness in his tone. "Just because your father did what he did, does not mean you have to wear a black hat. You can wear a white hat. Be a good, respectful, straight guy. Who your dad was and what he did had nothing to do with you."

This was a sentiment that was echoed to me repeatedly by some of the most powerful and feared men in the country.

The renowned and much-feared Rusty Rastelli once told me: "I wouldn't have made it to my middle ages if it weren't for your father."

He had been the head of the Bonanno Family and he was one of the bosses who got caught up in that whole Donnie Brasco sting. He had a reputation second to none when it came to gangsters. He was decidedly dangerous.

"Whenever I'd see your dad walking down the street, I'd duck into an alley way. Even though we were close, and he took care of me, I never knew who your father was looking for or what his intentions were. I was never afraid he was after me. I just didn't want to get caught in any crossfire. Your father was a type of man that when he told me something was going to happen it happened. And most of the time it was to protect me. If I had two or three of him, we would run the country."

Though it was strange to learn about my dad second-hand, I must admit, I soaked up every one of the stories about him. He was a hard man to get close to, but the tales made me feel like I understood him better than he allowed me to. They were my lifeline to the myth, the legend that was my father.

Willie Rudini, yet another powerful gangster, was very tight with Dad and proudly told me: "Your father was very special to me. He always looked out for me even though I was not part of his crew. I will never forget many years ago, I had a job to do. It was in a pool room. Your dad was sitting getting his shoes shined reading the newspaper. I walked in. Your dad immediately pulled up the newspaper to cover his face. I went upstairs and took care of my business. When I came down, your dad still had the newspaper up. I walked out."

Thirty years later, my dad and I were walking down 59th Street near the Coliseum. Willie was the dock boss there and upon seeing my dad, he acted like he had a newspaper in his hand and put his hands over his eyes. They both started cracking up. After all those years, neither of them forgot.

"Your father owned these streets," Willie told me. "He did things for so many people in this neighborhood, young and old. Geez, all of the old ladies loved him!"

Men from every corner of the mob echoed this sentiment, including Paulie Vario, who was portrayed by Paul Sorvino in the movie Goodfellas. Just like in the movie, Paulie, although as powerful as they come, was very soft spoken and full of wisdom. Whenever we'd talk, it was never about that life. He'd ask about mom and dad, then the conversation would change to life and golf. I even gave him a few lessons.

"Use your talent Chuck. That's how you are going to make it. You will make us all proud."

My talent for golf seemed small and insignificant to the titan my father was, but the support I felt from the men he ran with constantly reminded me that despite the many differences they shared, specifically in ethnicity and religion, they worked together.

They protected each other. And they respected each other.

The Combination Mob was specifically created for the Jewish mobsters and the Irish. The general feeling was that these men were valuable. They could help make money, provide much needed muscle and most importantly get the mafia into legitimate businesses. It gave the upper echelon ways to create direction. Over the decades, stories, mob folklore and gossip have solidified into fact, but I can tell you from first-hand knowledge that only a fraction of what people have read or heard is true.

The legend of Benny's hit was that he was gunned down because he and Virginia Hill were skimming money from the funds designated for building the Flamingo Hotel in Las Vegas. There was also a rumor out there about a love triangle gone wrong. The truth of the matter is, it had nothing to do with any of like that.

"I really liked Ben," Harold Konigsberg once confided to me while we were sitting in his hideaway office in northern New Jersey. He was leaning back in his brown, leather, swivel chair and his size 14 feet up on his cluttered dark oak desk. "We grew up on the streets together. We were very close and did a lot of things together. What happened to him was pure bullshit. It was his fucking temper that got him whacked. That's it. He broke a golden rule of the mob. You can't lay your hands on a 'made' guy without permission from the commission."

It had been ten years since Siegel's murder and the fire in Harold's eyes proved he was still furious over it.

"He beat up a made-guy?" I asked with a curious look.

Harold put his feet back on the floor, pulled his chair forward and leaned his huge frame on the desk. "Back in the mid 40's, a few years before he was whacked, Ben and I were hanging out at the Copa, having a great time. Girls, drinking, dancing, the works. I had to go up to the office upstairs to get some money, so Ben followed me. I opened the office door and there was this Italian made guy with this gorgeous dame and his pants down. Shit like that went on all the time with the show girls. Except this was no regular show girl. It was Ben's girl. He and Virginia Hill were on and off and he did what the hell he wanted anyway. But everyone knew this girl was with him, even the Italian guy.

Ben went out of his mind. The guy never got the chance to pull his pants up. He beat the living shit out of this guy. It was one of the most vicious poundings I have ever seen. I watched it with my own eyes and froze at first. I quickly realized, I had no choice but to step and pull Ben off this guy. If I didn't do that, he would have killed him."

Harold rubbed his hands hard through his thick, slicked back hair as if he was aggravated and shook his head. "That was his death sentence. He broke a major rule."

Stunned, I sat perfectly still and searched for the right words. I kept my eyes on Harold as he stared out the window. I blurted out the first thing that came to mind. "Yeah, but the guy was messing around with Benny's broad. Isn't there a rule about that too?"

Harold shook his head as his nostrils flared. "That only applies to wives Chuckie. You can't lay your hands on another guy's wife. Ben wasn't married to this girl. That's why the guy didn't get in trouble."

I always felt bad for Uncle Ben, but I now felt just as bad for Harold. I knew he was angry, so I respectfully kept calm and let him have his reflection of a horrid time. I knew he wanted to get it all out, so I asked. "So, what happened after that?"

"He put in a beef with the Commission, that's what the fuck happened." He shot back without moving a muscle.

"Wait. He didn't get killed until 1947 after the Flamingo was up and running." At least I got something right.

"At the first sit-down, Meyer stepped out for Benny, bought him some time hoping the whole thing would just blow over. He said something about getting the Flamingo done. The problem was the Italians, especially this guy, would not let it go. The beef was reinstated three years later. This time, it went his way. I don't know how or why, but he got the blessing he needed. Meyer was part of it, so was Charlie Lucky. If anyone could have called it off, it was Charlie. But for some reason, he let the decision stand. I guess rules are rules. No exceptions. There was nothing anyone could do about it."

I couldn't believe what I was hearing. In shock my mouth

opened, but I caught myself. I put my head in my hands but snapped out of it. "So, who did it?"

"Didn't ask." Harold shrugged. "Once I heard, I didn't want to know because if I did, I probably would have taken them out myself."

My mind rolled back to that time just after I found out the truth about dad. A few months later some gorgeous woman came to our house. I was outside playing in the yard, but Mom would not let her in. She wouldn't even open the door."

I mentioned the incident to Harold and he smirked. "That was Virginia Hill. Your mom called me right away. That woman was a total whack job! If anyone took money, it was her."

"Why did she come to our house?"

"Looking for sympathy maybe. She knew how close Ben was to your mom and dad, so I guess she wanted to talk to another woman or maybe have your dad and mom be on her side if something came of it."

"Why didn't Mom talk to her?" I began to realize there was a lot more to this than I ever imagined.

"Your mom always believed that somehow, someway Virginia caused it. On top of that, she never liked her to begin with."

On March 26th, 1966 Virginia Hill was found dead on a walkway along a brook in Salzburg, Austria. According to authorities, she over dosed on pills. I have my doubts about.

The Mob wasn't in the business of truth. But I couldn't help to want it, especially about my dad. I had amnesia for things I'd never experienced, but I wanted to fill in the gaps. Solving the mystery of my father came with learning other truths along the way.

As I did enough research and asked enough indirect questions, I drew my own conclusions as to what happened to Dutch Schultz. However, even I began to realize it was a moot point. What really mattered were the facts. However, I had to accept that the exact details would never be known because there were no eye witnesses and none of the men involved talked, especially my father.

This did not stop the media from fabricating their own versions of what happened. That was the only way they had a story at all. Tell a lie often enough and people will believe it. Even the authors who wrote about it drew their own conclusions and built them on innuendo. For example, there is a tall tale that my father bragged about doing the hit. I can tell you first-hand, that was not my father's way. It went against every fiber in his being.

I distinctly remember one of the last conversations I had with my mother about the whole Dutch Schultz debacle.

"Mom, I really need to know. Did dad do this thing?"

She stuck with the same answer she had been giving me for twenty years and always in the same loving tone. "I really don't know. All I know is there was no solid evidence."

That was about as true a statement as anyone ever told me. There was no evidence. Period. My researched proved that.

Her patent response did not stop me from pressing my luck.

A few months after dad returned from prison in 1964, I finally mustered up the courage to ask him the question that tormented me for so long. We were sitting in the backyard just taking in the sunshine on a cool day.

"Dad, did you really do what they say you did?"

He looked at me like I was stupid. Maybe I was.

His response was short and adamant. "I didn't talk about this to anyone for over thirty years. What the fuck makes you think I'm going to tell you?"

That was it. Over. Done.

This topic was never broached again by anyone.

I heard and read a lot of bullshit about my dad. These came from unreliable sources like books, magazines, newspapers, wannabes etc. I needed truth. My mind was so confused. I needed clarity: fact vs. fiction.

The only way to get that was from men, who were not only close to him, but loved him, my mom and me. Although, I was told many times to "just forget about it" when it came to the gory details about his past life, I know the stories I was told were exactly what happened: the truth. There is something to say about getting stories from the "horse's mouth". When there is genuine love and caring you know you are not being lied to. When you can look into their eyes and watch the expression on their faces, you know what you are being told is real.

The truth is not just words. It's a feeling. Just like the love that I had for men like Harold, Gyp, Rusty and the rest, who helped me understand not only who and what my dad really was, but reality vs. myth.

One of the toughest and most traumatic stories to accept, was the truth behind my father's arrest, trial and the years that followed.

18
LUCKY 16

My mom looked different that day, like there was less light in her eyes when there should have been more. "It feels closer than further away," she said in a near whisper.

We were sitting in the living room beside one another on the couch, talking about dad's upcoming parole hearing, his sixteenth consecutive review without any reprieve. The news played softly in the background. It was as if the house, which she kept neat as a pin, was full of an invisible energy that stuffed it to the rooftop.

"How so?" I asked.

She put her hand on top of mine and just smiled.

The landscape surrounding my dad's case had drastically changed over the past few years. The prosecutors who wanted to climb the political ladder had taken their shot, others had died. Most of the mobsters involved with the Dutch Schultz case were long gone and no one cared about it anymore. Besides, everybody understood my father would never talk.

When I got the call, I could tell just by my mother's tone the news was finally good.

"It happened," she said, relief and elation ringing in every syllable. "I just received a telegram."

"What does it say?" I was cautiously excited. My pulse started to drum in my entire body. We'd waited for this for ages. This was the closest we'd ever come to having him home.

"It just says that he has been released and he will contact us when he knows more."

I was torn between laughing and crying. It was one of the most emotional moments in my life.

For over a decade, Gyp DeCarlo and his associates had been on a mission to get Dad out. In the end, a friend's father, who had a special connection with Dad, agreed to help. The only thing I was told was that he was part of the Westies. He reached out to some powerful lawyers from Las Vegas. These men were heavy hitters with incredible influence and power. I truly believe that if it weren't for Gyp, Dad would have never come home. There is nothing I would ever be able to do to adequately repay what this man did for my father and me for that matter.

From what I was told, none of the four men at the hearing wanted to be the one to finally set Charlie Workman free, even though they all realized that enough was enough. They gave their recommendations. However, the final decision came from Harold Ashby, the Head of the Parole Board.

The phone calls back and forth between Dad, Mom and the lawyers were constant. Even though he had been officially released, weeks went by and he was still not home. Something was not right. Harry Sokol, Dad's lawyer, explained that there were all kinds of jurisdictional challenges. He served his time in New Jersey but lives in New York, so the Manhattan District Attorney and Parole Board needed to accept responsibility for him. I was living in Queens, which is a different county. It was going to be difficult to get him permission to go from county to county and the municipalities had come to an agreement as to how to handle things.

My mom was at the end of her rope, ready to do whatever it took to get Dad home. She threw everything she had at it – time, connections, phone calls, money. My mother was beyond tired. She wanted this to end for both of our sakes.

On Friday March 6th, Mom and I were having breakfast at her house when the call finally came. Sunlight was streaming in the windows like a celebration.

"It's done. I'm coming home," my father told her from a prison phone.

"What day?" Mom asked, nearly breathless with anticipation.

"Tuesday. I will get you instructions on what time and where to pick me up at Trenton."

All weekend long, details of his parole began to filter in. The one that stung was he would not be allowed to visit me at my house. My heart sank. "He can't even be in my home?"

"We are working on that. Be patient. Let's just get him home. You know your father. He will find ways." She winked. I don't think I'd seen her that happy in decades.

I laughed. "Okay, so what is the plan to pick him up?"

The night before Dad's release we drove through a chilling rain in my 1964 blue Ford Thunderbird to Trenton and stayed at a nearby hotel. We did not want to travel that distance from New York in the wee hours of the morning.

It was still cold and rainy the next morning when it was time to go. Mom had taken extra time with her hair and makeup. She wanted to look just so. I saw a schoolgirl joy in her that I almost didn't recognize. I wondered if this was the mom I would have had for all those years if my father never went away, a joyous woman who didn't have to be tough for herself and for me, a different person altogether. I didn't feel shortchanged for myself, but for her. Just before we left, I took a bunch of towels and hung them on the inside of all the windows including the back windshield, so no reporters or television cameras could get a look in. I wanted this to be for us, our family, not the world.

I cautiously parked where I was instructed to. Trenton state's front gates loomed large and imposing, razor wire twirling atop high fences glistened in the rain. The sea of people at the front entrance was mind blowing. Hundreds of reporters and on lookers. Three television trucks, camera crews, radio crews. There were also five cops and a handful of trustees at the front entrance armed with shotguns, riot guns and walking-sticks.

His release was being broadcast live on TV and radio. Thankfully, one of the trustees secretly pulled the plug on the TV trucks mid-stream, so the TV portion was very short and very quick. However, my sons did tell me after we got home that there was a car just like mine television, so the cameras caught what they could.

I zeroed in on a cop who was standing at the curb as my mother had instructed me to earlier. Meanwhile, she leaned forward in the passenger seat, anticipating jumping out of the car. I had the car in drive with my foot on the break. Finally, the wave came. I briskly pulled up to the front entrance. Another policeman stationed at the front door waved. Mom, dressed in a dark coat, with black gloves, sunglasses and a scarf over her head, pulled up her collar and practically bounded out of the car. They said she looked like Lana Turner. She went up the steps and stood by the front door.

Everything seemed to move in slow motion. The door finally opened and there was Dad. His first step of freedom. He kissed my mom, grabbed her arm and offered a triumphant smile for the cameras. He looked fabulous with an incredible tan, dressed in a gray shark-skin suit that complimented his now-gray hair. He looked like a movie star who'd flown in from a vacation in Palm Springs to play the part of an ex-con, not the other way around.

Mom led him down the stairs. As soon as he saw the crowd, his expression dropped to a scowl. Reporters were screaming questions. He did not say a word. They quickly made their way to the car. Mom opened the door and pulled the front seat forward for Dad to climb into the back seat. Someone tried to stick a camera in the car and Mom shoved him out then slammed the door shut.

Seeing my father in the flesh outside of prison was shear elation. Like a child seeing his father coming home from war for the first time in years. I wanted so badly to jump out of the car and hug him.

I pounded the gas pedal and tore out of there. As I did, I accidentally grazed a cop car. "Jesus, I hit the police cruiser, Pop!"

"Don't stop. Just keep going," he yelled.

I did as I was told, but immediately got lost. I was not familiar with the area. I saw Route 1, Route 9, the New Jersey Turnpike, and the Garden State Parkway. For some reason, I jumped on the Parkway, but in the wrong direction.

"Dad, I think I'm lost."

"Just keep driving. I don't care where you go, as long as you don't go back."

After a few miles in silence with only the sound of the road under our tires, I got us back on track. The feeling of relief was immense. I had to get him to the parole office first and fast.

Out of nowhere my dad said, "Pull over on the median."

I looked at my mother puzzled. She nodded. "Go ahead."

With the rain still coming down, I pulled up on to the median, which was in the middle of the highway. In his thousand-dollar suit, he got out of the car, looked up into the sky, held his arms out and shouted, "What a beautiful day!" The jubilation in his voice was unforgettable.

He got back in the car and took out a tiny scrap of paper and handed it to me. "Find where this is," he ordered.

"What are you talking about? We have to go to the FBI office to report in."

"No," he insisted sternly. "Go to St. John's cemetery. They made me wait all these years to get out. They can wait for me now." He had an agenda and wasn't taking no for an answer.

On the long, quiet ride there, I figured out the number on the piece of paper was a grave site. I pulled through the gates and went to the white, shingled house office. I looked around this sanctuary for those that have past. It was one of the largest and most well-kept cemeteries I had ever seen. Just about every grave had fresh flowers. The tombstones were bright and immaculate. It was more like a celebration of death.

I rang the doorbell. A tall bald, frail man answered the door, dabbing his nose with a tissue. "Can you please tell me where this grave site is?" I asked politely.

"Are you family?" he asked.

"No, I can't say that we are. We are just acquaintances that would like to pay our respects."

He stepped on to the porch and pointed to where it was, unwilling to even stick a finger out into the falling rain.

"Thank you, sir."

I drove where I was directed then got out of the car to find the tombstone. Once I did, I went back to the car. Dad pushed the seat forward to get out and I started to go with him when he growled, "Stay put."

We both watched closely through the squeaking windshield wipers as he approached the grave. He stood there for a few seconds then unzipped his pants and pissed all over the grave. My father bellowed: "I'm here and you're there!"

It was Bill O'Dwyer's tombstone, the final resting place of the man who helped put my dad in prison and who made him miss out 24 years with us.

When we arrived at the Manhattan FBI office, there were throngs of people waiting at the front door.

"Go around to the back," Dad ordered. He hadn't been there in 25 years, but he remembered where the service entrance was. Again, we waited in the car while he went inside and did what he had to do. He came back out about 15 minutes later. No one from the press or public saw him. We were finally on our way home.

Once we got home, Mom proudly led him to the kitchen table and pulled out dad's chair with an ecstatic grin. She had been waiting twenty-four years to do that again.

Dad sat down heavily in the seat he'd left vacant for decades. "Chuck, go get the whiskey. Let's have a welcome home drink."

Just then, my Uncle Red walked in greeted Dad with a big hug. "Good to have you home, Charlie."

Mom poured some whisky for everyone. She raised her glass and started to say something but the tears she held back for what must have been an eternity began to flow. I had never seen her cry before. It all finally hit her. Everyone politely waited. "It took a while, but we are back together. We're a family again," she declared then grabbed his hand. "I told you I would wait."

My dad smiled, squeezed her hand and nodded. His eyes said it all.

In short order, family, friends and neighbors started showing up at the front door, eager to celebrate. As the drinks flowed, my mom and dad became giddy like high school kids.

"I may not be able to sleep in our bed, Katie. It might be too soft" He said with a sly grin.

"Well, I guess you will have to sleep on the floor," she joked.

Dad laughed. "Oh, no I won't!

By 10 o'clock, there had to be 50 people at the house. The party did not stop until after midnight. The warmth and love that filled the house was like a wedding in a church. I didn't say much, just admired the adulation my dad received. I'd never felt anything like that in my life. My heart and soul were at peace, even if for just those few hours.

I visited dad every day for weeks after he came home. His body was free from prison, but his mind was not. He was programmed for a certain schedule. Twenty-four years of prison life will do that to a person. He struggled with the transition.

"I'm going to sit out on the porch," he announced one warm evening.

He got up, went to the front door and froze. He stood there for what seemed like five minutes. I thought something was wrong and went to get up. My mom stopped me. "Just wait."

She got up from the couch and walked over to my father. She lovingly put her arms around him and whispered, "It's okay, Charlie. You can open the door."

He would wake up at 5:30 in the morning and stand up waiting for the buzzer for morning chow time. He did the same things when taking a shower or sometimes just leaving a room. However, he was tough minded and in a short period of time he was able to adapt to the life that now belonged to him again.

His positive disposition amazed me. He was never a downer. "Tomorrow is another adventure." He would say just about every day. It takes an incredibly strong man to maintain that type of attitude after being away for so long. Through him I learned how to value each day and be appreciative of what I had; true life lessons.

All my father cared about after he got home was my mom me and my family. But, mom was his life and he let everyone know it. Any time he was having a conversation about the family it was always, "My Katie."

The love, respect and admiration he had for her, to me, was unprecedented. For her to wait for him all that time is just not something you see every day. He would tell people. "I went in while we were married. When I came out we were still married. That's my Katie."

Nothing bothered him. Not even the fact that he was being monitored 24/7 by the FBI, who watched his every move. Our neighbor across the street would call. "Katie, they're here again." She was referring to the Feds.

So, she made coffee and brought it out to them. She made sure they knew that we knew they were there. She had some serious brass, let me tell you.

The harassment was constant early on. They still wanted to see if he would break or do anything stupid. For weeks, every night, at ungodly hours, they would ring the doorbell with flashlights in hand. "Mrs. Workman, we want to see him in bed." She'd let them in and they'd find dad sleeping in his bed.

Besides the FBI, the cops from the 103rd Precinct would show up three to five times a day. My father didn't mind. "It's their job. Leave them alone. They're all good guys." He'd say.

Mom would invite them inside for coffee and they'd all sit at the kitchen table and talk. Everyone was on a first name basis. These police officers were supposed to be watching my dad to make sure he was staying straight. I guess, in a sense you can say they were doing just that.

I would walk in and they'd say, "How you doing, Chuck? You're playing golf? How you are playing? Hitting them any good?"

I treated them like friends. They'd ask me If could get them on to the golf courses I was playing at. So, I made a few calls and got them on. I didn't mind, and it helped keep things calm.

Dealing with the FBI and the police was one thing but dealing with reporters was something else. They were relentless. A few months after dad came home, an article appeared in the Daily News article called Over the River by Nick Kenny. He wrote, "There was Charlie Workman and Red Levine sitting together at Mendel's (a famous bar during that time), probably discussing old times about Murder Incorporated."

This statement ended with a question mark, meaning it was shear conjecture on his part. However, this wasn't good for my dad because he was not supposed to be seen with anyone in the mob. Thankfully, there were no pictures and the reporter never approached my dad.

At the time, I lived in a split-level house at 50 Craig Place in East Islip. Some reporter had been hounding dad, following him around everywhere. This guy kept coming to my house too. This ended abruptly when mom took a steaming bucket of hot water, opened the window and dumped it on his head. That's mom for ya. The crazy thing was dad wasn't even there.

The conditions and restrictions of dad's parole were understandable, yet annoying. He had to meet his parole officer once a week. Over time this decreased to every two weeks, once a month, once every three months and finally every six months. After several years his parole officer met with the Parole Board. "This is getting ridiculous. What are we wasting money for? Why don't you leave this guy alone already? He's done with that life."

Their answer was "That's Charlie Workman. Those guys are never done with that life."

The others were: No association with mobsters. The Garment Center was off-limits. He could only go to certain places; couldn't leave the county. He must work a legitimate job.

Another long-time friend stepped out to ensure dad had a good job. He got him into Local 829, the Stagehands Union, almost impossible to get into. 829 ran the Coliseum on 59th Street where trade shows were held. The workers would set-up the trade shows and then break them down after they were over. It could be boats, cars, trucks - just about anything. The work was arduous and back-breaking. My father did it and never complained once.

The FBI thought it was a no-show job. Every day they would have someone on the shake line wearing white socks, $90 shoes and $100 dungarees to see if dad was there. They'd go to the canteen and eat a few tables away. They even followed him into the men's room. My father didn't care. He just did his job in silence. He pretended like they weren't even there. This went on for two years.

At home, dad was cautious. He never spoke on the phone. Whenever friends came over the radio was turned up loud. He was paranoid that the FBI might be bugging the house. He rarely spoke, literally talking with his eyes and facial expressions. Those that knew him well would always know what he was saying. This is how he was kept up to speed on what was happening on the streets. Guys would come by all the time with messages. He was like a consigliere to everyone instead of a mafia family.

Many times, during meetings at the house, high-ranking mobster names would come up. In simple quotes he would let his feelings be known. If he didn't like the guy, his famous quote was, "He was a rat bastard when he was alive, and he'll be a rat bastard when he's dead."

He would really get upset when some knock around guy would claim to be something that he wasn't. He'd say, "That guy never even stepped on an ant. He did nothing."

Honestly, it was quite entertaining. Besides, I would learn the truth about certain guys, both in the mob and out.

Dad rarely went out. But, when special invites came from his friends, or my mom wanted to go out, he would make an exception. There were a few memorable nights.

"Happy's Bar and Grill was located across from the Tomb's Prison in downtown, New York. It had a bar about 90 feet long with some tables and chairs in the front room. In the back was a separate large party room. This unique establishment was considered hallowed, neutral ground for all mobsters and members of law enforcement. It was one of the only places where both sides of the law would be in the same building and just be men. The cops would sit at the bar. Mobsters hung out in the back room. No one bothered anyone, no matter what was going on out on the streets. Regardless of who walked in, they were acknowledged and greeted with respect. It's hard to imagine, but it's the 100 percent truth.

A few weeks after dad came home, he was invited there by his friends. Being the cops were there, he knew he wouldn't get into trouble.

When dad walked in, every single member of law enforcement, who was sitting at that bar stood up and clapped for him. Like a receiving line my dad approached each one. There were hearty handshakes, hugs, kisses. It was surreal.

"We're glad you made it." "It's good to see you back." "Welcome home Charlie."

If I wasn't walking behind him and seeing it with my own eyes, I would have never believed it. It was that awe inspiring.

After my dad greeted everyone at the bar, he went into the back room where his friends and associates were waiting for him, with the same reception he received from the bar.

Singer Jimmy Roselli was one of the most popular entertainers of his era. He was also a very dear friend of my dad's. He appeared regularly at a famous night club called the San Su San, on Hempstead Turnpike in Long Island. This famous spot was on par with the Copacabana, but smaller. It was owned by a connected guy named Johnny Evanzanno.

About two months after dad came home, mom announced she wanted to go there and have a night out. It was myself my mom my dad and my wife at the time. When we walked in the captain had a server set up a table right in the front of the stage. At one point, Jimmy Roselli dedicated a song to my dad and sang, Over These Prison Walls I Will Fly.

During the song, he came over to my father and gave him a hug and a kiss. He whispered in his ear, "Charlie, I'm so glad you are out. I'm so happy to see you again." He gave my mother a big hug and a kiss. It brought tears to her eyes.

Dad rarely wandered out of the house on his own. But, there were times when he felt like he had to let loose. Frank Sinatra was crazy about my father. He was scared to death of him, but he loved him. One day my mother called me – it was like four in the morning.

"Your father's not home! Where is he? His parole is going to get violated if they come looking for him. Where do you think he is?" She was a nervous wreck.

"He went to the city. I don't really know." I answered in a groggy voice.

"Go find him."

The first place I went was Toots Shor's on 56th Street. I got there at five in the morning. The bar had these thick, glass revolving doors. I looked in. Frank Sinatra, Toots Shore, my father and Joey Brown the comedian were sitting at a table with bottles of J&B all around them. I started banging on the door. They saw me and let me in. I started yelling "Pop! What the hell are you doing? You have to get home!"

Sinatra yelled "Have another one!"

My father stumbled up, I tried to grab him. "Get your hands off me. What do you think I am drunk?"

Although I was concerned, this incident was funny. I don't think he realized how entertaining he was at times.

Life was great. Dad was home. And golf was my life. What more could I ask for?

19
NO ONE TO BLAME, BUT ME

Golf defined me. I need it to breathe. It was all I had to maintain my sanity and to feel like I was making my own way.

By the fall of 1963, I was once again a full-time hustler. I didn't have a golf job per se, but I was winning big money doing it my way. I played in local tournaments just to keep my name prominent all the while hustling up and down the East Coast with guys like Mike Borsuk, Jack Mahoney and Lenny Bayline.

"Slow down your tempo," I told Jack once when we were on the practice range at his Innwood club. The blue of the sky and the green grass of the range met in a clear line about 350 yards ahead. I teed a ball up for Jack. "You're starting too fast."

He looked at me as if to say, "No, you need to slow down."

"Chuck, you have to pump the brakes," he warned. "You gotta fucking lose once in a while. And stop with muscling every guy you play. You're going to kill your rep. No one is going to want to play you anymore."

"Yeah, I get it," I snapped back, indifferent.

"No, you fucking don't. I told you this a long time ago. In order to win, sometimes you have to lose."

I was finding it difficult to lose to guys who had no business even being on the golf course with me. I wanted to show everyone how good I was. I wanted to be known as Chuck Workman the pro golfer, not Charlie Workman's son. The man who had stepped out of his father's shadow.

The warning fell on deaf ears. My ego was drowning out the message I didn't want to hear. I was relentless. Every now and then, we'd lose, but winning became paramount. I had to. And too often did.

But at what ultimate price?

On a cool spring morning, me and Mike Borsuk, a PGA Player and the pro at Commack Country Club on Long Island, packed up my blue convertible Cadillac, ready to set out on what we hoped would be an unforgettable, big money hustling trip. The plan was to go from town to town, playing our way south down the eastern seaboard, stop at some local tournaments to ensure our presence was known, then start with the scamming.

Right off the bat, we did well. We played a guy named Ronnie Marshall, a pro out of Long Island. He was a nice guy, but he just couldn't compete with our game. His partner was a known long ball hitter named Werner Teichman, who was also a PGA member.

We started out playing for $50. That turned into $100 then $200. We were beating their ass, I mean killing them. I was playing like a tour player. It got to the point where Werner and Ronnie Marshall started arguing over something called "Press," which in golf lingo means another bet from that point on.

Werner yelled. "You press your money, not mine. I quit."

Ronnie shot back, "I wanna keep playing and keep betting!"

"You do it." Werner said as he walked off.

It was game over. The problem was, they owed us a lot of money – about $4,000 and they didn't have it. We needed to get paid somehow. So, we drove my car up to Ronnie's pro shop. We took golf clubs, hats, shirts, balls – emptied out the store.

Most of the hats and shirts said Northampton Country Club on them. I took 50 hats, 30 shirts 20 pair of shoes, 15 sets of clubs and anything else I could get my hands on that I thought I could sell. The car was so full, Mike could barely get in. He had to sit on top of golf clubs. Luckily, it was a convertible or his head would not have fit in the car.

I told Ron, "If I sell all of this stuff and come up with more than what you owe me, I'll give you the difference."

Of course, that never happened. But I had to get paid somehow.

The further south we went, the hotter the weather got and the better we played. From Maryland to Hilton Head to Jacksonville, we just kept winning. We finally made it to our ultimate destination: Bay Shore Country Club in Miami. Bay Shore was regarded as the ultimate hustler's haven. Though the real owner was Meyer Lansky, it was run by a guy named Harvey St. Jean. Harvey, a former motorcycle cop. He went to college, got a law degree and then got hired by Meyer.

We cruised up and down the palm tree-lined streets of Miami with the top down, our sun glasses on, having the time of our lives. We felt like kings. Hot weather, hot women, beautiful golf courses and thousands of dollars to be made. There were mobbed up guys everywhere – great pros who were better than us, along with some of the biggest golf hustlers in the world.

Mike and I developed a winning routine. I'd play a one-on-one match and win. Mike would play his and either win or lose depending on the circumstances. Then we'd win the team match for the big money. This worked well until we hit Miami.

It had been about two weeks and all we did was break even. I loved Mike, but he was just not holding up his end. Maybe he was getting tired. Something had to give.

We were sitting on the balcony of our hotel enjoying a break with some cocktails, enjoying the warm breeze and a view of the sparkling blue ocean. I looked at Mike who had his feet up sipping a Pina Colada and said, "Mike, listen, don't play anymore. Stay in the clubhouse. We are still partners. Hit golf balls, do whatever you want, but don't get involved in any action or any games. If you do this, I guarantee we will come out way ahead. I will just play my singles matches and double up on them. If I can find another winner to play with, I will. But don't worry about anything. You will still get your end just like you always have."

He stared straight ahead as if he knew it was coming. "Okay, Chuck. I'm good with that."

The next day, I started to double up on my singles matches and we started winning money again. Nonetheless, I needed a good partner to get back to the three-match system we were using.

Within a few days, I found a new partner. Or should I say he found me. His name was Rocky Mafrice from Chicago. He never made games he couldn't win. He was my kind of player.

Rocky constantly increased the stakes, putting as much $10,000 on the line. We would usually win the team match and each of us would win our individual matches. Once again, I was raking in the cash. Sometimes he would put up more money than I had, which made me uncomfortable, but even if he put up extra on his individual hustle, he would still cut me in on half.

One blisteringly hot day, Lefty and I were playing two other guys at Bay Shore. Were in the middle of the 18th fairway about to hit our approach shots. I happened to look up and spotted Mike up ahead on the practice green. He was easy to spot because even though he was young, he had a shock of white hair. I started to line up my shot but didn't hit it right away because I zeroed in him trying to figure out what he was doing.

Then I noticed a guy about six-foot-six come over to Mike like he meant business. I jumped in the cart and tore down to the practice green. Lefty and the other guys started screaming at me. They were totally confused. I left them in my wake and kept going.

I drove my golf cart like a bat out of hell and jumped out, shouting, "Mike, what the hell are you doing?"

"I'm playing this guy," he answered with a shrug.

The giant he was playing was George Lowe – the greatest putter in the world. He made putters for Jack Nicklaus. He went to race tracks all over the country. He went to every major sporting event there was no matter where. He was known throughout the golf world, and across the country. He wore an ascots, black-and-white shoes and cashmere sports jackets. He looked like he stepped out of a Damon Runyon book.

Here he is kicking the ball with his instep into the hole more times from ten feet than Mike could make with his putter.

"Mike how far down are we?"

"Six hundred."

"Holy shit. Are you really that stupid?" I was furious.

I turned to George. "You can't do that to this kid. He's with me."

"Chuck, a bet's a bet," he replied respectfully.

"George, I'm telling you the kid is with me. You took advantage of him."

"He didn't have to say yes. I didn't break his arm. I didn't coerce him."

I kept at him. "George, we're going to have to get this straightened out. That's a lot of money and I'm not going to let him pay."

The guys I'd been playing against had already finished the 18th hole, which meant I was out the $200 I was going to win. I raced up to the veranda and saw "Trigger" Mike Coppola playing Hearts with some other fellas. The table was guarded by a bunch of big guys in suits.

I said to one of them. "Could you please tell Mr. Coppola that Charlie's son needs to see him?"

Mike had a wide nose with a crooked bridge from his fighting days. His dark hair was slicked to the side with shades of grey along the sides. He carried a menacing look that would scare anyone. When he saw me, he offered a twisted grin. "Hey, Chuck, come on up. What's the problem?

"My partner is an asshole. He's down $600 and I told him not to gamble."

"Who's he down to?"

"George Lowe."

Mike's expression snapped into a scowl. He nodded to one of his guys. "Tell George to come up here." He offered in a stern voice.

Within seconds George swaggered up, dwarfing the hulks that protected Trigger Mike, Mike simply glared up at him. "You see this kid? He's with us. You want the $600 or do you want to stay friends with me?"

George didn't even blink. "Tell your friend to forget the $600."

I liked George, but he took advantage of a friend, who he thought had no strength. I needed to show him what was what and who was who. As he walked by me he whispered. "Sorry Chuck. Meant no offense."

I felt kind of bad for the guy. He was just doing his thing. It wasn't his fault my friend wasn't so bright. "No problem. George. No offense taken, I appreciate it."

With that George disappeared into a crowd of golfers.

Mike had gone back on his word and I had to go back to my old connections to bail both of us out. It should have been an alarm bell to me. I still wasn't listening.

It didn't take long for my rep to catch up with me. I was still winning and having a great time, yet I noticed things were slowly changing. I was fine in small tournaments and would usually find good hustles at these events, but they were becoming fewer and farther between.

Guys I used to play against were beginning to decline. "I can't beat you Chuck."

I was welcomed with open arms no matter where I went, but the opportunities were drying up. Even at my favorite "go to" places that would always bring me big money were only yielding small money games.

Everyone wanted to play with me, not against me. Even though I was flattered, it was hurting my wallet as well as my ego. My partners had to find new ones because no one would even play a doubles match against me.

Things really hit home when I found myself squaring off against a pair called "The Grocery Boys." One was Irish, the other Italian and they were partners in the grocery business. One spoke with an Irish brogue, the other with an Italian accent. I played them several times a week for about eight straight months. Not only wasn't there anyone else to play, I had to get very creative to keep them playing.

I took them to the most prestigious golf courses around: Glen Oaks and Cedar Brook County Club in Westbury, Long Island. The greens fees for these places were well over $100. We played for free. So right from the get-go, they were ahead so to speak. They kept playing because they got on to courses they never could by themselves. They loved it.

However, I was cleaning them out. Now, I didn't win every time, but I took them for a lot of money. They were losing $2,000 to

$3,000 at a clip and getting upset.

I gave them handicap shots but the more I beat them, the more shots they wanted. It got to the point where I would have had to shoot sixty to win.

As the colors of fall began to dominate the scenery, I made another offer to keep the Grocery Boys on the hook. "I will bring in a partner. This guy is twenty years older than me. That should even things up."

They eagerly agreed.

I honestly don't even remember the guy's name that I tapped for the gig. He was in his 50's and with a handicap of about eight. I figured I'd lose a few times to regain their interest. Well, don't you know it, this older guy came in and shot lights out! We mopped the green with them.

These Grocery Boys went nuts, calling me a crook for bringing in a ringer. They walked away and that was that.

After that debacle, I was left with trying to come up with unique ways to hustle and make money. I played a lot at Commack Country Club where I met a guy named Augie, who dressed like he'd sauntered straight out of golf magazine. Truth was, he really couldn't play to save his life. However, he had a slick knack for cards. When it came to Gin, it was as if he couldn't lose. I set him up with big Gin games then he would clean up and I'd get a cut.

Though it was a sweet little side hustle, it was not what I was accustomed to.

The writing was on the wall. No one would play me anymore. I couldn't make a match and it was nobody's fault but mine.

During these times, dad was breaking his back at the Coliseum. He was proud of my golfing accomplishments because guys would tell me that all he talked about was me and how good of a golfer I had become. This is what he wanted from the get-go, when he forced me into golf lessons. Yet, all I could think about was letting him down.

I was taught to heed the advice of those where were wiser than I was. I didn't do that. I let my power and ego control me. I refused to look at the big picture. I had to win and win now. By 1968, I was completely out of golf and I had no one to blame but me. The worst part was I had to face my dad and tell him the truth.

20

THE GARMENT DISTRICT

My father was a big tough guy. But, when you spend so much time in the joint, you are never quite the same. Add to that about four years of arduous hard labor at the Coliseum and things being to take their toll. Everyone noticed. He still looked great, but he was moving slower. Concern began to spread to his associates. Something needed to be done.

Two dear friends Sol Orlinsky – Benzo's brother - and Julie Bernstein, stepped out. Although, he still never complained, they knew he wouldn't last much longer. Once again big-time lawyers were brought in, with their fees paid for by friends.

These lawyers garnered up petitions, testimonies, affidavits etc. They went back and forth with the parole board and the courts for about a year. Finally, the garment center restriction of his parole agreement was rescinded. He was allowed back in to be a salesman. This included what the courts regarded as the "hot bed" of mob activity": 29th Street up to 40th Street; 6th Avenue to 8th Avenue.

After five years, he was back home in the Garment District, where it all started. Once the decision came down Sol hired dad immediately at his company called S.O. Textile. S.O. was a major player in the industry. They sold poly bags, buttons and trimmings for the dresses and men's clothing.

It didn't take long for dad to make a huge impact. He first went to see his old friends at Trissi, one of the biggest dress makers in the world. His old friend Irving Cohen owned it. When dad showed up Irving went crazy.

Next, Dad approached Leslie Faye, a worldwide organization, which grossed about $60 million a year in business. At the time, it was impossible for salesmen to get in there. My dad did with one phone call. When he went to visit, it was like Jesus walked through the door. They gave him all their business as well.

Most of the industry players were his boyhood friends, so they weren't doing it out of fear or the unspoken mob connections. They adored him and jumped at the chance to work with him.

At the S.O. factory, they set Dad up in his own over-sized, black swivel leather chair in an office in the back of the warehouse, isolated and insulated – just the way he wanted it. He still talked to no one. He'd go in, spend a couple of hours, smoke a few cigarettes, and walk around the place. I'd meet him there sometimes to catch up and talk a walk. It was located on 40th Street between 7th and 8th Avenues.

One cool spring afternoon, around lunch time I met Dad outside. The smell of factory smoke and the banging of clothing machinery filled the air. We ambled along the street, side by side.

Things were going great for him, but not so much for me. It didn't take long for Dad to find out that I was out of golf. Word traveled fast.

"No golf today?" he asked in a cool voice as we walked slowly.

"No pop."

I was embarrassed because I knew I blew it.

"Giving it up?"

"Not totally."

"Good."

I was beyond relieved that he was not mad at me. And he was at peace and happy. This made it easier for me to seek employment in his stomping grounds. Though I knew I could ask for his help, I needed to do it myself. So, I started pounding the pavement for gainful employment.

Almost every day for about a week, I'd walk by the trucking company my father used to be partners in on 8th Avenue, owned by Yanni Satnick. The manager was Herbie Radler and I'd make sure I caught his eye.

Herbie would always say: "How ya doing?"

My usual response was. "Great." Then I'd just keep walking.

Finally, one day I asked. "Are you really interested in knowing how I am?"

He laughed. "Why the hell do you think I ask? Of course, I'm interested."

"Honestly, if I don't get a job soon, I'm going to jail."

"Why?" he asked, shocked.

"Cause I'm wearing thousand-dollar suits and I have no fucking income! Don't that look funny?"

He put his hand on my shoulder. "Come by tomorrow. I have a couple of guys who might be interested in helping you."

I showed up the next day dressed to the nines, hoping Herbie would come through. He shook my hand and said, "Go to Downe and Zier Knits. Ask for Al Silverstein."

"I don't know anything about knits."

"So, what? Just go see the guy. He makes all kinds of stuff for dresses. You know a lot of people. You'll be fine."

For a guy who made clothes, Al didn't dress very well. When I arrived, he had no tie or jacket. Just slacks and a white dress shirt and sweat on his brow. He invited me to sit down. After twenty minutes of talking, he announced, "You're over qualified."

"I'm over qualified for what? I don't know shit about this business."

"Well, you're too high priced."

"High priced? Look, I need a job. You sell these things I know a lot of people."

His eyes lit up. "You do, huh?"

"Yeah, just ask around about Chuck Workman." I finally had his attention. "Give me a draw against whatever the commission is. I don't know the first thing about it, but I'll figure it out."

He chewed the inside of his cheek, mulling it over. "I'll give you $250 a week against the draw."

With that, we signed a contract and he handed me a stack of fabric samples.

"Take these. Go into the different dress manufacturers in the district and ask them if they want to buy them."

I stopped him before he could say another word. "Oh no. I don't do that."

"Take these sample cases..." he continued, lifting a case to give to me.

"No, I don't do that either," I told him adamantly.

"I just hired you. How are you going to sell them?"

"I call people, tell them what you do, then you go see them"

He looked at me like I'd lost my mind. "I've never done that."

"Yeah, but you never met me before."

"No, I haven't. But that's not how it works." He was getting agitated.

"Name me someone you can't get into and would like to see."

He put his hand on his chin. "I've been trying to sell in the coat business for years and I just can't get in."

I shrugged. "How about Elliott Satnick?"

Al shook his head. "No way! Elliot Satnick is my neighbor. I've been trying to sell to him for 20 years and I can't sell him."

"Okay." I told him and started to walk away.

"Where are you going?"

"I'm going to see Elliott Satnick."

He laughed. "Right. Good luck."

About a half hour later, I called Al Silverstein on the phone. "I'm at Elliott's office. Bring the sample case."

Fifteen minutes later he showed up, even sweatier and out of breath. He must have run the whole way. I gestured for Al to open the case. Elliot glanced at him, then me, then perused the contents of the case.

"I want this. I want that. I want some of those. Some of these."

I didn't think it would end. There were beads of sweat all over his forehead. He was writing so fast, it was like steam was going to come out of the pencil point.

Elliott kept going. "I'll pay $2.50 a yard. I'll take a thousand of this, two-thousand of that…" He finished his order. "Chuck. I gotta run. Please say hello to Katie for me. Give me a call. We'll come to the house have dinner."

"Sounds great Elliott. Thank you." I gave him a hug and a kiss, and I left.

Al followed behind me. I turned back to him. "How'd we do?"

"Geez. I don't know if I can deliver this I don't have enough machines to cover the order." He went on and on, like this huge sale was a bad thing.

"What the hell do you mean you don't have enough machines?"

He started explaining it to me so fast I couldn't understand anything, rambling in a panic. "I gotta get the yarn, I gotta get this…that."

I just let him babble. When he stopped to gulp some air, I interjected, "How many machines do you have?"

"We only have 15." I thought he was going to have a panic attack.

"How many do you need?"

"For this we will need about 30!"

"Where can we find more?"

"There's a bunch in Brooklyn."

"Okay. I'll take care of it."

"You'll take care of it?"

I made a bee line back to his office, picked up the phone and called Willie Catone, who owned Brooklyn and was involved with the industry. "Willie, who do you know in the knitting business?"

"Everybody," he stated without hesitation.

"Okay. Take me to a guy where we can make a deal."

"A deal for what?"

"I have this big fucking order here and my guy can't fill it because he doesn't have enough machines."

"Not a problem. Meet me up in Brooklyn." He gave me the address.

An hour later we walked into this big warehouse with about ten of these machines, sitting there not being used. They were each as big as a house! I'd never seen anything like it.

I walked up to a husky, unshaven guy who I assumed ran the place. "What happens if I get all of these machines busy for you?"

"You do that and you're my partner," he replied with a half-smile.

"I think we're partners." We shook hands.

I handed him the order and he read it. "Holy shit! Are you kidding me?" Now this guy was sweating too.

"This is as real as it gets."

Within a few days, all the machines were humming. Al took half the business, whatever he could handle. I took the other half with the guy who owned the machines. And I did the right thing by taking care of Willie out of my end.

With the giant machines blaring, parts whirling, I asked Al. "Now what do you do with this stuff."

"Well, you gotta get it finished at Fisher Knits."

I happened to know the guy who ran the Union down at Fischer Knits and went to see him. "So, what do you do with this stuff?"

"Well, you stretch it, you do this, that...."

I cut him off midway. "How much do you get and how much would I get?"

"I get a quarter. You get a nickel."

I shook his hand. "You're on."

I soon learned that after the fabric is put in a roll, it's put in a poly bag then loaded on a truck and shipped to wherever it needs to go, so I went to a friend of mine who handled the rolling and the poly bags. I became partners with him too with a simple handshake.

Then I went back to Herbie and gave him the trucking business with a piece going to me. Before I knew it, I was in business myself with a piece of everything.

I put deals together like that for another week. I was amazed. I didn't even know I knew all these people. I mean I knew them, but I never connected the dots to create a deal. After making this all happen on my own, I felt comfortable enough going to dad for guidance. I'd catch him up to speed and the ins and outs of my deals, then he'd tell me: "Go see this guy. I grew up with him." Or "Go see that guy. I started him in business."

I had orders coming in left and right. This all happened in weeks. I hustled my ass off.

Following the deal with Elliot, I went to a place call San'Joe Knits. They made ladies dresses. I approached the middle-aged woman with silver hair and red lipstick at the reception desk. "Excuse me. May I see Mr. Feldman please?"

She smirked. "I'm sorry, sir. He's busy right now."

The door of the office was half opened, I looked in and saw a golf whiffle ball go flying across the office. "Can you please tell Mr. Feldman that Chuck Workman is here?" I knew Feldman knew my dad from when Garment Center since before I was born.

He overheard me and came running out. "Chuckie! Come on in! It's so good to see you."

He had his sleeves rolled, tie tucked in his shirt and was holding a nine iron. He started asking me about his swing. I gave him a golf lesson in his office. Within a half hour, I walked out with an order for about $10,000. That was how quickly and smoothly business got done.

About a week later, I walked into Al's office. "Am I doing good?"

"Good? You made yourself about $9,000!"

This time I looked at him like he was nuts. "What the hell are you talking about? I just started last week?"

To me, it was a game. All I really did was see some old friends and be myself. I'd go to dinner with this guy, to lunch with that guy, have a drink with another. Next thing you know I'm getting orders everywhere. They would ask me. "What do you know about the business?"

My standard answer was. "Nothing. I don't know a fucking thing."

They'd all laugh like hell, but they'd give me orders.

Within a month, I also got hired by a manufacturer on 463 Broadway. They had me watch over the stuff they purchased from other people. It all went to Fisher Knits and they paid me a nickel a yard to make sure nothing was getting stolen. I would go there once a week and tell them. "Now don't fuck around with me. Somebody could get hurt."

The business started to run as smoothly as the fabric machines, a steady hum. The owner was making thousands upon thousands of yards of fabric and I was finally making good money again, which helped me forget about golf for a while. But the best part was I got to spend quality time with my father, something I had longed for. We weren't working for the same company, but he was right there for me whenever I needed him. These times were priceless. He was the father I had always dreamed he would be.

Some six months or so after being in the industry, a guy who owned one of the largest luxury dress companies in the area reached out to me. I had been trying to sell him zippers, hangers and poly bags forever with no luck. So, I assumed he was going to give me some business.

"Chuck, I need some help."

"What can I do for you?" I asked puzzled.

"A truckload of my dresses was hijacked. Is there anything you can do?"

"Let me make some calls. I'll get back to you."

I immediately went to see Dad at his office at S.O. I gave him the story. He nodded expressionless. It hit me. He knew all about the heist. "Meet me here tomorrow at noon."

A cool brisk air filled the alleys of S.O. as I approached the back door to meet Dad. He came right out. "Where we going, Pop?"

"Huey."

The name alone said a lot.

My father had set up a meeting with Huey Mulligan, an Irish boss in New York, at one of their pubs a few blocks away. We walked in and were met with to the stale smell of beer and Irish décor all around the rustic joint. Huey looked as Irish as anyone I had ever seen, with screaming orange hair, long side burns and pale white skin. They greeted each other warmly with mutual respect and sat down at a table.

Dad spoke first. "That dressmaker is a friend of ours and we are going to get a lot of business from him if we can help him out of this jam."

"Charlie, for you I'll get it straightened out. But the kids have to make a few dollars." He said with a shrug.

Dad nodded.

Huey leaned in and whispered into my dad's ear. "Twenty-five large."

"Fair enough." They shook hands and we walked out.

A few days later we were told that the truck and all the addresses were returned. I went to see the guy. "Here's the agreement. You need to pay these kids $25,000. Those dresses have a wholesale value anywhere between and $175,000 $200,000. It'll be the best $25 grand you ever spent because they will leave you alone."

He glared at me. "No. They aren't getting shit out of me."

I got nose to nose with him. "You're wrong on this one. You can't do that to these guys."

"Watch me," he said with a smartass tone.

I gave him every warning I could think of to no avail. He would not pony up the money.

"This is your last chance." I warned him. "If I don't walk out of here with the money, I'm not responsible for what happens next."

He remained steadfast. "No is no!"

Calmly I left. I went straight to Dad's office and told him what happened.

Two days later they stole another truck of dresses.

Naturally, I got another call. "Chuck! They did it again!"

"I warned you! Now fuck off!" I slammed the phone down.

He never talked to me again. I still see him every now and then at one of the golf courses here in Florida. I ignore him. If he ever tries to approach me, I will tell him what I think of him.

For the most part, this new enterprise seemed like a harmless way to make a good living. It wasn't golf, but it was a job and I felt like I was accomplishing things without working quite as many angles in the process. Little did I know that working in the Garment District and having the last name "Workman "would unveil the nasty inner circles of this hoodlum infested area.

To me, I was finally making an honest buck. Others saw it very differently.

21
THE DARK SIDE

I was dead asleep on a steamy August night when the phone rang. I nearly jumped out of my skin. I looked at the gold-plated alarm clock on the bed side table. It was three o'clock in the morning. I fumbled to pick up the phone, heart pounding like a jackhammer.

"You better fucking pay up!" A gruff, unknown male voice screamed at me.

"What? Who are you?" I yelled back, racking my brain to try and place to voice or figure out what this could be about. "I don't even know you. But I do know I don't owe you shit!"

"I don't give a fuck what your last name is. If you don't pay us, we're going to have a big problem. We'll shoot your house up and kill you!"

"If you're threatening me, we'll see who's who and what's what." I slammed the phone down.

My mind went in to overdrive. I got up and paced the floors trying to come up with anything that could have prompted that call. I was certain I didn't owe anybody any money. I always made sure of that. I smelled a rat. My gut started to churn. Within an hour I was on the phone calling everyone I knew. I needed answers and I needed them fast.

At around six o'clock, I finally got a call from a friend of a friend. "There's some guy named Sandy betting at the Mousetrap in Huntington. He's using your name and he's about $20 grand in the hole."

I was stumped. I didn't know a single soul named Sandy, so I called Dad right away and told him what was going on.

"I can't get involved with this one," he told me solemnly and I respected his position. "Call Willie Catone."

Willie wheeled some serious power in the mob. Yet, very few knew about him. He was smart. He stayed out of the limelight and loomed in the shadows. You won't find him on the internet. But, as sure as my dad existed, so did Willie.

I met Willie in a little coffee shop in Brooklyn the next day. The aroma of piping hot coffee and fried eggs filled the air, thick as the summer humidity outside. He was sitting in a booth in the far corner. A fresh cup of espresso was waiting for me. For the first time, I felt some relief. With Willie in my corner, I knew this would get settled. "Hey Chuckie. Talk to me. What's going on?"

He nodded stirring his coffee slowly as I recounted the phone call and what I'd dug up. He tapped his spoon on top of the cup and placed it down. "Give me a day or two," he said calmly in a voice no higher than whisper.

"Okay, Willie. Thank you." I offered respectfully.

"You got it kid."

Like clockwork, he called me two days later. "Meet me at Post Time at nine o'clock tonight."

I showed up at Post Time, a restaurant and nightclub in Commack Long Island as directed. Willie out front in a dark suit, a dark grey fedora tipped to one side. A bright red, flashing neon sign lit up the front. He leaned into my ear, "Just follow my lead."

The place was empty except for two guys sitting at a long bar on the right. In tandem they immediately turned around to watch us walk in. "The one with the cheap hat on runs that gambling joint," Willie said under his breath as we took a seat at a booth. "The other dumb looking guy is his muscle."

Willie ordered a rare steak and a Scotch. I ordered the same, only with a Coke. Willie paid no mind to the guys at the bar, who were clearly keeping tabs on us while we exchanged some idle talk back and forth. The steaks were brought to the table and we started eating.

Just after our steaks were set down, the two guys came over to our table, sat beside each of us and grabbed menus.

Willie gave them the business. "I didn't call for you. You wait until I'm goddamned finished. Go back to where the fuck you were or go back to New York City, one or the other. But don't sit next to me until I tell you."

Stunned, their faces went flat. They both got up and went back to their bar stools.

"Wannabe punks. Neither are made guys. But they're acting like it. Dangerous proposition. Just enjoy your meal."

We talked, caught up, shot the breeze and enjoyed our food as if we had no other reason to be there than a good streak with an old friend. Maybe a half hour later, well after the waiter took away our plates, Willie waved the guys over.

His placid expression quickly turned cloudy and intense. He took his napkin off his lap and put it on the table, but this was no white flag of reconciliation. "See this kid here? He's with us. Understand? This kid catches a cold, you're fucking dead. If he gets a hangnail, you're fucking dead. You're talking about money? There is no money as far as this kid is concerned. Don't even go near him, it's over. And you tell your cocksucker friend that Willie Catone said so! Now, get out of my face before something really bad happens."

Just like that, it was over. I never heard anything about it ever again.

About a month later, I was walking down 6th Avenue. Out of nowhere Willie popped up behind me and threw his arm over my shoulder like a long-lost buddy. I jumped as he laughed then gave me a sideways hug. "Didn't mean to scare you, Chuckie! Came to tell you that situation is all done. Now let's go find that guy Sandy."

A wave of relief washed over me. Though it was a given that Willie's word was bond and I was no longer worried about any threats, the specter of someone using my name to rack up debts hadn't left my thoughts. "What's his story?" I asked curiously.

"He's a degenerate gambler. Somehow, he picked up your name and started throwing it around when he was at the joint playing cards. Found out he's at a bar in Hampstead as we speak."

Then like magic, three of Willie's enforcers appeared, intimidating guys each over two-hundred pounds dressed up in silk suits and ties. A gorilla in a suit is still a gorilla. There was no mistaking what type of men these were. We got in Willie's car and drove straight to a hole in the wall bar behind a dry cleaner. The place was a dive with sticky floors and the stench of old, flat beer.

Willie and I were barely in the door when his enforcers already had a wiry, hobo type by the neck. They checked his pockets as he struggled, eyes wild with fear as if he knew this day was coming but prayed it wouldn't. The problem was he didn't have any money on him. Not a dime. So, they gave him a beating right then and there in the bar. When other guys tried to make their way over, Willie turned and told them simply: "This is none of your business. Keep drinking."

It was fast and vicious. When the guy hit the ground, Willie looked over him and kicked him in the ribs. "I'm Willie Catone. My name you ought to remember. Chuck Workman's you better forget."

Sandy laid in a crumpled heap on the floor. There was blood from a cut over his eye trailing down his cheek like a single, red teardrop. The enforcers adjusted their suits and made a path for us toward the door.

Now, it was over.

With that a huge burden off my shoulders, my focus turned back to making money every way I could in the garment industry. I was good at it because it came naturally. But, the collateral damage was all around. I learned quickly why this was so mob infiltrated. Nothing happened without wheeling and dealing, conniving, manipulating – you name it.

The garment district had a wicked dark side. It was ugly, vicious and filled with malice. Every time I turned around somebody was in trouble and needed help. If it wasn't me, it was a dear friend or associate. I was getting paranoid and with good reason. Every wannabe wanted to make a name for themselves by hurting someone. It made me sick. I was constantly waiting for the next bomb to drop. Usually the ones in the crossfire were innocent guys, who didn't deserve it.

Barry Bernstein was a dear family friend. His brother, Julie, helped get Dad out of prison. Barry was a hard worker, salt of the earth type of guy. His only problem was he couldn't resist bet, be it hockey, basketball, horses, football, any sport, you name it. Unfortunately, he lost more often than he won. One day, he finally made a big-time score for about 65-large. The bookmaker told him. "Go fuck yourself. I'm not paying you."

"You're not going to pay me? Why not? I pay when I lose!"

"You're a Jew. I don't pay Jews."

Barry called me for help and I immediately turned it over to my father, who of course called Willie Catone. Dad was trying to stay away from situations like this. He was still on parole and had to be careful, especially when you knew there was a trusted friend who could handle it the way he would. It took less than a day for Willie to find out who the real bookmaker was. He had me and Barry meet him there. Barry was on edge – my world wasn't his world - but once he caught a glimpse of Willie's crew, he just blinked in awe.

The bookmaker's office was behind a stationary shop on Mulberry Street that you'd walk by without a second glance. They were in the paper business alright, just not the legitimate kind.

Willie's men busted in through the back door. A bald guy with suspenders nearly fell off his chair when we barged in.

Willie ushered Barry in and went right for the jugular. "Do you owe him money?"

The guy in suspenders was quaking. "He beat me for a few dollars. I'm not paying him. He's a Jew. He don't mean shit." Trying to sound tough to Willie Cantone was a bad move. The crew stood still but it was as if they moved closer just with the hardness of their glares.

Willie pointed to me. "Do you know who this kid is over here? He's his partner. That's Charlie Workman's son. You want me to go tell Charlie Workman you told his son to go fuck himself?"

The suspenders nearly fell off him with fright.

Willie got up in his face. "The number is $65 grand. Pay him now!"

"I can't," the guy blurted, his shoulders trembling. "I don't have it."

"You're going to pay him now!" Willie slammed his fist on the messy desk of papers which went flying.

I never saw a heavy-set guy jump up so high. He scuttled into a backroom then came back with a thick, envelope full of money. The bookmaker offered it to Barry from a quivering hand.

As if turning off a switch, Willie politely said: "Good. Now for my troubles you owe me $75 large. You will pay me tomorrow, same time, same place. Or else."

A look of agony washed over the man's face, but he resigned himself and just nodded. There were empty threats. Then there were threats from Willie Cantone. There would be no way around paying up.

Willie had his guys follow Barry home just to make sure he was safe.

The next day this bookmaker paid Willie the $75 grand.

A few days later Barry asked me to invite Willie to our office, where he handed him $15,000. "That's for helping me out. Thank you."

Willie turned around on the QT and handed me five. I shook my head. "Thank you, Willie, but that's yours."

He nodded. "If you want to give it back to him, that's fine with me. It's your business."

Nods of respect were exchanged. That was how business was done.

The thing of it is, my dad was not directly involved with any of these incidents. However, I knew deep down that he was aware of everything that was going on when it came to me. When it came to my life, he was the one orchestrating what guys like Willie were doing. The Garment District was dad's turf – his kingdom. Nothing went own without his knowledge or say so, especially when it came to me.

I never would have thought the fabric business would be as rough as it was, and I was yearning for a change as well as a break. This wasn't me or my passion. The one thing that ate at me though was disappointing my dad. We saw each other just about every day. Me getting out would change that.

Even though I was bored, he was back in his element; he was enjoying every minute of it. I'm not sure I ever saw him happier. However, the media would still not leave him alone. I remember the headline of a short story in the Daily News that read, "Charlie Workman is now selling buttons in the area where he used to kill people." There were many similar articles during those years. As a result, he had to insulate himself. At S.O. he was set up so that it was impossible to get to him. You had to get passed the two bodyguards out on the street, the banger at the front door, the guard in the hallway and then the secretary. Only the closest and dearest of his friends could make it through that many layers of protection.

I thought I met a lot of influential guys while he was away. But once my father was out of prison, being with him every day was like an adventure. I never knew who I was going to be introduced to. One who stood out was Milty Tillinger, a powerhouse Jewish Mob Boss from the Combination Mob. He was a generation or so behind my dad, yet they were very close.

Much like Willie Catone, Milty was shielded from the public eye. Very few knew him. Many didn't even know he existed. Look him up and you won't find him either. You might find a well-researched Jewish Mob book with his name it or some very old short newspaper articles, but that's about it. Only select men could get to him for a face-to-face.

My father was one of them. I became another.

As the story goes, when Milty was younger, he had a big problem one time with the mob. Years before I was born, he showed up at my parents' door and my mother hid him out for about two weeks. After things simmered down, with the help of my father, he left. However, he never forgot that. Whenever my mother or father, especially my mother would ask him for something, it was always an unequivocal "Yes."

My mom must have sensed my unrest in the Garment District and one day out of the blue, Milty called and asked me how work was going.

"Come and see me tomorrow," he told me. "I'll put you to work."

Milty had a piece of a big union on Long Island. Within 24 hours, I not only had a job, I was a member. I organized meetings, ran errands, entertained guys and whatever else Milty needed. I got paid far more than what the job was worth, that's for sure.

I learned quite a bit about union business, especially the inner workings. At one point, the Union President, an Italian guy, who was a friend ours, asked me to help recruit and sign up about 40 non-Union men from Brooklyn. The goal was that by increasing membership and having them attend meetings, that would improve their negotiation power at a big meeting coming up.

I busted my ass working these guys. I showed up every day. I took them out for meals. I bought them suits and stuff for their wives. It took a while, but I finally got all of them signed up. I felt great knowing I helped with such a big thing. Or so I thought.

Milty found out what I did. "Bring me the cards."

I was confused. "What for? I killed myself getting these guys on our side."

"Friends of ours have these guys." He wasn't mad, just adamant.

I thought I was in deep shit. I tried to explain, but he cut me off. "I don't want to know. I don't want to hear. Just bring me the cards."

A couple of days later, the President of the Union called me into his office. "Here's seven tickets to the Yankee game tomorrow night."

I was totally confused. "For what?"

"Because I caused you grief. You're a good kid. Just take yourself to the game."

He slid me an envelope. There were no tickets in the envelope. Just $500 in cash.

I saw Milty a few days later. "That was nice of him to give me those five baseball tickets." I told him with a knowing glance.

"Five? It was supposed to be 7!"

I shrugged. "I only got five."

Milty got on the phone and tore into this guy, who obviously took two for himself. He bellowed into the phone, "You don't know who you're fucking with."

It was as if couldn't do anything without this kind of thing happening. No good – or bad – deed went unpunished.

In the end, the job with Milty became a hassle. Because my last name was Workman, the Feds went to every account I had. They'd storm in to my customers' businesses and start firing questions at them: "Did he threaten you?" "What did he say?" "What did he do?"

The exchanges these guys had with the Feds were classic, sometimes even comical, but ultimately, they were wearing me down. I couldn't take being harassed all the time.

Finally, I had to tell Milty I needed to move on. "I hate to do this, but I have to do something else." I felt awful.

He nodded as if he knew it was coming. "It's okay, kid. I understand."

One thing for sure, it was my last name or dad's hand that saved me and many friends at every turn. No one knew it, because he remained in the shadows, just the way he wanted it. But, for me it was getting old and dangerous. I needed a huge change to break this cycle.

22
PUT A CANDLE IN THE WINDOW

It was time for a change. I just wanted to run a clean business and make an honest buck. So, I bought a place in the middle of midtown on 52nd Street. We served lunch, dinner and had a bar for late evening business. It was no white linen place, but it was clean and well kept. It sat about 75 people and 25 at the bar.

All kinds of people came in from all walks of life. One of the best things about it was the awning. It hung out almost to the street with the name of the joint on it. I changed the name all the time. If I was going with a girl named Janie, it was Janie's. Next week it was Sheila's. I had fun with it and the customers did too.

One afternoon, I was sitting at the bar with the manager and the bartender. It was around four o'clock in the afternoon and my dad walked in with Willie Catone.

They sat down at the long bar against the wall, ordered drinks and started talking. I left them alone. What they were talking about was none of my concern. If it was, they would have made that clear. A few minutes later, a woman walked in with a dog. The manager went running up to her. "You can't come in here with a dog!"

My father turned around and yelled back. "Let 'em in and give the dog a drink, too."

Everyone in the place had a good laugh.

The short, silver-haired lady her thanks nodded to my father as the stunned manager backed off, knowing better than to disagree with my father.

Business was good for a while. I was making decent money, but not amazing. It was a living. I left the night shift to the managers, bartenders and servers, so I got to go home at a decent hour usually at around 11 after the dinner crowd was done. I didn't care much for alcohol, so I didn't necessarily like being around the big drinkers. Everyone wanted to buy me shots or martinis, but I usually declined and stuck with coke. Occasionally, to be polite, I'd have a glass of wine, but that was it.

The summer and fall were great, but once winter hit, business started to decline. One day in the middle of January, the snow was pounding down hard. There must have been six inches on the ground with more to come. It was grim outside and even sadder in the empty restaurant with no business. At around 4:30 in the afternoon, I looked out the window and saw a figure in a heavy overcoat standing by the door.

I walked over to the door and opened it. It was my dad. My father always wore a hat. It looked like Abraham Lincoln's top hate because it had snow on it about a foot high.

"Dad, did you walk here from 40th Street? Why didn't you take a cab for Christ's sake?"

He looked at me flatly, snow dusting the shoulders of his overcoat. "Do you know how long it's been that I can walk as far as I want to and not have to walk in a straight line?"

I had never thought of that. I felt embarrassed that I didn't bother to put myself into his shoes, but it was a real reminder that even if I forgot what he'd gone through, he never did.

Within a few minutes, a few other guys came in, all friends of dads. They each threw $100 bills on the bar. They bought few drinks and left the rest of the money on the table for me. By this time business was terrible and they knew it. Dad brought them in just to help me out.

I sat down next to him at the bar, grateful for the influx of cash and business but feeling down about my decisions to open the place. "Pop this business sucks. Honestly, I hate it. I thought I was doing the right thing, a straight gig. But I gotta get outta here."

He stared into his double malt scotch. "Why don't you put a candle in the window?"

I had no clue where he was going with this. "What for?"

"That will make it a queer joint and people will come in."

I thought he was crazy. "Pop, you've been gone for 24 years. How do you know what's what with that kinda stuff?"

Straight faced, he remained adamant. "I'm telling you put a candle in the window."

That night, I put the candle in the window. And BAM! Out of nowhere people started pouring in. Each night was busier than the night before. Money was flying in. It was crazy!

At the time, all I focused on was the money that was coming in. I wasn't worried about trouble because I always had muscle in the joint. It was safe. I never had a problem with the crowds. The place was becoming well-known – but as a queer joint. I hadn't set out to open a joint like this, but I couldn't walk away from the money I was raking in.

At my now "gay" bar, I was charging five to eight dollars just to get in. No one complained. I was also selling hard liquor drinks for a buck and a half – big money in those days.

One afternoon before we opened, Dad stopped in and I pressed him about how he knew to put a candle in the window.

He looked at me like I had ten heads. "What do you think? I am some fucking dumbbell?"

Like always, my father understood business and the world in general with a vast scope that I couldn't comprehend. It was as if he had the inside track on all matters irrespective of where he was or how old he was. I shook my head, laughed and patted him on the back.

People would start arriving after 6:00 pm when it was dark. Many would come dressed in drag, many of them could easily have passed for real women. It was astounding to me. A brand-new world I wasn't the least bit acquainted with and a total one-eighty from the rough guys I was used running with. The irony always gave me a chuckle. But the fact was, while I might have loved the money, I didn't love the bar business. My heart wasn't in it.

Eventually, word started to get around about how well I was going. That was a good thing and a bad thing. Good because business was way up. Bad because owners of other clubs became jealous.

In the spring, I got a panicked call from the bartender in the middle of the night. "Chuck, you have to get down here now!"

I got dressed and flew over there. Some guy busted into the

front door with a machine gun and started firing all over the place. It was a mess of broken glass, bottles, mirrors, chandeliers, tables, chairs, all shredded from automatic fire. He didn't try to kill anyone. He just destroyed the place.

My brain was about to explode into pieces like the broken mirrors. I was beyond furious. No matter what I did, trouble followed. I talked to some of the employees. This guy had some brass. He didn't wear a mask or do anything to cover his identity. He thought he was a tough guy. Because of the bullets spraying all over, no one got a good look at him. I didn't know if it was my competition or some guy who didn't like gay bars. But I had to find out and put a stop to it.

After I helped clean up the place, I went straight to see Dad. His response was not one that I was expecting. He looked me square in the eyes. "What are you going to do about it?"

By then, I was in my forties. I was so accustomed to turning to my folks or my connections with things got tough that it was second nature. But this time, I had to take care of the situation myself. Without saying anything out loud, he was telling me I couldn't wait because that would make me look weak. I needed to act fast.

A few days later, Willie Cantone got me the name of the guy who'd set up the shooting. "It's a competitor. Here's his name and the name of his place."

I took a deep breath.

Willie slide me a piece of paper with the information on it, his message – like my dad's – was no nonsense. He got me the name. The rest was on my shoulders. "Now go show him who you are."

I got back to bar and made the call immediately. "You know who I am. I know who you are. And I know what you did."

"Yeah so what?" the guy on the other end of the line shot back.

"Now it's time to see who's strong. I will meet you at your place tomorrow before dark." I slammed the phone down. I was a nervous wreck, but my reputation was at stake.

The next day I got ready to go, ready for action. I packed two guns inside my under coat and jacket. I thought I was going to have a heart attack. I considered myself a tough guy, but I wasn't a real "tough guy." There's a difference.

I opened the door to this guy's joint and walked in slowly. My eyes surveyed the place. It was no big deal. Wooden tables and chairs with no table cloths or table settings. Rustic looking. It was one of your run-of the mill, hole in the wall local bars. The bar was in the back along the back wall, cheap bar stools lined up. No wonder he didn't have much business.

At a table right in the middle of the room was my new nemesis. Slicked back black hair, bulb nose. I noticed a small scar on his chin. He glared at me with a smart-ass grin on his face. Then I noticed to my right, there was a guy from 121 Mulberry Street, a friend of my father's. He was nursing a whisky at the bar. To the left there was another friend of Dad's with a beer, acting like he was reading the paper.

My father "salted" the place. He never told me he was going to do this. In total, there were about four to five guys in there all on my behalf. They just wanted to see if I was going to show up. That was my test.

I went straight to the guy at a fast pace. He quickly stood up. I grabbed hold of him by the scruff of his neck and went nose to nose with mean intentions. He tried to take a step back and almost tripped over his chair. The smooth ferocity of the motion made him put his hand up as if to call a truce.

"Let me buy you a drink," he offered, trembling under my grip.

He wriggled out of my grasp, walked back to the bar and poured a full glass of an expensive bourbon and set it in front of me. I turned it over on the bar. "This is what I think of you and your fucking liquor. The next time you come near me or my joint, you better bring an army, because you're going to need it."

I turned around and walked out.

Honestly, I'm sure if I would have done the same things or acted the same way if those guys weren't planted there. They didn't move a muscle. They just kept an eye out for me and made sure nothing went wrong. But I felt a lot more confident with them there, like I had training wheels on a bicycle. My father understood better than I did that I was no mobster, no true thug. I wasn't the life he wanted for me, but it was my life by blood.

Unbelievably, two days later, the bar owner I'd roughed up was killed, though not by my hand or any of my father's associates. It was merely the hand of fate. Nobody knows what happened to him. No one said anything to me about it – I just heard he was dead.

That was the life I was in, up to my eyes, whether I tried to go straight or not. People were alive one minute and gone the next. Days turned into months and I kept the bar business going. I was still making money hand over fist. But I just couldn't take it anymore. This wasn't what I wanted for myself or my future. I simply wasn't happy.

So, I sold the place and made some money on it because business was good.

I started trying to make money in other ways, so I had income when I let the bar go. Now divorced, I had to provide for my boys. Yet once again, I was lost and had no idea what to do.

I quietly yearned to get back into golf. It was what I was born to do. But without a steady stream of guaranteed income, golf was a risk.

There was a gangster element in every job I took. Every week I seemed to be in a different battle with someone. I kept using my dad to get out of jams that I was not even a part of. Like clockwork, I was caught up in a world I was not built for and soon enough I received a real dose of reality.

I got called to a meeting with the Gyp DeCarlo and a bunch of his crew.

In those days, Gyp found out about my every move. I didn't really know it at the time until he sat me down. All my running around, using my dad's name and utilizing mob power got back to him. I sat at a table across from him. He leaned in towards me with cold, steel eyes and stared me straight into mine. What he told me is something that I will never forget.

"You're running around trying to be something that you're not. Your father is your father. Not everybody is going to be like him.

There is only one Charlie Workman. You better stop doing what you're doing. You're going to find yourself in trouble and alone. We are always here for you and will always help you. However, if you get into trouble because of something you did, we don't know you."

This was the second time I received this warning from Gyp and third overall. Three strikes and you're out. This was that crossroads moment when I understood that golf was my destiny. Gyp was right. I wasn't my dad. I wasn't cut out for this. I was just wearing his name like a disguise. I had to figure out who I was irrespective of my father, my family name and my past.

For some reason, I couldn't seem to get there on my own. I needed help. A push. A spark. I was missing something. Then like a blessing from above, I met the person who would change everything in a heartbeat.

23
SHE'S WITH ME

There have been two women who have had a tremendous impact on my life. The first was, of course, my mom, Katie. The second is my current wife, Elyse. They taught me what true power and influence is. It is not by fear or obligation. It's through genuine love.

Elyse and I met in the early 1970s on a blind date. We got together at a little, family-owned restaurant, a red and white checkered table type of joint that was quiet and quaint. I was late as usual. But the second I laid eyes on her, I had a feeling in my gut. Between her bright eyes, her wavy red hair and her natural charm, I was at a loss for words. Which quickly became a problem.

We ate dinner with no conversation. It was awkward to say the least. The first thing she said to me after a gapingly long silence was: "Take me home."

Not a stellar start to say the least and I did as she asked.

Nevertheless, Elyse stayed in my mind. There was just something about her. I couldn't get her out of my head. A few days later, I called and invited her to my son Craig's Birthday Party at Jack Mahoney's Page Two Night Club in Island Park.

She left me hanging. She didn't say she was coming, but she didn't say she wasn't either.

Low and behold, she showed up. I was ecstatic. I honestly did not expect her to come. Lucky for me, she'd felt the connection too despite our rocky start. We went from not talking at all on that blind date to talking about everything that night. And my family loved her instantly. From that point, on we were inseparable.

I learned she was ten years my junior and a school teacher. She also reluctantly admitted that she was going through a horrible, ugly break-up with her husband. It got so bad, he locked her out of the apartment. She left with her two-year-old daughter and moved in with her girlfriend because of how scared she felt.

We went on several dates and I noticed she kept wearing the

same clothes. Finally, I got the clue; she didn't have any other options because when she got locked out of the apartment, she could not get back in to collect the rest of her things. To Elyse, her daughter's safety was far more important than her personal belongings.

But, there I was working in the garment district with open-ended access to clothes. So, I brought her up to different manufacturing warehouses there on our next date. I'd set it up, so my friend had a smorgasbord of dresses and blouses and pants all ready for her. You would have thought she won the lottery. She was thrilled, oohing and ahhing at everything in front of her, mesmerized at the vast options.

"Where do I try these on? Where's the Dressing Room?" Elyse asked, as she looked around the place.

"Just find your size, take whatever you want, and you can try them on at home. Whatever you don't like or doesn't fit right, I'll bring back. It's that simple. Don't worry about it."

She looked at me like a deer in headlights. "Well, how much will all of this cost?"

"Don't worry about it!" I was so happy to be able to do something for her, I was probably more excited than she was.

Fretfully, she walked out with a load of dresses and pant suits, asking, "You didn't pay for any of them?"

"No. I didn't have to."

"Why?"

"Because they like me."

Elyse couldn't get over it. She came from a traditional Jewish family, so she didn't understand how things worked in the garment district, let along for someone with my kind of connections. I understood and respected that. Every time I picked her up I brought her a new outfit. In no time, she had an all new top of the line wardrobe. She'd been a beauty to me in those same clothes night after night, but with every new outfit, Elyse seemed to blossom as did our relationship.

I brought her everywhere. I was proud to be with her. I was

genuinely happy for the first time in a very long time. I took her to all the best restaurants, night clubs and the golf clubs I used to work at. One night, we went to Middle Bay Country Club where I was the Assistant Pro years before.

The pristine restaurant and lounge overlooked the first tee, 18th green and clubhouse with floor to ceiling windows. The place was filled with members, eating dinner, having cocktails, smoking cigars. A man in a tuxedo played the piano just loud enough to hear the songs. It was a real classy place.

When I went up to the bar to get us some drinks, a man in a rumpled suit who I'd never seen before came over to me at the bar and nodded toward Elyse then asked, "Who's that broad over there?"

"She's with me." I announced boldly without giving her name.

"Oh yeah. I had her. I banged the hell out of her," he shot back.

Bang! I hit him right across the mouth and laid him out right in front of the bar. He started to get up and I stepped on his neck. The guys at the bar formed a circle around me, so no one would intervene. I had the power. This piece of shit didn't. He quickly learned.

"You want more of me. Try me. My last name is Workman. Ask around and you'll see what's what."

I took my foot off his neck and walked through the circle of men. Two security guys came over and politely asked me to leave, escorting me out the door. They knew better than to lay a hand on me. They were just doing their job. Plus, I deserved it. But, I didn't care.

Elyse, who was standing near the circle of men quickly came to me and grabbed my arm and walked with me.

In those days, I had a real chip on my shoulder. If you looked at me the wrong way, I'd knock you out. I was bad. Most of the time I was right, but I reacted defensively with violence. I took things too far. I had power with my name and knew I could get away with it.

If anybody approached me with respect and warmth, I had no problems. But if someone came at me with any sort of aggression or disrespect, they were going to see a side of me they were not going to like.

"Chuck, what the hell was that about?" Elyse in a panic.

I shook my head. "Nothing. Don't worry about it."

"I am worried about it. I know you. You wouldn't have hit that man for no reason. Tell me please."

I stopped walking, took a deep breath and looked at her beautiful face. "Honey, he said some very ungentlemanly things about you. He got what he deserved."

"Me?" She yelled "I don't even know that guy."

"Exactly. Let's just let it go."

Not a word was ever spoken about it after that.

There were times when that attitude helped, especially when Elyse was going through her nasty divorce. That side of me came out as protection for her and her daughter. Their safety was at stake. Let's just say, I did what I had to do. Then there were other instances when my temper backfired on me.

Around the time we started dating, I had an office in the back of a barber shop owned by Manny the Barber on 7th Avenue. Manny was 100% Sicilian, but a straight up guy. He wasn't a tough guy either. What for? Mob stuff?

Unfortunately, Manny got into a couple of headaches with some mob bullies. They weren't really that big, but to him, they were terrifying. Dad took care of a couple. I took care of a couple and eventually they all went away. In Manny's mind, we saved his life. As is Sicilian honor, if someone saves your life, you are forever indebted to that person. Manny made it his mission to honor his debt.

Even when Dad was sick, Manny took care of him. Although he lived in Brooklyn, Manny would bring his tools on the train then the bus, come to our house and cut dad's hair once a week. I can honestly say I loved him.

In his barber shop he had a shoe shine guy named JoJo. He stood only an inch or two over five-feet but, was as wide as he was tall with nothing but rock-solid muscle. JoJo also had a reputation as one of the best knife fighters around.

To keep Elyse safe, I hired JoJo to meet her every day after school at Penn Station. He would escort her to wherever I was at the time: the barber shop, the garment center, wherever. I knew no one would go near her. And they didn't. He would not allow anyone to even talk to her, much less look at her. I asked him to bring his knife with him every time he would meet up with her Elyse. His eyes were moving all the time. He could spot trouble before it ever happened.

Elyse adored him. She told me she never felt so safe in all her life, which was all I wanted for her. She'd had a totally normal childhood Her mom was a housewife and worked for a time as a secretary at a retail store. Her dad was a stockbroker and her brother was a doctor. Our upbringings were opposites, yet we clicked on every level despite our different backgrounds. It was nothing short of kismet.

Early on before we got married, I was still bouncing around the garment center, doing different jobs, hanging with mobsters. Although she did not like that at all, she understood and encouraged me to want more for myself.

She told me, "You can't keep doing what you're doing. You can't tell good from bad."

I knew she was right, but it would take a few close calls for me to finally come to my senses. She guided with genuine love and patience. We would be talking about anything then out of nowhere she'd say, "What about golf? Just go back to it."

"It's not that easy."

"What do you mean it's not that easy? Sure, it is!"

Elyse had incredible people skills, not just with how she acted and treated people, but how she read people. It was uncanny. I'd take her to Little Italy and a bunch of mobbed up joints and introduce her to everyone. She was completely unfazed. As a matter of fact, she had a hell of a time. The guys loved her, and she managed to blend right in.

What I didn't know was that she watched and learned about these men. She had a very keen instinct for bad situations and literally and figuratively saved my life more times than I can count.

She used to go down to 121 Mulberry Street and sometimes played cards. Usually there were as many as a hundred guys smoking, cursing, playing cards, drinking. When she walked in the door, heads turned. Everything and everyone stopped. You could hear a pin drop. However, Elyse was not intimidated by or afraid of any wise guy. She took the whole scene in stride. She didn't do anything other than be herself. I think they all knew she was genuine. That's why they liked her so much.

From the beginning, I'd been upfront with Elyse about who my dad was. She was not deterred. In fact, she and my father had a special bond. He respected her and that was saying something. My mother was grateful that I'd found my match and urged me to marry Elyse, who'd quietly confided to Mom that she was afraid to walk down the aisle again after what had happened with her ex-husband.

Mom's advice was simple: "You better marry my son, or you had better leave him alone."

I don't think my mother was being protective. I think she was telling Elyse exactly what she needed to hear the way she needed to hear it.

While the bond we had continued to grow, things with her family weren't going quite as smoothly. My background and how I earned a living concerned them gravely. Elyse's father would study me, as if appraising me every chance he got. I tried to undercut their misperceptions of me by being kind, generous, upfront and easy-going but it never seemed to work. Honestly, I got discouraged. I couldn't seem to win their approval no matter how hard I tried.

One night to try and break the ice, I took her father to a craps game in Queens. We walked into the joint, and I introduced them to a bunch of the guys who were running the game. When I told them he was with me, they automatically gave him $5,000 in cash to gamble with. The look on her father's face was worth ten times the five- grand! The guys gathered around him, all of them explaining how the game worked then we set him up to be part of the house. In other words, he was a shill. No one knew who he was or what he was doing except me and the house.

It turned out that Elyse's father was incredibly good with numbers and he wound up being a very good gambler. Hour after hour, he kept winning, a grin flickering on his face each time. He was having a blast but trying to hide it until he just couldn't anymore. We had a fantastic time! It was like he was a born gambler. In the end, he won about $15,000 for the house. Before we knew, it was 4 o'clock in the morning and her father went home with $1,500 more than when he started.

The only downside was that Elyse's mom had been sick with worry and started calling police stations and hospitals. She even started watching the television to see if there was a car crash. Little did she know her husband was having the time of his life and racking in more cash than he was accustomed to seeing in a couple of months.

When we finally got home at around 5 o'clock in the morning, he showed her all the money he had won. Standing there in a robe, she was as happy as she was stunned. Elyse's father turned to me and eagerly asked, "When are we going to do this again?"

I simply patted him on the shoulder and said, 'Let's not rush into anything just yet."

I was well-aware that I could not over-expose him to that element. Elyse was all over me as it was time to get out. And I still wasn't.

Elyse's parent's lack of trust and trepidation continued. They knew Elyse was trying to get me out of that scene and back into golf, but it didn't matter. It was my dad's and my history that outweighed everything. It was a battle, but one I was determined to win.

There was only one way to bring them around and win their trust. That would be with what I was taught by dad and mom. "It's family first."

24
STOP THE NONSENSE: DO WHAT YOU LOVE

I met Bucky at a dive bar on 10th Street in lower Manhattan. This was a place where the knock around guys hung out. They played cards, watched TV, smoked cigars, drank, told stories and cooked up their next score.

Bucky had connections and looked the part. He dressed sharp in high-end grey pin stripe suit and tie. He was a bit shorter than me, average looking, but he had a confidence about him that I liked. He knew the garment industry and that was obvious.

Like Milty said, it seemed like the perfect match. Within a few days, we were doing business together. Bigger money started pouring in. We were a good team. We found a small, no frills, office in the garment center with a few desks that we used to conduct business.

Other than working together, I never hung out with Bucky. I didn't want to because business was business. He just seemed to know his stuff. And that was good enough for me.

After a few weeks, I finally I introduced Elyse to him at dinner in the city. She was pleasant during the meal and did not say a word about him. That was until he left.

"I don't like this guy."

I was taken aback. "What are you talking about? I'm earning with him. We're doing well."

"He's going to cause problems for you." She warned me in a stern voice.

"Ah, you don't know what you're talking about."

Like my mother, Elyse didn't a press her point to prove it. She let time do that for her. Little did I know how smart she was and how stupid I was.

One day, Bucky and I were at the office when he confided something to me. "I'm in some deep shit. I'm in a lot of trouble for some big money. Can you help me?"

I didn't think much of it and replied, "I might be able to." Was my instinctive reaction. My partner was in trouble. What was I supposed to do?

"Please, Chuck. I'm gonna get hurt if I don't come up with the money." He was unnerved.

"How much we talking about?"

He looked down at the floor then up at me. "Twenty large."

"Man, that's a lot!" I scratched my head. "How are we going to come up with that kind of money to pay it back?"

"We're doing well in business. Take it out of my end. I just need the lump sum now."

It sounded reasonable with the money we were making. "Okay. Let me go to some people."

The next morning, I went to see dad's friend, Julie Bernstein. When I arrived, Dad was in the office with him, which I pretty much expected.

I approached Julie and we greeted each other with a hug and kisses on the cheek. Then I got right to the point. I didn't want lectures. "Julie, I need twenty-grand really quick for my business partner."

Dad didn't move or say a word. His face and eyes said: "Are you fucking kidding me?"

"I thought you were doing well? Are you starting something new?" he asked curiously.

I took a deep breath. "It's nothing like that. Bucky's jammed up. Says he needs help."

The silence was deafening, and it seemed to last an hour.

Julie and Dad exchanged looks. "Do you stand good for this money?" Julie asked with a stone face and serious tone.

"Obviously, otherwise I would not be here."

Julie looked at my father again, who just nodded. "The obligation is yours. No one else. Just you." Julie reiterated.

I looked at my father and let me tell you, I felt the heat. Without saying a word, he was all over me with his eyes.

Julie got up and went into a back room then came out and handed me an envelope.

"Thank you, Julie." I said." "I know my obligation and when it starts. Rest assured it will be taken care of."

He nodded. I left, the weight of my dad's stare like a sweat stain on my lower back.

I met up with Bucky about an hour later at a gin mill nearby. "Here's the money."

"Thank you, Chuck. I'll take care of it. What's the vig?"

"It's only 1 point."

"That's fantastic. Thank you again." He looked like the weight of the world had just been lifted off his shoulders.

He went to turn away. I grabbed his arm and pulled him towards nose to nose. "Don't forget where this money came from. We owe this money. It has to be paid back or we're both in deep shit."

I expected and assumed that whatever trouble he got into was now over. All we had to do was pay Julie back. As the saying goes, You should never assume.

A few days later Elyse called me when I was at the office with Bucky.

She was in a state of panic. "You better come home. I think we've got a problem."

I asked again, "What's going on."

All she did was whisper: "I can't talk about it."

I rushed home from Manhattan. It took me about an hour and fifteen minutes. When I got home, she showed me a strange, new wire hanging out of our living room window.

"I think we're being bugged." Elyse said into my ear.

I climbed out the window and followed the wire up on to the roof. Thankfully, it was a TV wire not something planted by the FBI, the cops or anyone else. I climbed back into the apartment. "It's just a TV wire. No problem."

She gave me a stare. "I don't care what it is. I am living in fear. I think it's time that you really started looking elsewhere for work. You're tough. But you're not a tough guy. I want you to go back to playing golf. That's what you're good at, that's what your passion is. That is what I want you to do. Stop this nonsense and do what you love."

I was reeling. I knew she was right. She was genuinely scared. I didn't enjoy making her feel that way. I was supposed to be her protector. Although, I knew no one would ever touch her, who knows what the Feds or cops might do. I'd seen enough of that with what my father went through.

I had gone long enough making every excuse in the book not to make the change. Now I had to figure out a way to get out of this life that was not meant for me. Elyse was right. I was no gangster. So, I started to lay plans to get out. I figured it would take about a month.

About three weeks later, I got a call at the office. "Your partner is gone," a voice told me.

"What?" I yelled into the phone.

"Yeah, he took a long trip. He's not coming back." Click. Then dial tone was all I heard.

In those circles, final is final, if you know what I mean. There had to be a legitimate reason, and somebody had to approve it.

My whole body turned numb. My heart began to race like an Indy car. My brain fired on all cylinders with thoughts, none of them good! He's gone and so is my money. We hadn't paid a dime back yet. I was on the hook for $20,000. All I could see was my dad's face when I left that day I took the money. I was the one in deep shit now. And I was totally alone.

Elyse and I weren't married yet. Our wedding was a couple of weeks away. I had to tell her we were starting our lives together with a huge financial problem.

We were driving to her apartment and I told her. "I have to come up with 20-grand because of the guy you didn't like."

She went bonkers and started screaming. "What? Stop the car! I want to get out!" She was trying get me to pull over to the side of the road.

"I'm not stopping the car."

"I told you he was no good. Your reputation is on the line. Take care of it now! I don't care if we postpone the wedding. We're not starting off $20,000 in the hole. What's your father going to say?" She was infuriated with me and rightfully so.

There was nothing I could say other than. "I know."

The reality was because of my dad's reputation and the fact that so many people respected him, I managed to get more time to get the full amount to Julie. I cannot say how or who from, but I got the money. As soon as I did, I went right to Julie's office and gave it to him. He didn't say a word. Just nodded.

Then I headed straight home. "I paid off the debt," I told Elyse with a sigh of relief.

"Now who do you owe it to?" she demanded, aggravated. Seeing the woman, I loved so angry with me hurt me in a way I didn't realize I could be hurt.

"It's not like that. I did it clean. It's taken care of."

"Good. Now get the hell out of that life!"

How could Elyse know a good guy from trouble and still want to be with me? It gave me heart and strength to know that she was sticking by my side. "How the hell did you know he was no good? Please tell me because I must be missing something. Tell me what you saw that I didn't see."

She just shrugged. "I just knew. What can I tell you?"

That was the first, but not the last time she was right when it came to certain guys and situations.

But, the Bucky incident was the straw that broke the camel's back. If I wanted to stay with Elyse, I had to get out of that world. That was that.

I sold whatever business I had in the garment center. Within days I was playing golf again at local courses, some of my old haunts like Middle Bay and Shackamaxon. I entered some local tournaments and hustled a little bit. I felt so much better, even lighter. It was cleaner. I still loved it and was still good at it with a born-again attitude. Although my reputation for winning was still out there, I still never forgot the art of the hustle. I was reveling in it.

A few months after, the bosses held a big meeting in the city with about twenty top guys around a long table in a swanky loft. The place was set up with finger foods, waiters in tails, fine china, the definition of elegance. The gathering was about Dad.

A top Jewish guy announced, "Charlie, we have decided that we're going to give you all the paper and twine business from 32nd Street to 40th Street and from 7th Avenue to 8th Avenue. Any packing house, any shipping house, anybody that ships any goods and uses paper or twine must get it from you. We're also giving you all the light bulbs in the same area."

My father turned to me with a blank, flat face. I said, "Dad, that's great. What are you looking at me for?"

"You're going to run it."

"No, I play golf now, remember?"

Honestly, he should have hit me with a right cross. Because if I would have taken all that business I would have been a millionaire!

My dad looked at his associates. "Well, my son doesn't want it, so you've got to come up with something else."

And just like that, an incredible lucrative offer that was on the table one minute was off 30 seconds later; because the stupid son – me – didn't want it. I was too busy hitting golf balls. I think he thought maybe we'd partner up in business, so we could spend more time together. I felt bad about that.

I was not always right. Frankly, I was dumb sometimes. But, my father would never embarrass me in front of people. I think at that moment he began to accept that I was finally beginning to find my own way. He hadn't wanted me in that life and now even with a huge offer on the table, I picked the life path he'd put me on from the start. I was a golfer.

So, golf it was.

Besides the hustling, I needed a steady job in the industry. At the time, I was playing with a guy named Lenny Marinello. He owned the Golf City Driving Range in Whitestone, Long Island. He also owned the famous Fulton Quality Fish Market. The entire Marinello family were dear friends of ours.

Out of nowhere he said. "I fired the pro at my driving range. How about you take it over?"

I was shocked. "You're kidding?"

"I'll give you the pro shop. Don't pay any rent. You give all the lessons. Bring in whomever you want."

"That sounds good to me!" I was ecstatic. On top of that it was only fifteen minutes away from where I lived.

"Just come on down and see what you can do with the place. It's yours." He sounded as excited as I was.

We needed equipment and supplies in the pro shop. I met up with Ted Galgano from the Ben Hogan Golf Company. He gave me $20,000 in golf clubs, supplies and equipment to put in the shop. I had no credit, no front money, nothing. He really stepped out for me. All of this was consummated on a hand shake. That's it. He believed in me and I will be forever grateful. We became very close after that.

My persona changed immediately. I was back doing what I was born to do. Golf City was huge and active. Once I got started, word started to spread to old friends of mine and my dad's. A bunch of them started coming for lessons. I would work from 10 o'clock in the morning until midnight.

Things were finally going my way and it felt like I was finally becoming the real me.

Besides Elyse and my parents, no one was prouder of me than Gyp DeCarlo. A few years earlier he had been arrested, stood trial and convicted of conspiracy to commit murder back to 1968. The details of this incident were kept from me on orders from Gyp. I tried many times to talk to him and visit him in prison. "Chuck, Gyp does not want you to see him like this," one of his crew told me. "He wants you to focus on you and rebuilding your golf career. He loves you and misses you, but he does not want you close to this. He knows any known association with him can hurt you."

"I don't give a shit," I yelled. I wanted to see the man who had been like a father to me, especially in his time of need.

"We know Chuck. So, does Gyp. But you must abide by his wishes."

I was dying inside. Other than Dad, there is no man that meant more to me than him. I was relentless in my pursuit to see him or even talk to him. It fell on deaf ears. Eventually, he called me from prison. The conversation was short and sweet. "Make us proud," he told me.

I had tears in my eyes and could hardly speak. "I will, Gyp. I promise."

Unfortunately, this was one of the last times I ever spoke to him. As my life started to come together, Gyp's began to fall apart. During his prison term he became very ill. More than ever, I wanted to speak with him. I was heart-broken. However, I had to keep my focus on golf.

Somehow, someway President Nixon pardoned Gyp, supposedly due to his illness. It was rumored a lot of money was exchanged. The word on the street was Frank Sinatra and Vice President Spiro Agnew had a hand in it. That's the kind of power Gyp commanded, even from inside prison.

Once Gyp came home, I again wanted to see him. I was turned down continuously with the same response. "His days are numbered. He wants you to remember him as he was."

On October 23rd, 1973 Gyp passed away, supposedly from cancer. At the time, it was the worse death I ever had to endure. My mentor, my voice of reason, my protector was gone. To say I was devastated would be an understatement. To this day, forty-give long years later, when I get up in the morning and shave, the first thing I do is I think of two people: my dad and Gyp.

I had no choice except to move forward. It's what Gyp would have wanted and what I needed. Business at Golf City continued to grow. Most of these guys, especially in the beginning, were connected. However, this time it was different. They came to me because of my golf expertise and because they were happy for me. I think they thought, "Well, let's go take lessons from Charlie's kid. Why would we go anywhere else?"

One powerful wise guy from New York City would come in twice a week. He always said the same thing: "Do you mind if I go into your office to put some stuff in there?" he'd asked respectfully.

"Not at all. Go ahead."

I watched as he took out his gun and put it in a drawer of my desk. Then he'd change into a golf shirt and take his lesson.

Five minutes later, an NYPD cop would come in and do the exact same thing. They were together but staggered their arrivals. When this odd duo was done, they would go back into the office, get rearmed and buy a new shirt. Then they'd talk about their lesson. "How is your golf going? Is he helping you?" This was their routine.

"Yeah. Chuckie is terrific. I'm hitting the ball better, scoring better."

"Yeah me too.'

It was like being with me at my place was neutral ground. I thought it was hysterical. I always got a kick out of the fact that a mobster and a cop were taking lessons together. Now where would you ever see that?

Even members of the Chinese Tong gang, who were in that area and ran their mob operations out of Flushing, started coming in. Some of these guys would spend the whole day there. They would bring their entire families along with their bodyguards. Their guards would have raincoats on with shotguns inside it and the coats stayed on rain or shine. The Tong families would stay all day and spend $300 to $400 at a clip. It was like a watering hole in a jungle where anybody and everybody put aside their differences and associations to take part in or watch golf lessons.

One sticky summer night, the place was empty when two legitimate, successful businessmen named Hy Kolinsky and Mel LeBow came to the driving range to see me. I knew who they were, though I thought little of it. I figured they were just coming for lessons.

"Chuck, we've heard a lot of good things about you." Hy began.

"Yeah, I love teaching. It's a blast!" I said with a smile.

"No, we mean about your knowledge of the golf industry in general. Would you be willing to meet with us at our offices tomorrow and discuss a golf project opportunity?" Mel inquired.

I had no idea how or why they came to me, but I had nothing to lose. "Sure!"

The next day I met them at their plush offices in midtown. It seemed like everything was trimmed in gold. The chairs were big enough for two people.

I was supposedly there for an interview, but it really didn't feel like it. Hy and Mel talked about building a club called Charter Oaks and turning into a very high-end, elite Men's Only Golf Club. Their problem was that neither one of them knew anything about golf nor how to even get started in the business.

They asked me how I would do it, where I would start, who I would contact, every question in the book. I told them the truth. And I relished that someone was taking my ideas so seriously. I didn't just love the game of golf – I loved everything about the industry, so I was thrilled to share what I'd learned with them.

"You seem to know a lot of people in the golf world," Hy stated.

"That I do."

"And you've run successful golf business in the past," Mel intoned.

"I have."

They asked a few more question, then swapped glances. Hy cleared his throat. "We'd like to hire you as an advisor for the golf side of the business."

I paused for a second. "What's my end?"

"We'll pay you $2,000 a month. All you need to do is meet up with us once a month, give us an update and let us know what else you need to turn this place into something special. You can even keep your job at Golf City and consider this a side project."

In my mind, this was too easy. "Okay, you got a deal. When would you like me to start?"

"Today."

In a million years, I couldn't have predicted how this advisor role would propel me back into the golf world nor could I have imagined that it would be in such a big way.

25

CHARTER OAKS: BACK IN BUSINESS

A golf club built around the former mansion of a multi-millionaire – that was certainly a step up for me as well as a step in the right direction. Charter Oaks Country Club opened as such in 1969 and overtook the 75-year-old, sprawling forty-room summer home once owned by oil tycoon George Brewster. Mr. Brewster sold the entire estate to Karlinsky and LeBow. However, the land was mortgaged through the Teamsters and controlled by the Central States Pension Fund. The goal was to cater to all types of members: golfers, tennis players, billiards lovers, card players and people who just loved that kind of atmosphere. The club featured a ballroom-sized dining area with vaulted ceilings, a lounge with long, marble bar that could seat 25-30 people at a time, a vast billiards room and several meeting rooms, all spread out over the 164-acre estate.

The biggest project was without question the golf course. That was where I came in. So, I reached out to the number one golf course designer in the world and a family friend, George Fazio. He was part of Bob Hope and Bing Crosby's sports and entertainment group, both of whom were dear friends of Dad's. When I asked him if he would be interested in the project, he jumped at the opportunity.

"I'll be there tomorrow," he said without hesitation. "But, I'll only deal directly with you."

"I don't make the final decisions," I reminded him. I did have two bosses to report to. "But whatever you need, I will make sure you get it."

In those days, George was considered unaffordable. However, because he was a friend, we made it work. To say he cut us a break would be an understatement.

When I informed the investors that George was on-board, they were ecstatic.

"Is there something we don't have that we need?" they asked.

"Most high-end country clubs also have tennis courts. You

should build some. Give the guys something else to do during the day with gorgeous girls serving them drinks from the outside bar. They need things to occupy their time while waiting for the course to get done."

"Girls?" the investors asked with a puzzled look

"Yes. Girls. You need good looking girls. If this is going to be an all men's club, you need gorgeous broads in here doing everything: bartending, waitressing, hanging at the tennis courts, greeting, hosting, whatever it takes. You're also going to need a billiard's pro. And I think I have just the guy for you."

Carl Zingale, who was better known as Cue Ball Kelly, was a famous billiards player and he was part of a crew at Golden Cue Pool Room on Long Island. Cue Ball taught Jackie Gleason how to play pool for the famous movie, The Hustler. Cue, like so many others, considered my father a close pal. I gave him a ring and asked him from a referral.

"That's easy," Cue replied. "How about Willie Masconi?"

"He's one of the best in the world! You can get him for me?" I couldn't believe what I was hearing.

"Willie is with us in Bob Hope's group. Now he's with you too. You want him, you got him."

"Wow! That's great!" I did not see this coming. "You sure he will agree to help out?" I asked just to make sure.

"Willie knows of your dad. I am sure he will be more than happy to do it."

I now had the greatest billiards player of all-time as our Pool Room Pro along with a world-class golf course designer. We put up huge posters with incredible preliminary drawings of course with Fazio's name in bold under them. It drew tons of attention. I can't tell you how many times we were asked: "This is going to be a Fazio course?"

Eight, stunning tennis courts were built within a few weeks. The billiards room was redesigned to suit a king, furnished with lavish, velvet furniture, gleaming brass fixtures and large photos of the titans of billiards with Willie's picture being the largest. He was incredible and did everything from putting on trick shot exhibitions to giving lessons to regaling members with hilarious stories. It couldn't have been going better.

Slowly but surely word started to spread, and membership numbers were increasing, but I had a lot of work to do.

I was still giving lessons at Golf City and doing legwork like making phone calls and visiting people if needed and putting them together for the country club. Little did I know how this would become a trademark of mine through the years. I had a blast watching projects come to fruition and become successful simply by connecting people. Say here about how wife/parents were proud.

When it came time to tap a tennis pro, my signature connection skills landed me the number one ranked men's tennis pro from 1953-1955, Tony Trabert. He won ten major titles, five singles and five doubles, including the French Open Champion in 1954 and 1955, the U.S. National Men's Singles Champion in 1953 and 1955 and a Wimbledon Champion in 1955. After retiring, in 1971 he teamed up with Pat Summerall as the CBS golf analyst and was world renowned in the tennis industry. There was such a natural crossover between golf and tennis that he agreed to take on the same type of role as Willie Masconi did. I couldn't have asked for a better fit.

Elyse and I started spending more and more time there, even before the golf course was finished. The food was outstanding as was the service and the overall ambience. It was like taking a vacation that was only a short car-ride away from home. All the patrons felt so too, which was what had our membership climbing month over month.

As the golf course got closer to being finished, I needed a big-time PGA golf pro. Though I knew quite a few myself, finding the right fit and one who was available to do it was another thing. I asked George for his input.

"What kind of guy are you after," he inquired.

"He's got to be popular. A name people will know immediately. Preferably a guy who has a few wins under his belt, maybe a major title. Full of personality and charisma. A salesman on the green."

"That's it?" George chuckled. "How about Ken Venturi."

I couldn't believe my ears. Ken was an ideal fit, but I didn't think he'd be available. George offered to make some calls.

While he was making his rounds, I decided I need to make a few myself to see if I could clinch a big name in boxing too. Since I was a huge boxing fan and my uncle had been in the fight game back in the day, this was a no-brainer. I called Rocky Graziano. By then the sales pitch was a cinch. Not that I needed one for Rocky. I knew he would say yes, but I was still respectful because he was a very dear friend.

"What do you want me to do?"

"Just be you Rocky."

"You got it, kid."

Now I had a beloved boxing champ on board, I eventually got a few other well-known fighters interested in the country club also. The next big name on my list: Toots Shor. Bernard "Toots" Shor was the famous owner of the legendary saloon and restaurant in Manhattan, Toots Shor's Restaurant. His place was one the places to be if you were in New York City.

Like Rocky, he was in. All he needed to know was what to do and when to be there. "Do I get paid?" he joked. "I'm just kidding, Chuck. I don't want anything from you."

"How about a car and a chauffeur to pick you up and get you home?"

Toots did not know how to drive. He didn't have to.

And just like that, the famous Toots Shor became Charter Oak's big name, meet and greet man at the bar. My star-studded lineup was almost complete. Except for Ken Venturi. I got word he was having some trouble out in San Francisco, so I asked my father to look into it.

Dad got word that Ken needed a friend in more ways than one, so I hopped the next flight out and was at his door by morning.

He met me at the door and when we hugged, I could feel his pain. After a few seconds, he pulled away, tears in his eyes. "It's been too long, and good friends don't go this long without talking. Even though I don't see you, there isn't a day that goes by I don't think about you."

"Same here, Kenny."

We sat down on his brown leather sofa in front of a sweeping brick fireplace, the crackle of the flames filling the silence.

"Talk to me, Ken. How are you doing? How can I help you?"

Once he began to open-up, we talked all day and through the night. I stayed with him for two days. The Kenny I knew and loved was still there. It took him a day or so, but his personality started to come back. I didn't do anything special. I simply listened and offered my two cents only when he asked for it. I waited until I thought the time was right before bringing up the opportunity I wanted to offer him at the country club. He needed to be smiling and feeling better.

With a smile finally brimming on his lips, I said, "Kenny, I think I have something for you that is right up your alley."

"Still the same old Chuck. Putting people together."

I explained my role and mentioned all the big names I already had committed to the project.

Kenny thought for a minute. "You offering me a job?"

"Of course. Why the hell do you think I'm here?" I laughed.

"I guess I could use a change of scenery."

"Consider it two friends helping each other."

"What about my family? I don't want to uproot the kids completely. This is home to them."

"Bring them out in the summer. Then send them back during the school year. If you need to get home for a bit, you go home. We'll let people know when you are going to be there."

"I think you have something, Chuck. I'm really intrigued. After what you've done for me here these past few days, it's the least I can do." He began to get emotional, but in a good way. "Okay, you've got me. Under one condition, though. I get to kick your ass on the golf course."

About two weeks later Kenny took like a fish to water as Mr. Meet and Greet for anybody and everybody who loved golf. His stories had people riveted or rolling with laughter. He was truly in his element and seemed happier than ever.

If Willie or Kenny wasn't wowing the members, I got actor Jack Kelly, who played Maverick on television, to swing by from time to time. He was another guy involved with that whole Bob Hope gang. All the women went nuts when he was on site.

Finally, after nine months of word of mouth and wooing potential patrons, we had enough money to start the construction of the golf course. It was about integrity creating reality. There was a ribbon cutting ceremony covered by the newspapers, radio and TV news shows. It was truly ground-breaking in every sense of the word and it felt like the beginning of a new era of elite country clubs. The public relations coverage was unbelievable. We really played it up, especially with our famous ambassadors attached to the club.

Then fate intervened and Ken Venturi had to leave when the course was about half way done. NBC recruited him to be their PGA Golf color commentator. No one was prouder for him than me. He deserved it. In my opinion, he turned out to be the greatest television golf commentator ever. Vision through the eyes of a player translated to a viewer. He was simply magical to watch and listen to.

As for me, I loved being at the club, but I stuck to what I was hired to do. I was still only an advisor and an honorary member. I never overstepped my bounds and maintained my job at Golf City, so I didn't really need anything else. I was in a very comfortable situation with very little pressure.

What I didn't realize was that what I had built up out of friendships and phone calls had set me on a path with much more to come.

26

CHARTER OAKS: THE KID IS BACK FOR GOOD

The last piece of master plan for Charter Oaks massive golf course remodeling project was barely through the design phase and memberships were spreading like wildfire. George Fazio passed the project on to his nephew, Tommy, to finish the project, so he could move on to other things. Then, I brought on famed architect, Bob Mazan, to draw up the final rendering. Next, I reached out to George Campanegro, also known as the Masked Marvel, a pro wrestler on television, to build the course. By that time, he'd retired and now owned a huge construction company. Although he had never built a golf course before, he eagerly accepted the challenge. Carl Simone, another friend, came and helped George with bringing the course to fruition.

Suddenly, to my shock and horror about halfway through, the investors ran out of money. Everything came to a screeching halt. We figured we were dead in the water.

After a big meeting with the investors, construction companies and board members, Carl Simone stepped up. He put a lien on the place and took out a second mortgage to keep the construction going. With that, came the passing of the torch to Carl to run the place. He not only finished building the course, he changed the concept from a men's only club to a family golf club. This was shear brilliance because it quickly brought in even more members.

He then managed to land Jack Oliver, a famous PGA golf pro from Long Island, as a partner and the club's golf pro. Carl Simone had wanted me for the job but fearing the stigma of collusion, with the Teamsters, it was decided that Jack was the smarter fit. That wouldn't be the last time I was passed over for such an opportunity due to my family name. As much as I wanted that job, I had to step aside and let Jack take the role.

The golf course was finished in 1974. As soon as the doors opened, it was regarded as one of the best and most elite courses in the area. It was nothing short of spectacular. There was action in every inch of the club from the golf course to the tennis courts to the billiards room to the card tables, right down to the bar and the restaurant. The money was rolling in. Everyone was happy. It was the place to be when it came to country clubs in that area.

However, sometimes success breeds over confidence and complacency.

When you rest on your laurels and stop doing the things that made you successful, it's a recipe for disaster. All the grunt work that it took to get the place on the map stopped. Not only that, members were getting away with murder not paying their dues and membership fees. Money was dwindling fast. The entire place soon fell into financial dire straits.

The Central States Pension fund was not happy. They sent someone down to scrutinize the set-up and figure out what was going on. They needed someone tough to make sure things got straightened out. They sent some muscle in the form of a man named Mike Lomet.

The first thing he did was put a registry book at the bar. When you walked in, you had to sign in. Mike would look up the member's name and check their payment status. If you owed, it wouldn't be for long. Mike had a patented system to make sure of that.

One member owed $2,000. When Mike gave him a killer look, the guy turned sheet white and swore: "I will have it tomorrow."

Mike pulled out some cash from a tin box under the bar. "Here's is your $2,000 for the fee. Now you owe me $2,000 and I want it by nine o'clock in the morning."

Sure enough, the guy showed up the next morning with the money. Why? For starters, Mike was a mountain of a man weighing over two-hundred pounds. Second, he kept a gun on the bar.

With Mike now at the helm, members began to get caught up on their dues almost overnight.

Nevertheless, the place needed an overhaul. Everyone heavily involved knew it, even my wife, Elyse, yet I had remained hands-off. One morning, she was at Charter Oaks having breakfast and started talking to Mike over coffee.

"I heard you're having a lot of problems around here," she

stated casually.

"Yes ma'am. We sure are."

"Why don't you talk to my husband? He knows all about the business, gives lessons and is quite charming."

"Would he be interested in taking over the pro shop and becoming the pro?"

"He might be. Why don't you ask him?" She was playing Mike like a fiddle.

Soon after, Mike called me at Golf City and offered me the position.

"Thanks Mike, but no. The current golf pro is a partner there. I'm not going to take his job. I don't do that." I was adamant.

Two days later, Mike called me back. "He's not a partner anymore. We gave him his money back. You interested now?"

I had a feeling this was coming. "Absolutely."

"Good. You're hired. Come and see me tomorrow?"

Even though Mike had hired me, it still had to be approved by Al Wolfson, the president of the club, and the Central States Pension Fund.

Based solely on my golf reputation, Al agreed to hire me. The Central States Pension blocked me for the second time to avoid any suspicion of bias.

Mike stood his ground and the Central States Pension team eventually gave in, but they made him sign a contract shifting liability to him rather than them. If something went wrong, Mike was on the line for me. That showed me just how much he wanted and needed me at Charter Oaks.

The pro shop was mine and soon my golf fire was turned into an inferno. I was back in a big way. I knew I could turn the place around, truly put it on the map. After all, it was my connections that helped get the place going.

I went right to work and made calls to every golf equipment sales rep I knew. In less than a day, shipments were pouring in. You name it, we had it. All high-end, state-of-the-art equipment. Within two days, the shop was completely restocked and reopened.

Word started to spread. While playing at a popular local tournament, manufacturers from all over the country approached me. They all wanted in. It was crazy. I was signing deals left and right.

That week I went to see family friends in the garment district and I approached the biggest manufacturers, who sold to Bloomingdales and Sax Fifth Avenue for merchandising. We received the same pricing as the big stores and sold them for less. We put our logo on everything: polo shirts, sweaters, jackets, windbreakers. In under a week, our clothing store was open for business too.

I didn't know it, but Walter Scheiber, who I had worked for back in the day was brought onto the staff. I found him sitting behind a desk one afternoon and we both looked at each other, stunned.

"What the hell are you doing here, Chuck?"

I leaned over his desk with a wink. "Now you work for me!"

We both had a good laugh. He was a good guy and an even better friend. He was a contemporary of Gene Sarazen, who he used to play with all the time. Walter stayed with me at Charter Oaks until the day he died.

As the club got back on track, so did the membership fees. On top of that, new members started joining. Legitimate businessmen from all over the area came aboard, many with their families, as did some of my old mob friends. They wanted to let it be known that they were proud of me because I was going legit doing what I was born to do.

As the club's reputation and success grew, my relationship with Al Wolfson blossomed. We became great friends with a mutual respect for our knowledge and insight of the golf industry. Although at times, we fought like cats and dogs about our philosophies, when it was over it was over. Our relationship remained tight despite our differences.

I started playing more, in both tournaments and hustling. Only now I didn't have to travel to do it. The action got hot. Big time players and hustlers were playing at Charter Oaks regularly and for vast amounts of money.

Lenny Marinello didn't join the club, but he started playing in big money games there. He introduced me to one of the best money players I ever met, Mike LoBosco. Mike and I teamed up and would often play against Bernie Berland of Berland Lincoln Mercury and a hustler named Harry "The Stockbroker."

At one point, they owed us so much money, I had to take them to a shylock, so they could pay me. Nevertheless, they kept coming back for more. Bernie lost his Rolls Royce. Harry lost another $12,000. Plus, he had to pay the vig on the shylock loan. After that he finally gave up.

Charter Oaks brought something out in people, a fever, a desire to be there and participate in the magic. Though it didn't always work out for some, like Bernie and Harry, most of the members and their families genuinely enjoyed their time there and made memories that they cherished.

Elyse was not a golfer when we met, but after spending so much time at Charter Oaks, she quickly turned into one. I gave her some lessons. She was a natural and fell in love with the game, becoming an avid player and a savvy one at that. I loved it. We played often and had the time of our lives. She was as low as a four handicap at one time.

The more we golfed, the happier we both were. We had so much fun. We played every afternoon. She would come home from teaching at the local elementary school and meet me on the golf course.

One afternoon I was short a player for a money match that I set up. Elyse and I lived right near the club. I called her up and told her I needed a partner.

I was playing against Al Wolfson, who was an impressive player in his own right and some guy I did not know.

When Al realized she was going to be my teammate, he said, "She'll play the men's white tee, and you cover the bets. She's not going to play the women's tee way up there while we are playing for money."

She shot 76. I played below average for me. But we still won $600. I laughed my way all through the golf course as she blew these two seasoned golfers off the course.

"When are we going to do this again?" she asked Al at the end.

He patted her on the shoulder like a gentleman. "Never!"

Elyse and I married in 1975. Our wedding was held at Charter Oaks. It was an unforgettable, magnificent day. The banquet hall was always extravagantly designed, designed in with white and pink colors, with touches of gold in all the right places. Tables were always white linen. But, on this day the entire room was draped in specially designed colorful flower arrangements with a special section for the ceremony.

Though her parents still didn't fully accept me due to my family's reputation and my ongoing affiliation with the mob, they were happy for us because we were happy.

My parents and my family were ecstatic. They all loved Elyse, no one more than my dad. My boys adored her. They all knew how happy I was and that is what mattered most to them.

I adopted Elyse's daughter from her previous marriage. She was only five at the time. She needed a good father in her life. I could never replace her paternal father and I didn't want to. However, I could provide her with the love and support she truly deserved. She was the same age I was when my father went to prison so there was an immediate connection there.

We may have been far from normal, but we were a family. That was all I'd ever wanted.

I was blissfully married, playing the game I adored and loving life. Everyone was proud of me. Suddenly, everyone wanted to play me again.

Big money golfers kept coming, looking for action. One time, I teamed up with Carl Simone to play a guy named Murph Projansky and a PGA Tour player named Ralph Johnson, who Murph sponsored. He also sponsored professional bowlers such as Mark

Lemongello and Dick Weber. Murph was no stranger to gambling. He would bet 10-15 football games a weekend.

We played three games of best-ball. The first game was for $5,000. Carl and I lost. Carl was waiting for me to find my game that day. Unfortunately, it never came around. On the second day, we played for or $10,000. We split, so we were still down five thousand. On the third day, we played for $20,000 with $5,000 presses. Today the total would be worth around $100,000.

A huge gallery formed. It was like the shoot-out at the O.K. Corral only with golf clubs. By the end, we had blitzed them for $25,000!

Murph went nuts. He said to Ralph, "How could you let a club pro beat us. He should be on tour not you. You should be selling shirts in a pro shop, you bum."

Ralph, a consummate gentleman golfer, simply shrugged. "He was just better than me today. That's golf. Next time you should make a better game."

To true golfers, that was the game. But Charter Oaks went beyond golf. That was its magnetism and its allure, like Las Vegas without the gaudy lights. That didn't mean it was free of sin. Golfers loved to gamble and vice versa. Nothing would change that.

I was always thinking of ideas to bring in more pros because they drew crowds. Crowds spent money. And I sure didn't mind playing them. It was mutually beneficial.

I decided to reach out to Doug Ford, a PGA Masters Champion and a good friend of mine, then together we brought in Roger Ginsburg, Joe Moresco, Larry Loretti and a bunch of other top players and some former tour players. We wound up with eighteen pros in all for a mammoth event intended to pack the place with fans as well as would-be members.

The night before the event, we invited everyone to the golf club. We created teams in what we call a "para-mutual," in other words we try to make them even, with each team having one current PGA golfer. Then I arranged to have one of my bookmaker friends, Barry Bernstein, put up odds on all the teams.

Once the odds were set, bids were made to own the teams, minimum being $500. The more a guy liked a team, the higher he would bid. Half of all the money would go into the pot and the other half would go into the para-mutual pool, part of which went to a charity. By the time it was all said and done, we had $35,000 in the pot.

I got teamed up with a knock-around guy named Nick Sofia, who was good lefty golfer. He carried a piece everywhere he went, even had one in his golf bag.

The winning bid for our team was $5,000. As part of the rules, each team was entitled to buy back fifty percent of the team. We put up the $2,500 then bought half the team back from the winning bidder.

On the first hole, Nick missed a short put. It was so short anyone could just kick it in with their foot easily. You could hear our whole team whisper, "Holy shit!"

On the second hole, he fluffed a shot. On the third hole, he fluffed another one. We started to argue under our breaths. I couldn't believe how he was blowing this for us.

With each shot, we bickered more. And more. And more. When we got to the fifth green, he pulled out his gun and shouted, "Go ahead! One more word, Chuck!"

I yelled back. "Wait a minute, let me get mine!" We both busted out laughing. Thankfully, nobody saw us, and cooler heads prevailed, all kidding aside. The real problem was that we played so bad, we finished dead last!

After eighteen holes, Doug Simone, who was teamed with Doug Ford were tied with two other teams. Ford didn't think he and Simone had a chance, so he left. Just like that, he got into his car, went to the airport, and flew back to Florida.

As per the rules, there had to be a sudden death play-off. With Ford gone, Carl, who was only an amateur, had to play two other teams by himself. On the third hole, Carl sunk a 60-foot putt to win the match. He beat the two other teams by himself and walked away with the $15,000.

The next day, Doug Ford called me at the pro shop and said. "Hey Chuck, I hear I won the tournament!"

"I think you better wait a minute. I'll get Carl, you talk to him. "

Without hearing the words, I had a feeling what Ford was saying because steam was practically coming out of Carl's ears. "What do you mean, we won the tournament? You were on a plane!" He went silent then said: "You want your cut? I'll tell you what you're entitled to. You're entitled to getting buried under the expressway." Then he slammed the phone down."

Charter Oaks was every bit a country club and a place where nobody could ever forget who built the place – men with a mob mentality, whether they were made or not.

We had a phenomenal run at Charter Oaks until 1979. The Central States Pension Fund was having trouble paying the mortgage on all their properties throughout the United States. In no time, the federal government stepped in. The Feds appointed overseers to every one of their properties.

Equitable Life Insurance company came to Charter Oaks and changed the name to Fox Run Country Club. They purchased everything, including the pro shop. They raised the rate on golf carts and greens fees. Fortunately, business immediately went up 20% across the board.

Little did everyone know, those who were appointed fiduciary were friends of ours. They ran all the properties east of the Mississippi for the Federal Government. However, when the balloon payment was due, the CSPF didn't have the money. They were being forced to close-down. Unwilling to watch all my hard work crumble, I came up with the idea to have the members buy the property.

The outstanding on the mortgage was around $3 million. The place had over 375 members. If everyone put up $20,000 to $25,000, we'd have $2.5 million. Any bank would have given us the other five-hundred thousand. We would buy the property and business. On paper it, was a slam dunk. And the members had the money. Except they were afraid. So, it never happened. And it's a damned shame too because the place is now probably worth over a $100 million. My idea would have made them rich beyond their wildest imaginations.

Yet again, it was my imagination that created an opportunity for so many to succeed, but fear won out. It was heartbreaking.

Though I stayed on, my instincts told me that when things were starting to go very wrong. There would be no turning back. So, I needed yet another new plan.

Only this time it wouldn't just be about golf. It would put family back in the forefront of my life for good.

27
REST IN PEACE

There is nothing more painful than the loss of a child. It is not the natural order of things. It is not something I wish on anyone. To this day, I still cannot get my head around it.

My son, Craig, died at the age of 31. We called him "Butchie." I understand the trouble that he was in. But, to me that never justified such a horrible, sudden end to the life of a young man.

Craig was a great athlete in high school, an incredible gymnast. His dream was to make the United States Men's Gymnastics Team. Unfortunately, that dream came to a screeching halt when he got into a bad motorcycle accident as a teenager. From that moment on, in his mind, he'd lost it all. He never got over it.

In my mind, I was responsible for it, not him.

When I got divorced, Craig came to live with me while his two brothers went with their mother. I was not around much, so he spent a lot of time with my dad and heard a lot of stories about that life. My mom tried hard to keep him on the straight and narrow. But Craig made a conscious decision to try and follow in my father's footsteps.

The problem was that Craig could not conceptualize the major differences between what my father did for a living at a young age and the fact that my father came from a totally different era and did the things he had to do to survive.

Between the onset of depression following his motorcycle accident and taking prescribed pain medications for the pain, Craig's personality changed completely. He was no longer the loving kid that we knew. He started making bad decisions, which resulted in him getting into trouble.

My father stepped in on numerous occasions and helped him. Regrettably, it was his protection that made my son feel invincible. I was all too familiar with that feeling. It is intoxicating. However, everyone has choices. Craig's continued to be the wrong ones.

My father was Superman to me. Now he was my son's

superhero. Except that was the problem.

My father had always been an imposing figure – in personality and in stature. By the time he reached his 70's, we noticed his strength started to decline. He also started getting hand tremors every now and then.

"Dad, what's wrong? Why are your hands shaking?" I would ask, concerned.

"It's nothing. Just war wounds."

He was referring to the residual effects of being shot four or five times in his previous life. In his mind, these wounds were causing the tremors. Whenever they would happen, he would just move his hands out of sight, so no one could see them.

Eventually, the tremors grew worse and lasted for longer periods of time. Other parts of his body began to deteriorate as well. His arms and legs were giving out, which affected his equilibrium.

One day, he was walking from his office in the garment district to a meeting and he collapsed in the middle of the street. Thankfully, his friends found him right away and had him rushed to the hospital.

When I got to the hospital, a young doctor was examining him. He asked my dad to put his arms up. He did then the tremors started again.

The doctor asked, "Why do you think they are shaking?"

"War wounds." It was his stock reply.

"You were in the World War?" the fresh-faced doctor inquired.

My father flew into a rage. "Get me the hell out of here. These are a bunch of kids! What would they know. Take me home!"

Soon we received a diagnosis. It was Parkinson's Disease. A cruel and debilitating death sentence for a man who'd been robust throughout his life. It was painful to see my Superman this way. It was even harder for Craig.

The physical pain from his motorcycle accident was real and intense. However, I have no doubt he was suffering just as much mentally and emotionally. I found out he was taking drugs. Whether he was involved in selling them too, I'm not certain and quite honestly don't want to know.

My instinct was to try and save him. I needed to do something. When I first found out, friends of mine told me where he was getting them from and who. I gathered up every guy I could and went to his school in Queens. We beat the living hell out of anyone and everyone who was dealing dope there.

The school was clean for about two months. But, they all came back. My attempt at helping failed miserably. If anything, it made the situation worse. Craig continued down a perilous path of darkness and self-destruction.

Right after high school, he disappeared for about two years. No one had a clue where he was. One day out of the blue, I received a call from my mom. "I just got off the phone with a cop your father knows out in Los Angeles," she said. "They have Craig."

"What the hell for?" I yelled.

"I don't know the details. All he said was, 'I have your grandson and I'll hold him, but send someone out here ASAP.' Your dad is already working on it."

When I got to my father's house, his face said it all. "You're going to California with the lawyer. First flight out." He ordered.

Things happened so fast. The next thing I knew we were outside of LAX where Mickey Cohen and some of his crew met us. Next, we arrived at the jail and the lawyers, cops and members of Cohen's crew held a long meeting. After a couple of hours, an agreement was reached. I will be honest. Money came into play. Where it came from and how much was involved, I have no idea. It was my son. Honestly, I didn't care.

Within an hour, we were back at the airport with Craig in tow, heading home. He looked like a shell of his former self. The muscle aspiring gymnast was lean and gaunt, his hair disheveled, his face was that of a ghost. It was hard to see my son that way.

As relieved as I was to see him and find him and save him, this turned out to be a huge mistake on my part. Now, Craig felt like he could get away with anything, that we would always save him. He arrived home feeling like nothing and no one could get in his way.

While Craig began to act like he was unstoppable, my dad's symptoms continued to worsen. He went out publicly less and less, maybe to dinner or for a drink with his family and closest friends. He could only hold a glass with two hands and struggled using utensils to eat. It wasn't something he wanted others to see. This became an increasing burden on mom. She was the only one allowed to help him, but Dad was a big man and she was a petite lady.

"I don't want anyone coming here to take care of me. We could be letting a killer in the door."

He didn't see the irony. "Dad you need help." I urged.

"If it's not a killer, it might be a reporter or law enforcement trying to get something out of me."

"You're being paranoid, Pop."

"Bullshit. They are still out there, and they still want me."

His suffering and refusal to get outside help went on for three years. Finally, he told mom. "I didn't expect to go out this way. Sorry to be such a bother."

He knew he was dying.

"I was never supposed to come home. So, whatever time I had was a bonus," he confided to me privately. "I fooled them anyway, what's the difference? Two days or ten years it doesn't matter. I fooled them."

He never ceased to amaze me. He accepted his fate the same way he accepted his prison sentence. He took it in stride as if it were just part of life.

Near the end, he told my mom, "Katie this is too much for you. I don't have long. I just want to be with family. I can't stay in the house. I can't keep doing this to you. Bring me to the hospital."

As sad as we all were, we abided by his wishes.

About a week later, in the morning, I was by his bedside. I was the only one in the room. Mom was home taking a much-deserved rest. He looked at me with glazed, tired eyes. "I'm really tired. It's been a long trip."

Those were the last words he ever spoke.

Within an hour, he was gone. He was only 74. He lasted five years after his health began to decline; 15 years after his release from prison and 34 years after he supposedly, took out the Dutchman.

When mom came to the hospital she said. "He is finally at rest."

He was. But I wasn't.

Craig's life continued to spiral out of control. At 20 years old, he got married. Soon after, he and his wife had a baby girl. We all hoped this might straighten him out. It did not.

He started disappearing for months at a time acting like a hoodlum. This was about a year and a half after dad had passed. I truly wish that I had dad to lean on during that time.

Frankly, I knew this was going to end badly, I just didn't know how bad.

The concept of fatherhood was complicated for me, mixed with strength and secrets and questions you couldn't ask or might never get answered.

The day my father died, the amount of people who came to the hospital in Long Island to pay respects staggered the imagination. It took forever for the hospital staff to take his body because there were so many people there. Each one wanted some time alone with him, to say good-bye in their own special way. I felt thankful.

No official notice was ever given to the press. Calls were made to people from pay phones. At first, not even law enforcement knew about it.

The news of his passing traveled like a hurricane across the county. The outcry of admiration and respect he received is stuff legends are made of. Countless friends and associates came in from out of state.

His viewing and funeral were private on Long Island. There were no pall bearers, which was his wish. The funeral home was packed with every kind of person imaginable, from the biggest to the smallest from all walks of life.

Many of my golf friends and associates came to pay their respects. Legitimate golfers who I met as far back as my first golf job at Engineers. I couldn't believe the admiration they had for my father or how much they cared about my family.

I was told by several of his friends, most notably, Harry Serio and Red Cerse "Remember your father for who he was, not for what he did."

After the funeral, some guys from New York and New Jersey came to the house to spend time with my mom and me. One of the bosses, Sonny Red, went up to my mom and said, "Let's talk."

After a few minutes, my mom called me into the room with them. "I want you to hear what they have to say."

Sonny Red spoke up. "As we told your mom, the only thing that changes is you have to come and pick up the package. Everything else stays the same. Just come every Friday."

A long-time contract was being honored. My father's legacy had that kind of holding power.

"Katie, you are one of a kind. We wish you the best." Sonny Red told her.

The meeting ended with hugs kisses and a few tears, but I was relieved that mom would be okay.

Then like clockwork, every Friday for eight years, I went where I was told to go and picked up the package. From whom, I never knew and never asked. It was part of our life that started when dad went away and continued right until my mom passed.

These guys meant the world to me. They took care of me and my mom in every way possible and they made sure I stayed on the straight and narrow. They watched me become my own man, and they were all proud of me. This is the side of the mob people just don't know about.

Little did I know the generous, caring and giving side of my dad were traits that began to define me as a man. I found myself being able to help people out of whatever trouble they were in. It made me feel good doing it.

But the person I couldn't seem to help was Craig.

He had disappeared again for about three years and we hadn't heard a thing from him until one afternoon when I was playing golf with my friend Mario Posillico at Huntington Country Club. My wife called in a panic.

"Chuck, you have to come home!" she yelled frantically.

"What's wrong?" I was panicked.

"Just come home. Please. Now!"

When I walked in the door, her face was streaked with tears. "Chuck. Butchie is gone. He was killed in Tucson, Arizona."

I lost it. I have never cried so hard in all my life. I was grief stricken and furious. I wanted to kill someone, and I meant that literally. I had to find out what happened and why.

The only story I could get from the police was that the Hells Angels were after him. They had surrounded him, and he barricaded himself in his house. Before the police could intervene or the Hells Angels got to him, he turned his gun on himself.

I wanted answers. I called Willie Catone. In a measured voice he told me. "Let it go."

"Let it go?" I yelled. "Are you fucking kidding me?"

"There are many things you don't know and many things you do not want to know. Just let it go."

I wanted retribution. I wanted an army. I wanted these guys hurt. I wanted them to bleed. I want them to die. I wanted a war.

Willie remained calm yet steadfast. "We are so sorry that your son is gone, but we don't think you should be doing what you're doing, and we cannot help you. You can do whatever you feel you have to do. However, we cannot stand behind you. This is a path your son took. He knew what the risks and what the repercussions could be. Nobody is invincible. Even the guys at the top of the heap are not invincible. I know you want revenge and pay back. I strongly advise against it. You'll end up in jail and how does that help the rest of your family?"

Steam was coming out of my ears. This was not what I wanted to hear. If it were anyone else but Willie, I don't think I would have listened. If it wasn't for him, my mother, and my wife, I probably would've started that war. And it could have very well ended with me either dead or in prison. I couldn't do that to my loved ones.

What reverberated with me was the fact that the most feared gangsters in the country, who helped keep me on the straight and narrow, were still doing it.

I didn't love my son any less, regardless of the path he chose and there is not a day that goes by that I don't think about him. He will always be a part of me. From the moment I lost him, I made a vow to try and help in some way and not let the adversity get to me.

We decided to try and raise money for some children's charities. Along came the United Jewish Appeal. A few years later, they named me "Man of the Year" for the USA. I was in Tucson, Arizona of all places when I found out about the honor.

My dear friend, Quinton Gray, a regular tour player who I traveled with, said. "Let's do something special. We can set something up when the tour heads back to New York, do a charity event and raise some money in your son's memory."

We set a date for when the tour would be on Long Island at the Northville Invitational Tournament at Meadowbrook Country Club.

In June, we proceeded to ask about 16 pros in Tucson to commit to play New York on a Tuesday at the Tam O'Shanta Country Club in Brookville L.I. close to Meadowbrook. We guaranteed each of them $1,000 for their appearance plus prize money. Jim Dent, Tom Joyce, Joe Jiminez, Reeves McVee, Gary Player, Jack Keefer and others committed to play in the event. Their standard appearance fees were upwards of $100,000. They came for a grand guaranteed fee.

In the end, the pros not only gave back their appearance fees, those that cashed in gave their prize money to the cause as well. We raised $140,000. The money went to opening a camp in Israel for children who lost their parents in the conflicts there.

Shortly after the loss of my father and son, I suffered another emotional blow when Milty Tillinger died of a sudden heart attack. While at the viewing, I was ushered into an anti-room. There was a man in an ill-fitting gray suit sitting in a large chair like a king's throne, his hand dangling off the edge of the armrest. He did this on purpose. It was an old Sicilian thing. You were supposed to kiss the ring out of respect to a top boss. I did not do it. I wasn't familiar with this guy and knew better.

He sized me up with a cold stare. "You're with me now."

"I don't know you," is all I offered.

"Everything you had with Milty, you now have with me."

I turned around walked out.

When I told Elyse what happened, she spun on her heel to face me, her instincts kicking in. "No, you are not," she whispered so as not to disturb the other mourners. "Stay away from that guy. He's bad news."

My mom said the same thing. "Leave it alone, Chuck. Let it play out. Just stay away from him. He's overstepping his bounds. Keep him at bay until something happens."

After the funeral, we all met at Milty's apartment. The guy asked me to take a walk with him.

Before I left, mom told me: "Walk on the inside."

"I'm making a move," he insisted as we strolled along the street. He was cocky, so I stayed quiet. "You are with me now. I'm taking over."

I got out of there as quickly as I could without a word.

After that, the guy hounded me with phone calls for a meeting. I always made an excuse and never went to see him.

Not long afterwards, the guy ended up dead. The police found him chopped up into pieces in a wicker basket.

In a flash, so many of the men who had played pivotal roles in my life were gone. I wasn't sure what to do next or who to turn to, so I dove into golf. It was my sanctuary and my salvation, so I set my eyes on something special. Something huge. The greatest undertaking of my life. I owed it to my son, my father, all those men, but especially to myself. I had to prove that their investment of time, love and protection was not in vain.

28
BETHPAGE: THE PATCH

Before Bethpage Black became one of the most historic and challenging golf courses in the country, it was a hustler's haven, a who's who of the country's top golfers. It is said that almost every private country club member on Long Island cut their teeth there. Bethpage often attracted PGA players like Jimmy Wright, Mal Galetta – who shot a 62 on the Black Course - Sal Ruggiero, Ralph Camerlingo and Jay Morelli. With guys like these hanging around the course, it never took long before someone would drop a challenge. They'd swagger in full of bravado, willing to play the money out of everybody's pocket. It became a laughably routine after a while.

One dreary afternoon when the action was slow, some kid in his twenties sauntered up to a table I was at, boasting that he would take anybody on, no matter who they were. He announced that he played on the PGA tour and that his name was Farrell Furst, as if he should have been on the five-dollar bill.

"I don't need any shots and I don't give any shots. Who wants some?"

This wasn't the first or last time a gauntlet was thrown down at Bethpage. I simply smirked. "Okay, Mr. PGA Tour. Let's go."

I didn't ask to see his money. That was my mistake. But we made our bets and hit the course. There must have over fifty guys from the clubhouse following us, making their own side bets.

Farrell and I went out to play the Black. I was kicking his ass. By the time we finished the fourteen hole he was down two thousand dollars. His ego in smithereens, he didn't want to play anymore and sullenly offered to write me a check.

The onlookers braced themselves for what was coming.

"Are you out of your fucking mind? I play for cash not for a piece of paper! Its cash, or we have a problem!"

Farrell didn't have it. So, I escorted Farrell to the parking lot, took the kid's car, his keys and ownership papers. I then gave him enough money to pay for a cab home. "When you come back with the cash, you will get your car back."

I put Farrell's car out in the greens keeper's shack and covered it up. This was on a Friday. On Monday, I got a call from a friend from the club named Teddy Macaluso. "Chuck, I'd like you to come and see me. We have a situation I'd like to talk to you about."

When we met at Teddy's office, Farrell was sitting in a chair outside the office door. I just ignored him.

Teddy asked me point-blank: "Did you play that kid?"

"Yup. He owes me two grand."

Teddy called Farrell in. "How much did you lose?"

The kid fumbled over his words. "About $1,5000 to $1,800."

"No, you didn't. You fucking lost two large," Teddy yelled. Then he reached into his drawer and took out that exact amount in one-hundred-dollar bills. "Give this to Chuck," he ordered Farrell.

With that, I got the keys and ownership papers and gave them to Teddy, who handed them to Farrell, stating: "Now you owe me $2,400. I want the money tomorrow."

And that was the end of that. I never saw Mr. PGA Tour Farrell Furst again. One thing about hustling, you either paid, or you really paid. Come hell or high water the winner gets his money, no matter what it takes. This was no business for the faint of heart.

While it was fine to hustle up a few games on my own, I eventually racked up a crew of regulars that I would hustle with. We always sat at a table near the kitchen in the clubhouse, shooting the breeze to find out which players were there that day and if there were matches and money to be made.

My group of players consisted of Art Silverstone, whose nickname was "The King," a PGA Tour player and top tier earner on the course along with a guy named Fluffy, who was a mediocre golfer but a phenomenal match maker. He won with his set-ups. Then there was Fat Jeff, the bartender. He'd shoot 80 with only a sand wedge – it was one of the damnedest things I've ever seen. Last was Tex. He called himself "George Kent" but went by several monikers and claimed to be part of the Eastern Airlines Riddle family, claiming he did not use the family name because he was considered the black sheep. He was built like Mr. Atlas, a natural athlete, but also completely, certifiably nuts.

There were a few other men who would drift in and out of the crew whose names I have forgotten. One would play both lefty and righty. Another would let his opponent play his "best ball" of two and he would just use one ball. By the fifteenth hole, his opponent would be exhausted from playing two balls on every hole.

Back in the day, we called Bethpage "The Patch." It was a simple nickname for a not so simple course. It was a play on words. It was one of the toughest courses in the area.

Out of the entire crew, Tex was the biggest wild card. Given the goings on at The Patch back them, which was saying something.

He would come in with green hair on a Tuesday, red hair on a Wednesday and a shaved head on Friday. One day he'd show up in a limo, then a Caddy, then a Mercedes. There was just no telling with Tex. He was good enough to win his fair share and would distract his opponents with crazy antics. People often came out to just see him and play him.

On a slow Tuesday morning, he threw out a challenge. "I will bet anyone I can do a finger-tip handstand and walk up to the upper floors of the clubhouse backwards."

There were more than two dozen guys standing around and only a small fraction of them knew Tex the way I did. "No fucking way!" one guy yelled.

"Put your money where your mouth is!" hollered another.

The bets began to fly. My crew put our money on Tex. The rest went against him.

Within no time, Tex was not only in a finger-tip handstand, but he was up the stairs! We cleaned up! He must have been practicing that trick for months before he pulled the hustle off. That was typical Tex.

After a few weeks of slow going, my crew decided to head to the Nassau Country Club in Glen Cove, Long Island to play for some big money. This is where the golf term "Nassau" originated. That day, Tex drove up in a four-door Lincoln stretch limousine.

The course was gorgeous, manicured right down to the grass lining up perfectly with a six-foot-wide gravel walkway that ran between the back of the 18th green and the tennis facility. That's where we were when Tex had six-foot putt on the line for $3,000. As he was pulling the trigger on his putt, a young guy walked down the gravel path and the crunching of his footfalls on the gravel was deafening.

Tex missed the putt. He dropped his club and screamed, "Damn it!"

We all thought he was going to kill the guy. We were ready to jump on Tex to stop him from attacking.

Instead, he yelled to the kid. "You play golf?"

"Yeah," the stunned kid replied.

Tex pointed to his caddy. "Caddy, come here!" He yanked the bag off the caddy's shoulders. "Give that kid the whole bag of clubs." The caddy froze, dumbfounded. So, Tex grabbed them then dropped them at the kid's feet. "Now get the fuck out of here!"

The kid grabbed the bag and took off as fast as he could. Before he got fifty feet away, Tex yelled again. "Hey kid! Come Back!"

Reluctantly, the kid returned and Tex took off his shoes and threw them at him. "Here take these too. I don't need them anymore!"

Now totally freaked out, the kid took off like a bat out of hell.

Tex just stood there for a few minutes barefoot with no clubs. We were all in shock.

Tex started walking away, muttering, "I'll see you guys on Monday at the Patch."

The following Monday when I showed up at Bethpage, my crew was sitting there with strange looks on their faces.

"Jeez, did someone die?" I asked stupidly.

"Yeah. You heard?" one of them piped up.

"Tex is dead," another said.

"Got shot busting into a house in Hicksville. Somebody caught him between the eyes with a 22."

We started to put the pieces together. Tex, it turned out, was a second story man – a professional thief. The different cars were because he'd jacked them. The different hair was to keep from being too recognizable. Here we were thinking he was a kook, but he was crazy like a fox.

They were crazy times. Truly unforgettable. Unfortunately, despite the steady stream of accomplished golfers as well as accomplished hustlers, the condition of Bethpage's course, clubhouse and pro shop all went downhill. It seemed like everyone stopped caring. The prestige of the Black Course began to fade due to a lack of maintenance.

It doesn't take long for golfers to stop coming. If you don't care, neither do they. There are thousands upon thousands of courses to play. Good players – be it pros, hustlers or hackers – prefer quality courses, clean club houses, up to date pro shops and decent food. All of that had gone by the wayside, a distant memory like the crazy tales about Tex. In no time, the place was unplayable. Though it was a shame, the glory days of The Patch were gone.

In the mob world, this was nothing new. Change, although at times uncomfortable was a necessary part of their evolution. When the opportunity to make money disappeared it was time to move on. And that was costly to who or whatever lie in their wake. Once a door closed it rarely reopened. They just looked for the next place with action and to make a score and never looked back – usually.

But, as the saying goes, one man's trash is another man's treasure.

29
THE NEW BETHPAGE

As soon as Charter Oaks was taken over and changed to Fox Run, my gut told me it was the beginning of the end. My instincts said "run" as clearly as the new name on the front sign. I started poking around for other opportunities. A friend of mine Davey G., and I were sitting in the clubhouse having a drink and shooting the breeze with my friend, Davey, when he came up with a bold plan.

Davey asked. "What about us getting some money together and fixing it up?"

Though the glamour and prestige of an elite club was completely gone, muddled down to stained carpets, tired-looking drapes and a staff that didn't care as much as they used to the crown jewel, The Black Course, which was designed by A.W. Tillinghause, one of the most famous golf course designers of all time, remained. The problem: it was just buried, weedy, overgrown in a mess. I stared out the window and pictured in my mind's eye what was once had been a magnificent golf course.

"I know the contract is up for renewal," Davey added with enthusiasm.

Beyond the aging veneer, the problem was not Bethpage itself. It was the current management team. Not one member had a golf background. They had zero knowledge on how to create or maintain a prestigious golf club. Maybe Davey was right. It was a golden opportunity.

"Let's look into it." I finally replied.

A few days later, we met back at Charter Oaks. Davey pulled up a stool close to mine at the bar as I stirred the ice in my soda.

"So?" he asked, excitedly.

"I can get a lot of people involved. Put this place back on the map."

Davey got all jacked up and nearly popped off his stool. "I knew it! This is going to be a great score, Chuck!"

To me, this was way bigger than a score. I wanted to get the course back in the top fifty world-wide. However, I realized, this whole deal was on me. Davey did not have any golf experience. But, being it was his idea I had to bring him in as a partner. We went in 50/50.

Because the course was owned by the state of New York, we were mandated to give a presentation on how we would get this done. As much as I wanted success, so did the state. I gave a sweeping presentation to the board; my excitement wasn't only genuine, it seemed to be contagious. A few days later we got the news that we won the bid for the pro shop and the driving range operations. We were on our way.

I immediately secured credit from a bank for a million dollars and lines of credit from all major golf manufacturers. However, as required by the contract, we needed up-front cash to refurbish the pro shop and driving range. Davey and I agreed to split that cost down the middle. Elyse was all for the idea. As long as I did it legitimately. That's all she cared about. Other than that, she had more faith in me than I did.

We set up a meeting at our lawyer's office to pay the money, sign the documents and finalize the deal. I paced, anxiously waiting for Davey to arrive. Then the lawyer told me he had Davey on the phone.

"Where the hell are you?" I demanded under my breath as the lawyer looked on over the tops of his glasses.

"I am not putting up any cash. I found you the place. You put up all the money and I am your partner or else."

"Take a fucking walk. You've got no chance!"

"We'll see about that!" he shot back.

I never saw this coming. Davey had a decent rep and his father was a nice guy with some connections. I was furious and crushed. I felt stupid, because again, I trusted someone I did not know. But, it was too late to turn back. I was too close. I had to come up with the entire amount by myself. I would deal with Davey later. What I really needed was a break.

A few days later at Charter Oaks, I was giving a lesson to a guy named Al Bart. I only knew him from teaching him the game. However, he had a reputation as a stand-up guy and was always gentlemanly to me. He was also very honest.

My mind was not on the lesson. All I could think about was Bethpage and the money. Al caught on. In his khaki pants, light purple shirt and cigar in his mouth, he addressed the ball with his nine iron as we were working his short game. He stopped mid-swing. I didn't even notice. "What's wrong Chuck? You're not yourself."

I told him about the whole ordeal.

He listened closely as he mimed his next swing. "You really need the money?"

"If not, I lose the deal and it's a slam dunk."

I had not told Elyse yet and I told Al that. I did not want to admit to making another mistake with someone I didn't really know; like that whole Bucky ordeal before we got married. I could just hear her saying, "I told you. You trust too easy." I didn't want to hear that or admit that I made another mistake. I knew I had to fix this without leaning on my mob friends. That wouldn't work anyway in this situation. All I did know was this idea was a "no brainer" and Elyse agreed.

Al grinned and nodded. "Come to my office tomorrow morning. I'll help you. You just tell your wife it's a loan."

The next day at his office, he handed me a check for the amount Davey was supposed to put up. I couldn't believe it. I was speechless. "Al why are you doing this?"

He grinned. "Let's just call it paying it forward. Your dad was a straight up guy and always helped people. He was good to several friends of mine. You are his son and a chip off the old block. You just need a break. I can give that to you and am happy to do it."

I was lucky to know a man like Bart. They just don't make many like him. I was and will be forever grateful.

After winning the bid, I met with the Chairman of the Long Island State Parks Commission, John Sheridan, to sign the official contract. John was a stand up, Irish guy with ginger hair and a hard, blue-eyed gaze. "We've heard a lot of stories about your history, that you are with some connected guys. Word has it that you are part of different things that some people don't take kindly to. Even though you won the bid, we need assurances that element will not a be part of this operation."

His statement was fair. I respected that. Quick on my feet I came up with an idea to put his concerns to rest. "I will sign the contract. You don't sign it. Put it in your drawer. If I don't get Bethpage back on the list of Top 100 Public Golf Courses in the United States in two years, rip up the contract. Throw me out. I will walk away with nothing. But, if I get it done, this three-year deal automatically turns into five years and we will go from there."

He raised an eyebrow and grinned. "That's a deal I'll take."

"Don't sign it." I reiterated. "If I don't produce what I said, I'm out."

John believed in me so much he even tweaked the agreement to a flat rental rate forever, instead of giving a percentage of sales. If it weren't for his open mindedness, I don't think I would have convinced the committee of anything.

It came to pass, that even after signing that contract, the deal still was not consummated. The New York State C.I.D. (Criminal Investigation Department) conducted their own investigation on me. "Where did you get the money? We need proof that all the money came from acceptable sources."

Thanks to Al, I provided them with a legitimate paper trail for every dime. Then with that, the deal was finally done. Now all the higher ups were behind me. They wanted it to succeed.

With my entire golf reputation on the line, Bethpage was now my baby to nurture. I oversaw everyone and everything. I knew what I had to do. It was my way or the highway. There was no other way to get this course back into shape. I'm the first to admit that I was demanding, my standards high. But, I had to instill pride back into the workers. They were good people and just needed direction and enthusiasm. Everyone seemed to want the change as badly as I did, so they followed my lead.

Their habits and attitudes changed. They were once again proud to be part of Bethpage. We cleaned up and manicured all the golf courses, without any outside help, so it did not cost the state a dime. The grounds keepers took care of the fairways and greens like it was their own backyard. They looked out for each other and for troublemakers. It was an amazing transformation.

The clubhouse and restaurant received a full professional cleaning, with the carpets professionally shampooed, the drapes washed, even the chandeliers were meticulously cleaned by hand.

After the clean-up of the inside and the courses were complete and to my standards, I went to work to bring in some big names. At first, I brought in PGA players like Joe Moresco; Jimmy Nichols, the one-armed golfer, and Nat Roscasco from Chicago, who owned the Northwestern Golf Company, that still exists today. I also got PGA tour players like Bob Murphy Andy North. Jerry Pate, Tommy Bolt, Mark Wiebe, Jim Dent and John Cook to come in to give clinics and exhibitions.

On Labor Day that first year, I ran a tournament with sixteen pros from the Metropolitan area, which eventually turned into our "Skins" Game. We paired up into two-man teams and played Best Ball on the Black Course. Teams were formed by simply picking names out of a hat on the first tee. Fans walked the golf course along with the players.

The first time we played it, there was about three hundred fans in the gallery. We played the first, 15th, 16th, 17th and 18th holes for $500 per hole. The rule was: one ties, all tie. There had to be an outright winner. If not, the money would carry over to the next hole. One year, the money got up as high as $5,000. The fans and the players loved it and had a great time.

This event was not only the shot in the arm we needed, it became a mainstay and eventually drew over three thousand fans. Bethpage Black was once again garnering attention.

About three months into the contract a friend of mine, Danny Kapilow, who I had known since I was five years old, called me up in a panic. "Chuck, I need to see you. It's urgent."

"Why and what for?" I asked a bit startled.

"We have a claim against you. Some guy is making a beef."

I knew right away it was about Davey, probably with help from his father making the claim. However, they had no idea how well and how long I knew Danny.

I agreed to meet him for breakfast at a joint in Queens at nine o'clock Sunday morning. I took a seat across from Danny in a booth. Describe to set the scene. Danny got to the point. "Do you know a guy named Davey?"

"Yeah. He brought me to Bethpage."

He glared at me. "He claims he's your partner."

I glared back. "If he would have come up with his end of the money, like he agreed to, he would be my partner. But he reneged." I leaned across the table. "Danny, I've known you since I was five. Have I ever lied to you?"

"No. Never, Chuck," He paused and took a deep breath. He pushed his coffee cup to the end of the table cup and the waitress filled it immediately. Politely she refilled mine as well. She reached into her front pink apron pocket to pull out her pad. But, before she could get it out, he shook his head no. She took the hint and walked away.

"Well, I'm not now. You tell Davey get a gun, get an army, I'm ready to go to war. That's my message to Davey."

Danny shook his head again and put his hand up. "I will take care of this Chuck. This not the time for you to be strong arming anyone. Leave that to me. Okay?"

I breathed easier. Danny got up. I followed suit. He gave me a hug and walked out.

Danny called me back two days later. "Forget about it. It's over."

In that world, what's right is right and what's wrong is wrong. There's nothing else left after that. I never heard from Davey again.

With that weight off my shoulders, I was more determined than ever to take Bethpage to newer heights, beyond what it was before. My next project was the pro shop, a specialty of mine. Most of the new equipment didn't come out until after the holidays; so I figured if I could get that stuff in before anyone else, which would put us way ahead of the curve.

The first guy I approached about this idea was sales representative from Ping. At the time, Ping irons were one of the most popular brands the world. The demand for their clubs was through the roof. They even had waiting lists. Countless pros were using them.

When he came into the pros shop, for his usually weekly visit on a Wednesday, I asked him, "How many sets of new irons do you give to each golf course." Is this in person or via phone? Set scene here.

"They all get four to start," he replied flatly.

"Well, I have five courses. If it's four per course, then how about I get twenty, four for each?"

"I never approached it that way before, Chuck.'

"It only makes sense. Right?" I told him. "We have five times as many players coming through here, I can't just have four sets. You know me. I'd sell them all in a day."

"Okay Chuck. You convinced me. You get twenty."

I wasn't finished yet. "The new ones don't hit the market until after the new year, right?

Why not bring some sets in before then? You can do some demo shows here and sell a ton of clubs before the year even starts."

He smiled and nodded. "I think I can make that happen. We can have a Ping Demo day at Bethpage."

That started a new trend, which at the time, was exclusive to Bethpage. I soon convinced every major golf manufacturer to do the same thing. That meant that during the deadest time of year – October through December – we were packed because of demo days!

Thanks to those demos, the number of clubs we sold before Christmas was staggering. As years went by, this became another staple of ours. We were open 364 days a year. The only day we closed was New Year's Day. During the holidays, we sometimes stayed open twenty-four hours. We served hot cocoa, pastries, cookies to people who came in late to shop and we gift wrapped at no charge.

Pro Shop sales sky-rocketed from close to nothing to a million dollars per year. Through our vendors, we stayed one step ahead of our competition and found ways to beat supply and demand.

After the first full year, the pro shop won the prestigious Merchandiser of the Year Award for the Metropolitan Section of the PGA, an honor we won three years in a row. Not only that, the course shot up to number 88 on Golf Digest's Ratings of the Top 100 Public Golf Courses in the United States. Being the most read golf periodical in the country, their word was gold.

However, I knew I still had a hell of a lot of work to do. I had the big names and the pro shop. Next, I needed major golf events. Although the autograph signings and events produced great turn-outs and high sales, it would be name tournaments that would really bring the people.

In 1982, we obtained the Etonic Golf Company's Pro-Am Tournament. This was the start. The following year, we acquired The Izod Metropolitan Open. This event became our springboard back to PGA prominence. For fifty years, the Met Open was usually played at well-known, private golf clubs. We were one of the few public courses to host it.

We even managed to get a television deal with local channel 12. All four rounds were televised, an historical first for Bethpage. I did the color commentary and had a blast. My kids, Elyse even my mom thought it was out of this world, seeing and hearing me on TV.

Riding off our resounding success, bigger and better events lay ahead. My ultimate prize was the U.S. Open.

In two years, my staff and I accomplished one of my main goals. We were number 46 on Golf Digest's Top 100 Public Golf Courses. We eventually reached number 39. I delivered everything I promised John Sheridan, so my contract was immediately extended to five years. Bethpage was reborn and it's shining star was "The Black" course.

Tony Insolia was the Editor and Chief of Newsday, one of the top newspapers in New York at the time. He was also a dear friend of mine I played golf with. He had his people write a flattering article about the rejuvenation of the Black Course. The impact that story had was indescribable. It covered every part of the club, even the demo days. With that, we increased membership and our media presence continued to rise.

Even the driving range became an attraction. When I took over, the cost for a bucket of golf balls, was $1.50. As a pro golfer, I knew the quality of golf balls and the range itself could make a huge impression. We wanted our customers to know that we cared about every part of their golf experience. We upgraded the golf balls and installed new green mats that were replaced on a regular basis. The range was set up to compliment the beautiful courses. With that approach, the price for a bucket of balls quickly climbed to five dollars.

We treated our golfers like they were members of a private club. We had designated lesson areas as well as private teaching areas, led by top-notch pros giving lessons. The higher we rose on the golf course charts, the more in demand our course became. We started getting calls for tee times from pros all over the country. Tommy Niaporte, the Head Pro at Wingfoot Country Club, would call saying he was bringing in other pros to play a few rounds on the Black. We did everything possible to make their days memorable. Most pros play for free at clubs, but not Bethpage. It's not allowed because it was owned by the state. These guys didn't care. They just wanted to play The Black course and talk about it. That's how special it was.

Almost every PGA pro that came by would sing praises about us to the PGA, which helped get us esteemed events and starting in 1984, we held several prestigious Junior Tournaments. That way, everyone got to see what the PGA future looked like.

With the support of great pros like Gene Westmoreland, who was Head of the Metropolitan Golf Association, Dr. Richard Silver, the Head of the Long Island Golf Association, Tom Meeks, a member of the U.S. Golf Association, and Rabbi Mark Gellman, a passionate and influential golf devotee, we hosted our first major tournament: The Metropolitan Open Championship. This was a prominent event going all the way back to the 1920's.

As soon as we attained the rights, I made a call to some guys I knew at Sports Channel on Long Island. For the second time, we struck a deal to have all four rounds televised. I had the honor of color commentating again. I was no Ken Venturi, but I think I did okay.

I had so much fun. Again, my whole family got a huge kick out of seeing me on television. Mom was so proud. "Your dad would have loved this." She beamed. That made it even more special.

"You were great dad." My kids told me.

The PGA was ecstatic at how we hosted the event. So, in 1988, we started hosting the qualifying rounds of the National Long Drive Competition too. We held this for seven or eight years.

With all the success came the need to give back. If guys that were good to me lost their jobs, I would give them one. At times, I even created new jobs. Good help was always needed anyway. The driving range had to remain immaculate. The golf course needed to be extraordinary every single day. The pro shop had to be spotless every morning before we opened our doors.

Joe Malloy was the pro at an upscale country club called Southward Ho, where I used to go every now and then to hustle for big money. Whenever I won, I gave Joe a few dollars.

After thirty-five years, they fired him out of nowhere. He phoned me in shock to break the news.

"Go back to your shop get all your stuff and I'll put you to work. I'll pay you $300 a week. You start tomorrow."

He came in that Monday with a lot of garbage clubs, balls, clothes equipment. It really wasn't worth much, maybe $200. I gave him $1,000 for all of it, just because of the way he was treated. He didn't deserve that after over three decades of loyalty. It was the best thousand dollars I ever spent. What he did for us at Bethpage, paid me back thousands of times over. He was a class act, hard worker, consummate professional and always knew the score.

I didn't purposely help guys to mirror how my dad helped people. I think I just heard so many stories, that it became ingrained in me to help those in need. As dad always told me, "Everyone has the right to make a living."

A wise guy friend of mine had to go away for a couple of years. He asked me to take care of his son. He was a very nice young man, well raised, impeccable manners and a good golfer.

I took him under my wing and did the best I could for him for five years. I made sure he had a job and kept playing golf. Most importantly, I made sure he was taken care of and protected. If he did get in trouble, I would straighten it out. "Don't tell your father." I'd tell him. "I'll take care of it. He's got enough problems of his own."

Five years later, the kid's father was released from prison. I had a job waiting for him too. Like clockwork, the cops or the Feds would show up to make sure he was there, and they would ask, "Where is he?"

I'd tell them, "He's out on the range, picking up golf balls." And there he'd be.

"This is the best job that you could get for me? Picking up golf balls?" he joked with me.

"Yeah but look at the great tan you have now."

Dad didn't tell me to do things for people. He showed me. That's how he taught. By doing. That and his little anecdotes. "If someone is good to you, be good to them."

By the late 80's, the value of Bethpage had sky-rocketed. When that happens, big corporations get interested. They see easy big money when millions are already being made.

It was fun to bask in the success, to truly take pride in my accomplishments, but in the back of my mind I knew it knew it wouldn't take long before someone would come knocking.

END OF AN ERA

Bethpage began to draw interest from potential buyers. I was so proud of the fact that I was able to accomplish everything I set out to do. I loved the place. It was like nurturing a deathly sick child back to health and watching him grow into a wonderful young man. I was pretty sure of myself into this project, but by this time I as confident as ever. There is a fine line between confidence and arrogance. I took a lot of pride in not crossing it. I still respected the business and the game. There was always something to keep me humble. I truly believe you never stop learning.

I had a great kid named Jimmy Lee working for me. He spoke several different languages, mostly Asian dialects. As a result, he helped bring in a whole Asian contingent, who played there regularly. If it weren't for him, these guys may never have come around. He sold them everything! The loved him and so did I.

After being there for over a decade, a Japanese group – some of guys Jimmy brought in - wanted to buy my operation. This was just the pro shop and driving range. I always listened to offers. I had nothing to lose. So, I had a sit down with these guys. Even with translators, I couldn't understand anything they were saying. They talked so fast, sometimes in English, mostly in Japanese. Yes, means no. No, means yes. It was crazy. My head was spinning.

It got to the point where I had to come up with not only the price, but my terms. I was willing to sell them part of the business. However, it had to be worth it to me not only short term – a nonrefundable retainer and purchase price – but over the long haul.

Unbelievably, they came up with the large retainer and handed me an agreement just the way I requested it. I would also stay on as a partner, manager and Head Pro.

Well, I waited and waited. Nothing ever happened. They were full of shit.

Weeks later, this Japanese guy called me. "I want my retainer back," he demanded.

I let him have it. "You aren't getting your money back. Are you kidding me? First off, it was nonrefundable. Besides that, what you put me through with this whole thing was bullshit. Not a chance."

He started shouting at me in Japanese. I had no idea what the hell he was saying. Then, conveniently, he changed to English and said, "We'll see about that."

I had feeling what was coming. He called in the Japanese Mafia. I countered with none other than Willie Catone. I told him the whole story, detail by detail. He made some calls and we agreed to another sit down.

Immediately, the guy started playing stupid. He acted as if he didn't understand or speak any English. We all knew what was said. I spoke, and he understood it perfectly. He'd say something to one guy, who would say something to the big guy, who would say something back to us.

When Willie finally spoke up, you could hear a pin drop. In the end, the guy didn't get back anything. I got to keep the retainer.

I learned you never show anybody all the cards you're holding. Because whatever happens, good or bad, they will know where you came from, what you have, which leaves you wide open to be taken advantage of. That was a valuable lesson.

In retrospect, mom and dad were both like that. They wheeled a lot of power. But were patient. They never played their hand until they absolutely had to. As dad told me, "Don't show your strength until you know you have the power to back it up."

That wasn't the only major bump in the road.

In 1995, Bernadette Castro – the same Bernadette Castro of Castro Convertibles – took over as the Head of the Long Island State Parks and Recreation. Unfortunately, we never saw eye to eye from day one. I understood right then and there that my days were numbered. It was just a matter of time. I kept doing my thing and stayed away from her as much as possible.

While playing on the PGA Sr. Tour in 1996 at the Northville Tournament in Brookville, I thought of a great idea – I wanted to have Chi Chi Rodriguez come up early in the week and visit Bethpage. We'd get some nice media exposure for the tournament, put on a show and do something fun for the kids. I figured we'd get several thousand people there.

So, I called up Eddie Elias, Chi Chi's manager, who insisted that Chi Chi got $50,000 for any guest appearance.

I set him straight. "Not for me he doesn't pal. You tell Mr. Rodriguez that Chuck Workman called him. Here's my phone number."

Two hours later the phone rang. It was Chi Chi. "When do you want me to be there?"

He did not take a nickel for appearing. He performed trick shots, did demos with new clubs and gave some lessons. As always, he was wildly entertaining. The day was phenomenal, a huge success. About five thousand fans showed up and they all received Chi Chi Rodriguez hats, which a local hat maker donated. He was even happier because his hat company was imprinted inside the hat. He was fantastic. A lot of state dignitaries were there along with Bernadette Castro. She saw the interest I could generate. That was the beginning of prominence for Bethpage in everybody's eyes.

Discussions and negotiations to bring the U.S. Open to Bethpage had been going on for five years before Bernadette came on. We made it our mission back in 1990 to make it happen. However, we had to keep pushing for another couple of years.

Finally, in 1997, the contract was signed to have the U.S. Open at Bethpage Black in 2002, something no one ever thought was possible. All totaled it took seven years of working with the USGA to make this happen. It paid off.

The U.S. Open had never been played at a public course before with the exception being the phenomenal Pebble Beach. They were usually held at prestigious private clubs. We proved that a public course was worthy, and the facility could handle all that was needed by both the players and the gallery.

I will give credit where it is due. Bernadette was part of the final negotiations and signed the contract. The problem was that she claimed all the credit for acquiring it, which was not true. She carried on like no one else had anything to do with it. Yet, numerous people had paved the way for it to happen. This whole thing became inevitable long before she ever stepped foot in the office door. All she did was sign the contract.

I did my best to let her know in our first meeting after acquiring the tournament that many people did the hard work for this big win. She just ignored me. I said what I felt needed to be said. I knew immediately things were changing.

Her father Bernie, founder and owner of Castro Convertibles, was a nice guy and was regarded as an honorable man. I had even given him golf lessons twenty years before, back in Huntington, New York. Based on our relationship, I never saw this coming from his daughter. I tried to keep my head down, hold my tongue and stay focused on the tournament.

Taking on the U.S. Open required major renovations. This meant big money had to be thrown into the course. In the blink of an eye, my old skeletons reared their ugly heads once again and right in the middle of it was Bernadette Castro.

They put the whole thing up for bid, included were the renovations for the course and grounds as well as the pro shop and the driving range. I was told the price was $2 million dollars. The money was available to me from my banks because of the great success I had over the years. I also had several tour pros that were going to become my partners in hopes of expanding the place even more. The odds were against me, but I did everything I was asked to do. I knew the door was closing on me. She was just too strong politically.

During the bidding process, some big corporation came in to take on the renovations, the pro shop and the driving range. Losing Bethpage became inevitable. It was a done deal.

Even though I knew it was inevitable, it still hurt. I carried a heavy heart. I just didn't outwardly show it, especially to the workers or our customers. Everyone knew what I accomplished. I wasn't asking for anything except a little acknowledgment and respect.

My whole family felt for me. Elyse was frustrated, but she didn't want to make things worse. I give them all credit, they were careful with the subject and very supportive. But they all reminded me, "No matter what happens no one can ever take away what you did."

The icing on the cake would come somewhat unexpectedly from

an unknown source. A kid, who was with the Westies up in Westchester New York, overheard a conversation while bartending and my name came up. He got close to make sure he could hear what they were saying.

One of the men said: "No matter what, he can't get the bid again. Workman is not going to get the contract when this deal goes down."

The kid immediately made a few phone calls, first to make sure I was Charlie Workman's son, then to relay the message to his bosses.

I received a phone call from a friend of ours. "Are you having trouble at Bethpage?"

"Yes, the contract is coming up shortly."

"Well, someone's got it out for you. A reliable source overheard someone saying you are out."

Though I was not surprised, I was pissed. I thanked him respectfully for letting me know what the score was. I thought I was strong enough to handle the challenge, but obviously I wasn't. What I didn't realize at the time was that I was also being sold out by some of my so-called friends.

At the top of the list was my assistant, JR, who had been with me for twenty years going all the way back to Charter Oaks. He sold me out. He made his own deal with the new people who were coming in to replace me.

I was furious and had the mind to do something bad. Then I took a step back. I was told by some friends of mom and dad, who had looked out for me for years. "Let it go Chuck. You had a great run. You will tarnish your legacy. It's not worth it and you can't win."

Word got out to all my wise guy friends about the whole conversation at the bar that the Irish kid overheard. Out of nowhere, I received a phone call from a dear old friend, an old school mobster who loved my dad and took care of me as a kid.

"I want to see you," ordered a gruff voice over the line. It was Jack, who I called "Cuppy" since I was a kid. He was one of my father's associates – a banger and a good one. "I'm at the Hicksville train station. Come get me. And come alone."

Cuppy was not a man to make small talk; or a man whose request I would ever refuse. I jumped in my car and drove to the station. It was sweltering hot summer afternoon in the middle of July, well over 90 degrees. When I got there, Cuppy was wearing a long raincoat, which I recognized immediately. It had a special lining. Inside that lining was a shotgun. I greeted him with a hug and felt his weapon of choice under the material.

I held his shoulders and looked directly into a pair of tired eyes. "How can I help you my friend?"

"Take me to this guy who's busting your balls and I'll take care of it."

"No. Please. Don't do that. There's no need," I respectfully pleaded.

He pushed. "Take me to him and your troubles with him will be gone."

Part of me wanted him to do it, but I knew it was wrong. We sat in my car and talked for a while about the old days, when he used to take care of me. I don't remember exactly what I said, but somehow, someway, I talked him out of it.

I drove him back to the city. When we arrived at his place, I reached in my pocket and pulled out all the money I had then handed it to him. "This is for your troubles my friend." I gave him a kiss. "Thank you for looking out for me."

The next day I got a phone call from another friend. "Did you hear what happened to Jack?"

"What do you mean? I drove him home last night."

"Jack died, Chuck."

"That can't be right. I just saw him! I dropped him off at his doorstep."

"We know. That's why we're calling you. That's where he was found, right on his front steps."

I couldn't believe what I was hearing. The man literally died as I drove away. My heart sank. It took a while for it to sink in. I don't know, but I guess I was meant to see him one last time before he passed on. Cuppy was up there in age. It seemed like he wanted to do this one last thing for me. I was the last person he saw and talked to.

As the months went on, the end drew near. I had given almost twenty years of blood, sweat and tears into that place. I put it back on the map and I knew it would be kept there. Just like that, I was out.

I packed up all my stuff and got out of there as fast as I could. There was no reason to prolong things. It was a tough time for me. I think what bothered me most was that almost all the people who I helped get me there along the way disappeared. It was like I had the plague or something. Where were all the people I helped along the way? I felt betrayed.

Dad must have been rolling over in his grave. Lack of respect is one thing, but betrayal was a death wish in his world. If this were 40 years prior, I don't think this would have ever happened. Too many old school guys, would not have allowed it. What's right is right, what's wrong is wrong. This was wrong.

The only guy who stepped out for me was a kid named Billy LaPosa. He was a good guy, who I didn't even know very well, from Suffolk County. He gave me a place to teach and hang my hat, so I could make some money before Elyse and I moved away. He will always have a special place in my heart and in my thoughts.

The ironic thing is, after it all was said and done, and I was gone for good, some reporters from Newsday conducted a research article about how the whole Bethpage sale went down. It turned out, they were working with the Attorney General. They were digging up details on the entire bidding process and specifically how this corporation won the bid, included in that was acquiring the U.S. Open.

The last word I received was that the people who bought into Bethpage were not who they said they were. They were not in the golfing business, which is how they portrayed themselves. They were in the nursing home business. Problems arose. Eventually, they got what they deserved.

But by then, I had stopped caring. The damage was done.

When I think about it, I probably should've left Bethpage about five years earlier. Running Bethpage and playing on the senior tour at the same time, like I said was rough. But hindsight is twenty-twenty. I wouldn't change a thing.

There is no question it was tough on me, more so because I was good at what I did, and I enjoyed every moment of it. What made it even worse was it seemed like every time I turned around someone else had something negative to say. There were people who didn't like the idea of me being synonymous with Bethpage. There is a book by John Feinstein called Inside the Ropes at Bethpage Black. The entire book was about the U.S. Open at Bethpage in 2002. In that book, he did not speak kindly of me.

The author started off with how Bethpage was built back up from nothing to one of the top forty public courses in the country and how it was finally awarded the U.S. Open. You would think I would have been given some credit. Unfortunately, this guy, who wasn't even there, came up with his own ideas, which were not only wrong, they were pure fabrications. He had no idea what the place was like when I took it over. On top of that, he never called me to get the truth. My contributions to the course are both well-known and well-documented, so reading nothing but lies was downright infuriating.

In the book, he states that there were signs everywhere reading: "Welcome to Chuck Workman's Bethpage Black." He even went so far as to say that on every bench and every tee box my name and signature was there. All that nonsense is so far-fetched it's laughable. There was only one sign with my name on it. It was over the front door of the pro shop. It read "Welcome to Chuck Workman's Bethpage Pro Shop." My name wasn't anywhere else on that property.

Despite that book's slander and lies about my history at Bethpage, my experience there was memorable, a point of pride. Anyone who had visited or played there during my tenure knows the truth. It is these people who matter.

It was and still is a majestic place that will go down in golf history. The Black as it is still called, remains one of the most famous and challenging courses in the world. No, I didn't design it or build it. But, I gave it new life and brought it back to the prominence it deserved. That is a very satisfying feeling. I am proud to have played a major role in its rebirth. Not only that, it was while working there that I finally fulfilled my life-long dream and became a fully exempt PGA Senior Tour Player.

As Frank Sinatra sang, "I faced it all and I stood tall and did it my way".

31
THE PGA SENIOR TOUR: FULFILLING A DREAM

Ever since I became hooked on golf, it was my dream to become a PGA Tour player. I took my first shot at joining the tour in the late 1950's. I researched and learned the numerous PGA requirements that had to be met, one of which was to complete an apprentice program at a golf club under a PGA professional. The apprentice qualifications included: your quality of play, the amount of time of being under the pro, your knowledge of the game regarding the rules and regulations, your personal history and background, whether you were a gentleman and thought of as such, all of which was scored on a points system. I started my apprenticeship while working at Shackamaxxon Country Club, under their pro at the time, Alex Ternyie.

I also attended a PGA school in Dunedin, Florida, with another pro named Horton Smith, a PGA Masters Champion and the President of the PGA. Based on the points I accumulated, I was told by Horton that I earned my card. I was so proud, and I knew that Dad would be too. I couldn't wait to see the beaming smile on his face when I told him that I was now an official PGA Tour Player.

A few weeks later an envelope from the PGA offices came. I thought: This is it! My card! Finally.

Inside the envelope was just a letter. No card. My heart sank.

The letter read: "You don't meet certain requirements. The process of your application has been terminated."

I felt like someone smashed a sledge hammer into my stomach. I sank into the kitchen chair with my head in my hands. Back came that raging fury that used to burn inside of me. I knew I belonged. I proved it.

I had lost my job at Shackamaxon because of my association with mobsters and Dad being in prison. The PGA review board didn't have to say it. There was little doubt that's why they rejected me.

Other than finding out the truth about my Dad, this was one of the most devastating blows I had ever suffered.

In 1977, while the pro at Charter Oaks, I went through the process of earning my PGA card. Without it, the members in my club could not play in any PGA co-sponsored event. Mind you, a playing card is not the same thing as a PGA Touring Card. They are two very different things. With a PGA card, you maintain your status as a PGA Member and can play in certain small, local events. With a Touring Card, you can play in every event.

After going through the process of getting the PGA member card, I decided to try one more time get the tour card. I went back and researched all the new guidelines. There was a litany of new requirements including: attending classes, taking a playability test and attending the PGA school again.

I was determined to give it another shot. I did everything I was supposed to and followed every protocol and rule. I even went to the classes in Binghamton, New York in the middle of a winter snow storm with drifts over six feet high.

Every night, Elyse helped me study. She was a teacher so, she really put me through the paces, night after night. She pulled out every teaching trick in the book, including flashcards, memorization tricks, relating one thing to another. She would make a pot of coffee late at night just to keep me going and stayed up with me until I was too tired to study.

You'd think golf tests would be easy, but they were not. If it weren't for Elyse, I would've struggled. With her help, I passed every test.

Next up was the playability test. They wouldn't let me take it. After 20 years, they still did not want me in. However, at the time, a gentleman by the name of Jerry Coats, the President of the PGA Metropolitan Section, stepped in. I met him in passing a few times at some local events, but I cannot say I knew him well at the time. The bottom line was, if I couldn't get accepted by my own regional section I had no chance nationally.

Jerry attended a special meeting to review my case at the Wykegel Country Club in Westchester, New York. He read through my files and became familiar with my case. He stood up in front of both the Metropolitan Section and National Committees.

It got back to me that he told his fellow board members: "We're not the C.I.A. Let's let this guy in, for crying out loud. I'm getting a hernia carrying his file around. Give him his card in the Metropolitan Section, and let's give him a try. We can always change it, but why hold the guy back? Let's see what happens and go from there."

Jerry carried some serious clout, so the panel agreed to let me take my playability test down in Dallas, Texas.

There's nothing like pure, dry Texas heat. Even though I arrived early in the morning, as soon as I stepped outside, sweat started to stream out of my pours. I had to ignore it and play.

There was a sign at the entrance next to a folding table "Playability Test". I approached the pretty, blonde haired receiving girl who was sitting behind the table. She couldn't have been more than 18 years old. I gave her my name and stated why I was there. "They are waiting for you at the driving range just down the path to your right." She said politely with a sweet Texas accent.

Like most courses, the practice green, driving range, first tee and eighteenth green were all close to each other. That first hole looked like a bear. Hard dog leg left, with huge sand traps on both sides. In my mind I started to play the first hole.

I headed to the driving range and was greeted by an old friend of mine, Irv Schloss. Irv was a well-known PGA player and teacher. He was running the playability test.

He looked at me cross-eyed with his wavy white hair. "Chuck. What the hell are you doing here?"

I smiled, sheepishly. "How are you Irv? I'm here because they told me I have to be."

"You've beaten these guys already." He said with a huge smile.

"I still have to do what they ask Irv. It's fine."

"All righty, Chuck. Go ahead and hit one."

"Hit one? I don't even have my golf shoes on," I declared.

"Just tee one up and hit it," he repeated, knowingly.

So, I did.

Irv shook his head and smiled. "Go home Chuck. You earned this a long time ago. Go do what you do best."

We shook hands and hugged. "Thank you again Irv."

Now, the PGA Board had to review my tests and approve my application. During the assessment, a board member from California called me. "Mr. Workman, we are reviewing and discussing your application. We want to get some facts straight," he stated curtly.

I answered his initial questions politely. Then he dropped the hammer.

"Tell me," he began in a sarcastic tone. "Would you do the same thing today that you did years ago with Tony Marco? Or have you gotten smarter?"

He was referring to the time I went after Tony at Middle Bay Country Club, because he bad-mouthed my father over 30 years prior.

"I'm the same guy. I might be a little smarter, which would lead me to do it even better." I fired back. "What would you do if someone said something awful about one of your parents? Would you take it lying down or would you stand up for your family?"

After a second of thinking, he admitted, "I'd make the guy sorry."

"Well, you just answered your own question. I handled it my way. Where I come from, he got off easy. People can assume whatever they want. I know who I am. And I have nothing to be ashamed of." I slammed the phone down.

This was the final straw for me. I called Billy Mariano, a lawyer and friend of the family. He agreed to take my case. He sent an affidavit to the PGA Board with official letters and transcripts of phone calls from legitimate professionals who went on the record for me, such as Jerry Coats. He threatened to take the PGA to court with a law suit. He warned the General Council: "This will not bode well for an organization that is supposed to give everyone a chance."

The whole process took a few years, but finally it was over by 1980. I was in! I was a PGA Player.

Without Jerry and Billy, this would have never happened. I will forever be in their debt. Jerry and I became friends over the years and we still connect every now and then. I have the utmost respect for his integrity. He always did what he thought was right.

Even though I had my card, I didn't get the opportunity to do much with it. I was too busy at Charter Oaks. Seven years later, while at Bethpage, that all changed.

PGA Tour Player Art Silvestrone and I were good friends going all the way back to the old Bethpage. I respected him as a man and as a player. His success on the tour spoke for itself. By then, I had taken my fair share of matches against him. After beating him, on a brisk, blustery morning at the Black, he asked, "Why aren't you out on the tour? You're playing the best golf of your life. I know you have to keep an eye on this place and not many could pull off doing both, but you should try."

Though it was a cloudy day, it was as if Art had brought a little sunshine into a part of my memory I'd shut down, a reminder of what all the struggle was about – to play on the Tour.

I started practicing diligently for four to five hours day, practiced my short game and putting religiously and devoted myself to the sport, both physically and mentally. I officially started playing at The Great Syracuse Sr. Classic at the Lafayette Country Club, which I had to qualify for. I will never forget the start date: July 22, 1985. I shot 72, 73, 70 for a 215 total. I finished ninth. My check was $3,400.

The great Peter Thompson won that event. Nevertheless, I beat guys like: Fred Haas, Jimmy Cochran, Al Balding, Charlie Sifford, Sam Snead, Doug Ford, Bob Toski, Tom Nieporte and even Art Silverstrone. I was on my way.

Later in 1985, I played against 90 golfers on a Monday for two spots in the Sun Tree Classic in Melbourne, Florida. I won one of the spots. Right after, I went to the putting green to practice. Out of nowhere, Art Silverstone, came up to me, asking, "Do you have a game this afternoon?"

"Nope."

"We do now. We have John Kalinka from Hawaii and another guy. Okay?"

Well, that other guy, was Peter Thompson. Peter made an eagle on the first hole. From there he went on to shoot a twelve under par sixty.

Art and I shot a combined nine under par, but we lost $500 each. Playing that guy was like fighting Joe Louis. We couldn't win no matter what. Not only did Peter take our money, he took first place in the tournament, along with a check for $24,000.

As things started rolling in 1985, I signed a contract with DeFini Golf to wear their clothing while playing in tour events. Their logo was a four-leaf clover, which made no sense because the clothing was made by a bunch of Italian kids. The owners were Joe Defini and his brother Jack. The Head of Sales was a Jewish guy named Jack Lust. If this wasn't an old familiar tune, nothing was. A smart Jewish man working for Italians, coming off as Irish. Very ironic. Maybe that's why I signed the deal.

Jack Lust was a Hasidic Jew, who spoke with a heavy accent. He was a concentration camp survivor from WWII, who still bore the prisoner numbers burned on his arms. We had a special bond and signed me to a medium-sized contract. I wore their clothes, used their bags, golf club covers and every accessory they had. When I played on weekends, I would wear knickers with their huge logo on one of the pant legs. My outfits were sharp, just the way I liked to dress.

My whole family got a kick out of my unique golf attire. They all knew how important it was for me to show off my personality. Elyse just shook her head "Yep, that's you alright." Even other players loved it and talked about my clothes all the time. As the saying goes, there's no such thing as bad press. I figured it was a nice tribute to dad, who always dressed sharp. My professional attire was just a little bit louder and brighter.

Once a month, I would go up to their factory in the Bronx. They called it Fort Apache. It was not a good neighborhood. If you left your car there for more than five minutes, it would be gone or totally stripped. They had a huge fence with barbed wire fence around their parking lot.

One time when I was visiting Jack, he said he got stuck with hundreds of sweaters from the Bob Hope Desert Classic because he delivered them late. Each one had the logo of Bob Hope's face and nose on it and read: Bob Hope Desert Classic, Palm Springs.

I asked him how much they were wholesale and he rattled off that they were $39 a piece. I told him, "I'll give you $10 each." He sold me three-hundred. I took them to my Bethpage store and put one on a mannequin with sign: $39.95 down from $89.95." Every single one was sold within a matter of hours.

Another time, I bought an entire boxcar load of Footjoy Golf shoes for $10 a pair. There had to be over a thousand pairs in all colors, styles and shapes. Wholesale they sold for $80 to $100. I charged $29.95 and sold out in a month.

That's how I did business. That's how you made good money back in those days. I did stuff like that all the time. It was fun. It was a win-win for everyone. He got rid of inventory he was stuck with, I sold expensive merchandise for less than half price and made money.

I was keeping up with both Bethpage and the tour. I was having a blast. In 1986, I set my sights on one of the PGA's Major events, the U.S. Open. Doing well in a major could define your career. The 1986, USGA Sr. U.S. Open was held at Scioto Country Club in Columbus, Ohio. This club was considered Jack Nicklaus's home turf. It was a private club and he was a member since childhood. He knew that course like the back of his hand.

I played my ass off on Monday and made the cut. I was in my first Sr. Tour Major event. All I could think about was dad. How I wished he could see me now.

At the U.S. Open, they have everything you could think of for the players: doctors, dentists, tailors, physical therapists, you name it. I was in golf heaven.

The amount of people at this event, from fans to executives, to volunteers to officials to players was beyond comprehension. You could not make a move without running into someone. I had never seen so many people at an event in my life. Autograph seekers were everywhere. Security controlled the crowds, but nonetheless it was nerve wracking. It took everything inside me to maintain my composure.

As I approached the first tee, I was shaking. I kept saying to myself, "Breathe! Just get through the first hole."

I have never teed off in front of so many people. When they announced my name, a shiver went through me like a ghost. I smiled and waved. I was so nervous. I took a deep breath and took in the familiar aroma of fresh cut grass to try and calm myself. I teed up my ball and stepped back to visualize my shot. The first hole was straight out, over three-hundred yards. "Just keep it straight and your fine." I said to myself.

The crowd fell deafly quiet. I could hear birds chirping and my heart pounding. As soon as I started my swing, I knew I was off. I duck-hooked it and almost killed two spectators. I ended up with a double bogey six. The second hole was a dog leg left. Afraid I was going to hook it again, I pushed it so far right I couldn't hit the green in regulation. I bogeyed it. After two holes, I was already three over par.

My caddy asked in a whisper, "You have tickets to go back to New York?"

I said. "Not for you."

As crazy as it sounds, that's exactly what I needed: a challenge. Suddenly, it all clicked. All the years of lessons, while my father languished in jail were all for this. He was with me. Over the next fifteen holes, I nailed eight birdies. I played the way I knew I was capable of playing. My confidence rose. I walked with my head up and chest out.

I called home as soon as I found a phone. When I told my kids how I played, they were so excited. It was heartwarming. Elyse, who now loved the sport as much as I did, was playing her own tournament at the time. So, we shared our scores and excitement. It was fun.

But, I still had work to do. I barely slept that night. I never slept well in hotels to begin with, but I was just too revved up.

On Friday, I had laser focus and stayed on fire. Every part of my game was firing on eight cylinders. My play was crisp, my swing mechanics smooth – it was like an out of body experience. I just played. I kept my eyes off the scoreboards and focused on the only thing I could control: my play. By the end of the round I added seven more birdies. When all play finally ended sometime in the early evening, I found myself tied for second!

I was on cloud nine, flying high. I made calls back home, but I honestly cannot remember what was said. I was numb. But, their love and support meant everything to me. Elyse called my hotel room at night to talk everything through. Our passion for the game fueled each other.

I called the guys at DeFini and they were jumping for joy. For them, this meant I would get TV time on Saturday because I was in the final pairing. They immediately sent out four pairs of pants for me to wear over the weekend, specifically for television exposure.

When I arrived at the course at around 11 o'clock on Saturday for my one o'clock tee-time, people started cheering and clapping for me. I was the underdog and fans love that! All I could do was wave, say thank you, and shake hands. People were screaming. "Good luck Chuck!" "Go get 'em Chuck!' "Make New York proud Chuck!" I had never experienced anything like that in my life outside of my home area.

I made it the locker room and found the package from DeFini with the new pants. I immediately had Randy take them to the on-sight tailor to alter the inseam. He was so happy to be among the leaders, he happily obliged. "No problem, Chuck! I'll take care of it."

Playing in the afternoon was unusual for me because I was not used to being among the leaders. I didn't know what to do with myself. I was trying to waste time. I opened my locker, which was covered with telegrams from top to bottom from people wishing me good luck including one from Sounder Golf Company, with whom I had just signed a contract a month prior.

I wanted to wear the pink DeFini pants with the logo around the knee and no back pockets. I looked in my locker, but the pink pants I'd asked Randy to have tailored were not there. So, I put on a different pair and went back outside. I immediately saw a big crowd of caddies and players in a circle and heard Randy in the middle of all this chaos. He had my pink pants, which were hanging on to his body for dear life, tucked underneath his stomach because he had such a big belly.

"I knew I had a pair of pink pants!" I told him, cracking up.

He said, "Boss, don't you want me to look good on TV?"

I laughed. "They look better on me than you but go ahead."

Every time the TV cameras were pointed at us, Randy made sure he was in the picture. It was hysterical. "Randy! I'm the player. I'm who they want to see."

"Yeah, but I look good on TV!"

Jack Whitaker, the main television announcer, loved all the swag I wore. He reveled in it and always had something flattering to say. I guess Randy wearing the pink pants worked.

I continued to play some of the best golf in my life. Hundreds of fans started following me. I couldn't believe it. The pressure of being amongst the leaders in such a prestigious event began to rise. I seemed to thrive on it. I think a key was once again not minding the scoreboards. This helped me play my game. I knew I was playing well and so did my new-found cult following.

Saturday is known as moving day, when good players make their move to the top of the leader board. I could feel the tension and the intensity from the players as I passed each one by. I kept to myself but smiled and nodded respectfully.

As I walked up the 18th green, the crowd went crazy. I putted out for a par and finished with seven more birdies. The thunder of the spectators was deafening. Randy gave me a big bear hug as we walked off the green. He looked back at the scoreboard. "You're in the top five boss."

I finally looked up at the board myself. I was in second place. I had a shot to win the U.S. Open! There are no words that could due justice as to what I was feeling at that moment. I thought of dad and knew he was looking down on me with a proud grin on his face.

The media swarmed me with microphones, cameras and questions. "How are you feeling?"

"How did you pull this off?"

"What does it mean to you?"

I don't remember what I said to anyone. I was shaking in my

golf shoes.

Between the phone calls back home, trying to stay focused on my game, coming to grips with a dream come true, trying to keep calm and enjoy the moment, knowing my entire round would be televised, should have been enough to give me a coronary. My emotions and nerves were in overload.

Again, I talked to Elyse later. She was intent on telling me about her game that day. I listened, busting at the seams waiting to share details my round and they day. Then she said. "Oh yeah, I saw you on TV today."

"That's it?" I questioned, disappointed.

I don't remember the rest of the conversation. Thinking about it now, it was kind of funny, but I didn't think so at the time. I was hurt. But, we both loved the game so much, it's easy to understand how she was excited too, I tossed and turned all night. I just wanted to get to the course. Morning could not come fast enough. Sound sleep was not part of the equation.

From the moment I arrived the media was once again everywhere. It was continuous television coverage alright and I hadn't even teed off yet. But, this is what I dreamed and yearned for, for so long. The whole thing was surreal. It was far more exhilarating than I imagined. It was and still is one of the most amazing experiences of my life.

I headed to the practice area and went through my normal routine of shots and clubs. I was relatively calm that is until they called my name to head up to the first tee. "Okay Chuck." I said to myself. "This is the real deal."

I looked at Randy, as he was wiping off my clubs and putting them in the bag. He could see I was nervous. "Just play your game boss, like you've done a million times before."

"Okay buddy. Let's go."

With each step I took, the more nervous I became. This was not what I had imagined over the years. I was supposed to be cool, calm and collected. But, the cold, hard reality of it was I was a nervous wreck. My whole body became numb. I could tell you the weather was perfect, but that's it. I couldn't feel a thing other than my nerves, which were at a fever pitch. I tried to stay in the moment and enjoy it. I did love being there, don't get me wrong. It was not only a lifelong dream it was a once in a lifetime thing. I imagined mom's warm, loving smile and dad with his arm around her waving me on.

Other than being there at that moment, in second place with a solid shot at winning the Open, my 35 years of imagining this went by the wayside. I wish I could say fantasy matched reality that day. The only exception was the enormous roar of the crowd when my name was announced to tee off. That was one of the most magical moments I had ever experienced.

As I addressed the ball, I felt the weight of my father's presence like a hand on my shoulder, leading me onward. A surreal calmness came over me. I crushed the tee shot, splitting the fairway in half. I let out a huge of relief as my nerves settled a little. I managed to par the first two holes. I felt pretty good about that.

On the third, I hit the green in regulation – two shots. I approached the green to a round of applause. I waved and nodded feeling good. This is what I worked so hard for. All the battles to get my playing card. Proving so many people wrong. I was here. I belonged. I was proving it. Randy gave me a nod and helped me line up the putt.

I have no idea what happened or what came over me. In the blink of an eye, I three-putted for a bogey. As I reached in the cup to retrieve my ball my heart started to pound.

"It's okay boss." Randy comforted me. "We got this next hole. We'll get it back"

I wish I could say that's what happened. It just didn't. It was downhill from there. The numbness returned, my nerves sky-rocketed, I stiffened up and my game went right to hell.

Before I knew it, I was four over par and spiraling down into oblivion. There is only one way to describe it. I choked. Plain and simple. I shot a 78 and wound up finishing 12th. If I had finished in the top 10, I would have been exempt for the next year. I missed it by two.

For my 12th place finish, I won $3,500. Big money back in those days. But because of the contract I had signed with Sounder, I received $1,000 for qualifying, $1,500 for making the 36-hole cut and another $1,500 for making the Top 20. Along with that, me and fifteen other guys put up $100 a piece to see who would make the most birdies in the first 36 holes. That list included Art Silverstrone and Gary Player. I won. In total, I walked away with over $10,000. Not bad for my first US Open. I could picture my father's eyes telling me, "You made us proud."

I still have this round on video tape. It was amazing, unforgettable and a dream come true. Jack Whittaker said on TV, "It's great to see Chuck playing where he belongs."

Davey Marr, a great name in golf and one of the color analysts, said. "When he gets back to Bethpage, they will want more shots."

What he meant was, when anyone was playing against me, I would have to give them more shots as a handicap. That's not something you want to do when you are playing for money, like I always did. But, I had finally graduated from being a hustler who was great at the game, to a true golfer shooting for greatness on a larger playing field.

The one thing I loved about the sport, the solitude, having everything on me, and no one to blame but myself is what comforted me. I was proud of myself for making it that far. Even though it did not turn out the way I had always dreamed it would, it was okay. It just wasn't my day. My solace was my family. I knew no matter what they were all proud of me.

I guess you can say, even though I did not win the tournament, it was an exhilarating triumph. Even in defeat, sometimes you win. My journey to that moment was an indescribable conquest.

32
THE TOUR

Although I had my PGA playing card, I did not have my full-fledged Touring Card. The Touring Card meant I did not have pre-qualify for every event, which I had to do every Monday before a tournament. From 1987 through 1989, I tried to qualify for thirteen tournaments. I made the cut eleven times. In six of those events, I finished in the top hundred. My winnings came to $7,589. For, not playing full time, in having to tend to Bethpage as well, I was happy with what I was accomplishing. In every tournament I was finishing ahead of some of the greatest golfers in the world.

I tried two times to make it through tour qualifying school, which was the last requirement to gain a touring card. The process had two stages, the first of which was called "Pre-qualifying" and I made it through that both times. The second was the "Actual Qualifying." That is where I missed both times. I played well, but not great both times. I was frustrated, that I came that close two times and fell just short. That stuck in my craw for a long time.

In 1990, I tried for the third time. This time it was different. I felt as confident as ever. I was already playing in tournaments and probably playing the best golf of my life. The day I left for Qualifying School, I told Elyse, "This is a hanger. I'm going to nail it this time."

On November 30th, 1990 at a PGA course in Palm Springs, Florida. I was one of over a thousand golfers playing for the same goal. I have never seen so many golfers at one course in my life. It was mind blowing. It was very difficult to find areas to practice either on the driving range, chipping area or putting green.

I could see the panic in so many players' eyes. Nerves were at a fever pitch. There was not a lot of interaction amongst the players, unless they were already friends. Being we were all vying for the same prestigious goal, everyone was an opponent and in a sense the enemy.

No one was rude. It was still a gentleman's game. However, there were no long conversations. No one had the time or inclination. It was game on. Period.

I was confident, but not arrogant. I showed respect and it was given back. I knew I was facing some incredible talent.

I played my heart out and shot some of the best scores of my career: 73, 69, 70, 69. Only eight cards were given out that day. I was the eighth. What an incredible relief! It was like the weight of fifty full golf bags was lifted off my shoulders.

Soon after earning the tour card, I became partially exempt. Eventually, I was totally exempt, which meant I could play in every tournament and did not have to pre-qualify on Mondays at all, which was also a relief.

From 1950, when I first started to learn the game, it took 40 years to achieve my childhood dream. If it weren't for my father, I would have never picked up a golf club. All I ever wanted to do was make him proud. How he knew I had it in me, is something I cannot comprehend. It is one of the few things that brings tears to my eyes to this very day.

While in pre-qualifying school, I met a wonderful guy named Quinton Gray, who was a Cherokee Indian. At one time, he was a catcher for the San Francisco Giants, so he was an all-around incredible athlete as well as a straight shooter and a genuine gentleman. He epitomized a true PGA Golf professional with his dress, demeanor, likeability and how he carried himself both on and off the golf course. He was one of those people that you could never get mad at. We had an immediate connection that lasted.

One day at the qualifying school, some guy, with gangster wannabe look – expensive watch, chain, pinky ring – a bad attitude and an expensive set of clubs, was giving Quinton a hard time. The guy had done some improper things on the course, so Quinton would not sign the guy's scorecard. I wouldn't have signed it either. I stepped in immediately and went nose to nose with the guy. "You see this guy?" I pointed to Quinton. "You leave him alone. He's with me. Understand?"

This poor act for a wise guy, knew who I was. He promptly walked away. I am not saying Quinton could not take care of himself, but to me stepping in was the right thing to do.

Because of our friendship, we decided to travel together. Let me tell you, traveling with me is no picnic. I used to bring my own pillows and tons of luggage. I hated to drive and made it a point not to. We would sit on the curb together with him trying to convince me to drive. After a while he would just give up and say, "Okay come on. Get in the car. Let's Go."

Then, just to piss him off, I'd say, "Okay chauffer, time to hit the road."

On one of our trips, he got on the phone with my wife, Elyse and went on a rant. "Chuck doesn't need a travel partner – he needs a nurse maid! He is an absolute pain in the ass. Jesus Elyse, I have to walk on his back. I have to put cold towels on his shoulders...." This went on for about fifteen minutes. I sat in the background and laughed my ass off because it was all true!

At a tournament in Dallas, Texas, we were staying at an upscale hotel. While we were in town, I gave my old friend, Al Bart, a call and he invited Quinton and me to dinner.

We arrived at the restaurant and were escorted into a private room in the back. There had to be thirty mobbed up guys in there. Describe a bit here. A typical gangster dinner.

For me, this was nothing new. It was a different story for Quinton.

"Are we in the right place?" He looked petrified.

I grinned. "Oh, we're in the right place alright."

When I introduced Quinton, Al stuck out his hand and gave him a hearty handshake then a slap on the shoulder. "Welcome! A pleasure to meet you. Please sit down. Eat and enjoy yourself."

As soon as we sat down, typical gangster conversations about that life started: who whacked who, who went to prison, who stole this, who did that. I looked over at Quinton and as he sat there with his hands tucked underneath his legs nervously. When his steak came, he was too afraid to move and barely ate. When it was time to go he said thank you in a nervous voice. I never saw him move so fast.

"Oh my god, Chuck!" He whispered as he darted for the driver's side of our car. "That was the scariest dinner I've ever had!"

I busted out laughing. "For one big tough guy, you sure are one hell of a baby!"

On Sunday afternoon after the final round we went back to the hotel to check out. The clerk shook her head. "Mr. Workman, you and Mr. Grey do not have a bill."

Al Bart had picked up both of our tabs.

Quinton remarked how kind that was of him, really taken aback by the gesture.

I said. "Before you were afraid of him, now you love him?"

Quinton just shrugged. "Maybe we can do this again next year?"

The next week Quinton sent Al Bart a driver and a putter as a thank you. He began to understand my life a little bit and wasn't quite as afraid anymore.

I am very sad to say that Quinton passed away in early 2018. The world needs more men like him. I was honored and privileged to have called him my friend.

As my relationship with Quinton proved, playing on tour was not always about me. Whenever I played near home, I got to witness Elyse blossom into a good player. Around 1992, when I was competing in the Northville Classic at the Meadowbrook Club, a made for TV event on the Senior Tour.

She was playing in her club championship at Tam O'Shanter Country Club in Brookville. After the second round, she was down by ten shots. She was dejected and started to complain about how bad she was playing.

I encouraged her, just as she had always encouraged me. "If you shoot seventy-eight and the leader doesn't break ninety, you can win."

She rolled her eyes. "Yeah. Like that's going to happen."

"That lady is going to be under tons of pressure – pressure that she has probably never experienced in her life. Just keep playing and don't worry about her. I guarantee you will win."

The next day, my tee time was at seven-thirty in the morning at Meadowbrook Country Club. After my round was over some guy came running towards me on the practice range "Where's Mr. Workman? Where's Mr. Workman? Your wife won the club championship at Tam O'Shanter! She shot seventy-six and won by two."

Miller Barber, a PGA Tour Champion, was hitting golf balls next to me on the pristine driving range that was 400 yards lone. Miller had distinct look about him: beak nose, receding hair line and dark glasses. "Man, you have this town wired," she remarked. "Your wife plays too?"

I laughed. "Yeah, you want to play her for some money? "

"No, thanks. I want easier games."

Sometime around 1996, I came home for a few weeks to rest. Tony Darrow, the actor who was in Goodfellas and the Sopranos, came to Kutcher's Hotel and Country Club in Monticello, New York to play in a charity event that Elyse and I were playing in. Tony came from a family of connected guys, so we knew each other.

I pulled up to the first tee in my golf cart. There was Tony waiting for us. We couldn't tee off because we were waiting for our fourth.

"Where is this guy?" Tony grumbled.

"Don't worry," I assured him. "Our fourth is coming."

Elyse drove up in her golf cart. Tony's eyes bulged. "What the hell? I don't play with women. She should be home taking care of the sauce."

"I'll tell you right now, she'll beat your ass."

Tony grudgingly gave into playing. In the first nine holes, Elyse shot thirty-four. Tony's tune quickly changed.

It started raining so play was stopped. After a while, the officials were talking about canceling the event. Tony went crazy. "You can't cancel this tournament. I'm going to win. I got a great horse in this race. We're unbeatable!" He turned into Elyse's biggest fan.

From 1985 to 1997, I flew all over the country playing full time on the Senior PGA Tour. I'm pleased to say, I had a pretty good run. I was the first club level pro to ever qualify. I competed and finished ahead of some of the biggest names to ever play the game. I had several articles written about me in most of the golf magazines, including the most prestigious, Golf Digest. The whole experience was equal parts exhilarating and humbling. I think this is what dad had in mind, when his instincts got this journey started. He pulled a lot of strings and called in some major favors to not only get on this path but stay on it.

However, going back and forth became a two-fold problem. I played about every other week, taking a week off to tend to Bethpage. This created inconsistencies in my game. I wasn't getting in the repetitions I needed to play my best. That comes with playing week after week. I honestly believe I could have done a lot better and maybe even win a tournament or two if I didn't take breaks.

I received many phone calls form the PGA offices telling me I had to play in the next tournament or I would risk losing my playing card. That meant I had to find a flight at the last minute and scramble to get there. This included playing in the Pro Ams on Thursday, as required by the PGA, then playing the tournament Friday, Saturday and Sunday. The schedule was grueling. Elyse was patient with me, but it took a toll on both of us. I was never home. If I wasn't at a tournament, gone for four to five days at a time, I was at Bethpage working 15 to 18 hours a day. I was not available physically or emotionally. That wasn't fair to her.

Even though I tried many times to play back to back tournaments, it became too difficult. While I was away, business at Bethpage dropped by as much as 25%. Yet, while I was at Bethpage, I wasn't getting my competition rounds in. I was damned if I did and damned if I didn't.

Despite the ups and downs, I always did what I felt was right and whatever needed my attention at the time. I wouldn't trade any of it for anything in the world! I lived a dream. I'd do it all the same all over again if I had the chance.

I have incredible memories and stories with legendary players like Ken Venturi, Lee Trevino, Chi Chi Rodriguez and Arnold Palmer. But, my most unforgettable experiences were when I played with the pros who accepted me for who I was. In other words, they knew about my dad, his past and my history and it didn't bother them one bit. Because of them, I truly had the time of my life.

The great Tommy Bolt, a U.S. Open champion, always used to marvel at me. He would shake his head in amazement and say, "I never met anybody like you before. You tell people to go fuck themselves and they laugh."

John Brodie, the former NFL quarterback for the San Francisco 49ers, transitioned into a pro golfer and was enamored with the whole mob thing. He knew that my dad was friends with the people who owned the San Francisco 49ers back then. He was a good guy. I had the pleasure of playing with him a few times and hung out with him quite a bit.

Another good friend was the late Charlie Sifford, a terrific, African American PGA pro. He was a wonderful, stand-up guy, who really looked out for me. One time at a tournament in Texas, I was so ticked off at a player that I went to hit him. Next thing I knew Charlie grabbed me and pulled me back. "What the heck are you doing? If you hit him you're done." He yelled.

He was right, and he saved me from getting myself into a serious situation. It just goes to show how tight we were.

Jerry Barber, a two-time PGA Champion, was another guy I loved playing and hanging with. "You look bigger and bigger every time I see you," Jerry once told me. "You don't talk about yourself, you make other people talk about you. And your clubs do the talking for you out here."

I knew I belonged because of the quality of my game but being accepted by my peers was just as important. It all came down to respect and honor. Two things my dad had his entire life. "Respect the game. Respect those in it. With that comes honor."

There are many stories about tournaments I played in, one more bizarre than the other. I played the New York State Open at Grossinger's Hotel in the Catskills one year, a place where my dad's history with that family go back a half a century. During the tournament Paul Grossinger, the owner, came out on the golf course, right in the middle of the tournament and gave me a hug and a kiss in front of everybody. I did not see that coming! It was a bit unusual, but who was going to stop him?

He set me up in the executive suite and I never received a bill. I wasn't allowed to pay for dinner. I couldn't pay a bar bill. It was amazing. I asked him. "Why? Why are you doing all of this for me."

He said. "Are you kidding me? What your father did for me. There wouldn't be a Grossinger's if it weren't for him."

Again, I felt dad's presence. He was with me every day. He never wanted credit for anything. He just believed some people deserved a break and to make a living.

Another time, I was back at Scioto in Columbus, Ohio where the 1986 U.S. Senior Open was held when I received a call at my hotel from a man who was only identified as "Roger." I assumed it was Roger Ginsberg, who was the pro at a club in Muttentown, Long Island, across the street from Charter Oaks Country Club.

"I saw your score on television," he began, "and called to congratulate you. I'm coming out tomorrow to watch you play."

"Geez, that's great Roger. I appreciate that. I'll leave tickets for you out at the will-call."

The next day, I was in the locker room when the attendant came over. "There's a guy outside asking for you."

"Okay. Let him in." The player's locker room is an exclusive place. You had to be someone or know someone to get in.

In walked Roger Wilkenfeld, a total blast from the past. We'd gone to grade school together in Queens and I hadn't seen him since graduation. He lived in Columbus at the time and came out just to see me play. We wound up having dinner together and had a terrific time swapping old stories and catching up. We were both die-hard New York Rangers fans. I was good friends with the famous Ranger goaltender, Ed Giacomin. I also knew John Davidson and the "Captain," Mark Messier.

When the Rangers won the Stanley Cup in 1994, a few of my Ranger friends sent me a jacket, which I happily mailed to Roger as a gift, a small token to thank him for reminding me that people remember you for the good things too, not just the bad things from your past. That stuck with me.

When Roger passed away, his wife gave the jacket back to me, now a token of her appreciation. Roger had died young and I wound up taking care of his kids, who couldn't stay out of trouble. His wife asked me several times to straighten a situation out and even straighten them out if they were headed down a bad road. I clearly remember telling the oldest: "Your father, would be heartbroken, if he were here. He had better things in mind for you than this road you are traveling now. Unless you are willing to pay the piper, you better be willing to change your ways." It was like I was regurgitating the words both Willie Catone and Gyp DeCarlo said to me so many years before. "We will always be here for you. That is unless you created the problem. Then you are on your own."

The older I got, the more my father's traits came out in me. I would often look up into the heavens and ask: "Okay, Dad, what do I do now?" Even though I knew what to do, I needed to feel a connection to his spirit. When I did the right thing, it was as if he was standing at my side, patting me on the back.

Fortunately, my run on the tour allowed me to play in amazing, faraway locales such as Portugal, Spain, the Bahamas and even Japan with Arnold Palmer, where I had the distinct honor of getting to play a round with him. It was like meeting Babe Ruth when I was a kid. Arnold was my idol. There is no one in golf I respect more. He revolutionized the industry with class and dignity. If it weren't for him paving the way, golf would not be what it is today. One of my prized possessions is a framed picture of Arnold, Lee Trevino, Elyse and myself.

In the end, I made believers out of a lot of people, many who did not want someone with my background on the PGA Tour. These are the ones who fueled my fire. They made me determined to prove them wrong. I competed against and beat some of the greatest players the world of golf has ever known.

Ken Venturi once told me: "You fooled them all, Chuck. Good for you!"

The bizarre thing was that some of my biggest detractors eventually became my staunchest supporters and friends. My play and how I carried myself as a pro turned them around. I was very proud of that.

Dad always used to say, "Respect the game." He was right.

Respect made all the difference.

In 1997, I was diagnosed with kidney cancer. My PGA playing days came to a screeching halt. I went right into treatment. It took time, but eventually I went into remission and beat it. However, my full-time playing days were over. I could not compete at the highest levels for an entire tournament anymore. My skills were still there. My competitive juices were still flowing. I could play top-notch golf, but only for a day or two. The endurance I needed was gone. Sadly, the cancer took too much out of me. I was never the same.

As tough as it was to face, it was time to retire. Elyse was concerned for my health too. "I think it's time Chuck. Your health is more important. You've achieved everything you set out to do. You have nothing more to prove."

As I always did when facing a crossroads, I had my own private conversation with dad. "No one said you have to leave the game. Just don't tour." I imagined him saying.

Just like he did when he got back into the Garment Center and semi-retired. He hung out at the S.O. offices and only went out if he had to.

For me, it was time to hang out at golf courses, play a little, teach a little and just be me.

33
FLORIDA: JUST WHEN I THOUGHT I WAS OUT

After recovering from cancer, which ended my PGA career, and losing the bid to buy Bethpage in 1998, it was time to close that chapter of my life and start another.

I poured my heart and soul into the PGA and Bethpage, accomplishing everything I set out to do. I had a nice run on tour. I competed with the best and held my own. Although, I never won a tournament, I cashed-in at just about every event and finished ahead of some of the greatest golfers the world has ever known. As for Bethpage, I'll let the record speak for itself. I put it back on the map and kept all my promises to bring it back to prominence and beyond.

These are, by far, my two greatest achievements in golf. I am proud of my accomplishments and I wouldn't change a thing. As these two major accomplishments came to an almost simultaneous close, I thought about Dad and Mom quite a bit. I would like to believe I made them both very proud. I had become the type of man they wanted me to be. I was finally comfortable in my own skin and had come to accept things that I had grappled with for decades. I was at peace for the first time in a very long time.

As I turned my attention to what to do next, the first dose of reality hit when I tried to get another job. Because of my name and my age, no one in New York would hire me. Potential employers in the golf world were once again leery of me. Although I couldn't play the full three rounds to stay on tour anymore, I could play in shorter, easier tournaments for money. I also still loved giving lessons.

Elyse's tenure as a successful teacher had come to an end in New York. She wanted to retire. Who could blame her? She loved golf too and wanted to play more often. We both agreed there was only one place for us to be: Florida. Where better for the both of us to live out our golden years, doing what we love in a climate where we could do it all year long?

Some friends I knew had already moved down to the east coast of the state so that's where we decided to start looking. Our thought process was this would be our final home, a place where we could retire and really enjoy life for a change. My plan was to find someplace to give lessons, play as much as my body would allow and continue pursuing business opportunities as they arose.

When Elyse and I first moved to Florida, we rented a house with a big backyard for our dog. It was right behind a 24-hour gas station. It was so bright, we never had to turn our lights on at night. This was just a start to get us there. We knew it would take time to find our final home.

Once we got settled in, we started looking at several different golf course housing developments. We finally decided on a quaint community called Del Aire Country Club. It had a magnificent 27-hole golf course as well as a luxurious club house and restaurant. We thought we found our dream home. In the beginning, just about everyone there seemed to like us. We were accepted warmly and started to make friends quickly. It was perfect.

Or so we thought.

After a few months, the club was having issues with one of the members who lived there. I guess he wasn't carrying himself like a gentleman. It got to the point where a few club members, mostly those on the board with power, wanted him gone.

One day while in the clubhouse, one of the board members approached me. "Can you help us get rid of this guy?" he asked me in a whisper. "Maybe set him up in some way. Then we catch him, and we can kick him out."

I couldn't believe what this guy was saying. "I don't know what you're talking about."

"Well, we know that you can do certain things."

"I don't do things like that. I don't set people up. I don't know who you think I am, but you have the wrong guy. If you want him out, then do it the right way. I will have nothing to do with it."

I stuck to my word and stayed out of it. Eventually, they ousted the troublemaker, but the whole episode stuck in my craw. My instincts told me that my refusal to help them would come back to haunt me.

About eight months later, a member came up to me in the

clubhouse. "Did you see the article in Gentlemen's Quarterly about your dad?"

I shook my head. "I don't even read that magazine."

"I will put a copy of the article in your locker," he offered.

When I was done with my round, I went to my locker expecting to find the article. It wasn't there. I approached the guy in the clubhouse. "Where's that article? I wanted to read it."

"I showed it to the president of the club. He has it."

This was not going to end well. "Well, let's go get it," I challenged him. "What the hell does he have it for?"

He headed towards the President's office and I followed right behind him. We found the President of the club at the copy machine making copies of the article. It showed he was making sixteen copies.

My temper started to climb. "Why do you need sixteen copies of an article about my father?"

The President never took his eyes off the copy machine. His bald head never moved to face me like a man. I would have broken his five-foot nothing body in half and he knew it. I could sense his fear and his self-righteous attitude "There are sixteen members on the board. I want them all to read it. So, we can discuss it."

I said to myself: Discuss it? Really? Here we go again.

Now that my father's name was in print once again, the community wanted nothing to do with me. Suddenly the Workman name did not fit. They started to build a case against me to get rid of me with a bunch of trumped up lies.

What they wanted me to do in the beginning – help get rid of a member by doing something - was fine. They were looking for someone to do their dirty work. My last name was fine then. Now it wasn't because I didn't comply.

Even the golf pro, who I considered a decent friend, turned on me. He accused me of selling golf equipment out of my house and garage. He even accused me of giving lessons there, which was false because I was working with someone else at another place.

The board members interviewed the salesman, who sold to the

pro shop, and he stated unequivocally: "I sell the equipment to the shop. That's it. I do not sell any equipment to Chuck Workman. But he was helping me get some LPGA tour players to use my equipment on the tour."

They didn't care. His word meant nothing. Their minds were made up.

I was not going down without a fight. My professional reputation was on the line. I had well-respected friends write letters standing up for me and assuring the board I was not doing these things. I even got my lawyer involved and asked that he speak at one of their meetings. They would not allow him to attend, let alone speak. The board held a special meeting just to discuss my personal standing in the community. I never stood a chance. They accused me of being a bad member. One by one, they laid it on me. "Mr. Workman, we have a huge file on you filled with wrongdoings that very well could lead to your dismissal."

"A file, huh? You been spying on me? Infringing on my personal privacy?" My temper and my voice rose quickly.

That file was filled with pictures of me. They hired a private investigator who took photos of me everywhere, going everywhere from the club to my home. There were even pictures of me with my grandkids and my dog on my golf cart. It was insane. It's one thing to accuse me of something, but you bring my grandchildren into it? I could not believe it. I'd known real-life mobsters who weren't as low-down or dirty as this and these people were from an upscale country club!

Tensions continued to rise when Elyse and I went to club's annual New Year's Eve party. The President of the club came up to me, stuck his finger in my face and started accusing me of all these things that I was supposedly doing, right in the middle of the party.

I was furious. "Take your damned finger out of my face or I'll break it and punch your eyes into the back of your head."

Stunned, he stepped back a pace. "What did you just say?"

"You heard me! I don't just talk about it. I do it." I growled loud enough for everyone to hear. Like a coward, he tucked his tail between his legs and walked away.

At one point, during the evening, they wanted to take a picture of the members. We were told: "Chuck and Elyse, please step aside. You cannot be in these pictures. This is for members in good-standing only."

Elyse had then barred her from playing cards or golf with her friends. Coming after me was one thing. But coming after my wife was another.

We were being railroaded. There is no other way to put it. The whole situation was the opposite of what we'd hoped for when we decided to move to Florida.

Sadly, we had to sell our house, leave the club and start over. They did return our initiation fee, but not the membership fee. We took a huge loss on our house too. When you get to be a certain age, you can't replace that. I wasn't in New York anymore. I wasn't at Bethpage anymore. I wasn't playing on tour. I wasn't hustling. At that time, it was a horrible situation to deal with, which brought up a lot of old wounds. It took quite a while for me to come to grips with the whole thing. However, in retrospect, I think it happened for a reason. I was with the wrong people, at the wrong place.

Ironically, many members who played at the golf course, including people on the board, eventually came to me for lessons at my new club, Marina Del Ray, once I'd moved on. The hypocrisy was mind-blowing. What really incensed me was that the GQ article that had started this whole firestorm was totally fabricated from top to bottom.

A few years after the story came out, respected writers and researchers vetted the article's author Owen Moritz and his supposed source, Joe Stassi, who claimed to have set up the whole Dutch Schultz murder. They proved beyond a shadow of a doubt that Joe Stassi was an inveterate liar with zero connection to the murder case or my family. Respected mafia writer Rick Porrello wrote an article on his website, Mafia.com, proving Stassi was another wannabe trying to make money and a name for himself on his death bed. In another day and another time, this Joe Stassi would have been taken care of. Both Moritz and Stassi were now a part of the long list of people who had dragged my father's name through the mud and made money off it.

My last name was like my shadow, something I couldn't out run. In the end, Elyse and I wound up buying a beautiful two-bedroom house at Wycliffe Country Club in Wellington, Florida. With Elyse's touch, it was beautifully decorated and filled with memorable photos of our loved ones, even an almost life-sized photo of my father and Benzo together all dressed up in tuxes from back in the day when they were in Hot Springs, Arkansas. It makes me smile every time I passed it!

From day one, the members of Wycliffe accepted me for who I am. Most know both my and my father's background and don't care. They are more interested in my golf than anything, which to me is refreshing and flattering. We have warm, friendly neighbors who all look out for each other. It is a wonderful community. We are exactly where we are supposed to be.

There is nothing I can do to change my past or my dad's. But, I have learned to accept the fact that either you accept me for who I am or stay out of my way. I am who I am. That's it, end of story. When I was young, so many people fought for and stuck up for me. They taught me to be who I am. If I didn't learn that from them, none of this would have been possible.

34
K.O.

Harold Konigsberg was the epitome of a wise guy. His nickname was "KO," for his initials but also because like a knockout punch, he was an incredibly dangerous head breaker and hit man. Standing over six feet three and weighing over 250 pounds, he had a look that would send most running. During his heyday, he was one of the most feared gangsters on the east coast.

However, he was also one of the most respected and well-liked men in that life. Notorious mob boss Frank Costello loved him. He drove Frank all over the country before he was even twenty years old, acting as both chauffer and body guard. Though many mafia writers have claimed he was unhinged or downright crazy, KO knew exactly what he was doing. He was a capo, who did what he was told, no questions asked.

That loyalty spilled over to the other side of his life too. Much like most of the gangsters of his time, KO had two different sides. He was genuinely caring to those close to him and would do anything for them with my family at the top of the list. His dedication and respect for my father was unwavering. I do not know when they first met. All I do know is that K.O. was about 12 years younger than Dad.

In 1956, I had a golf store in Woodmere in Nassau County where I sold equipment and gave lessons. Sometime during the coldest part of winter, out of nowhere, a huge menacing looking man walked in with an overcoat and no hat on. He walked right up to me.

"Is Chuck here?"

I tried hard to not show fear, but I did not have a good feeling. "No, he's not here. He'll be back in about an hour."

He glared at me with ominous eyes. "I'll be back in about an hour."

In a flash, he left.

I immediately called my mother. "Mom some guy came to see me. I don't know who he is. He's huge and scary looking."

Calmly, as usual, she said, "Oh sure, that's your father's friend K.O. He's fine. You have nothing to worry about at."

I hung up and breathed a huge sigh of relief.

In exactly one hour, Harold came back. "Where's Chuck?"

I smiled. "That's me."

"You son of a bitch! What did you make become back for?" He went on a long curse-filled diatribe. He really handed it to me. This is how I met Harold for the first time face-to-face.

I took what I had coming to me. Then I smiled. "Sorry Harold. I honestly didn't know who you were. I had to call my mom."

His entire demeanor brightened immediately. "Oh yeah? How's Katie?"

"She's good. She said to say hello and come by any time."

Like a light switch Harold's expression changed again, back to business. He slowly looked around the store. "Okay close the store," he demanded.

"What do you mean close the store? I'm here by myself. I won't make money if I close the place."

"Close the store. And were going to take your car," he stated.

What choice did I have with this hulk of a man standing before me? I sighed heavily. "Okay. Where we going?"

He handed me a small piece of paper. "Just find this address."

I drove into a private upscale development and circled several streets. I finally found the house then slowed down.

"No. Keep going," K.O. ordered.

I did as I was told, and I drove back to the store. I had no idea what the hell was going on. Harold got out of the car before I could even turn it off.

"Bye Chuck." That was it. He was gone without another word.

A couple of days later at work I was reading Newsday. There was a story about a multi-million-dollar jewel heist in the neighborhood I had driven him to. It mentioned the owners of the house were tied up in a chair. It didn't take me long to figure it out. Harold had me find the house for him. He did this job.

A week later K.O. busted through the pro shop door. He put an envelope on the counter. "Give this to Katie." With that, he turned around and left.

I opened it and there was $10,000 in it. I guess that was a finder's fee. However, I did what I was told and gave it all to mom. This is the type of guy Harold really was.

After work, I went to see mom and handed her the envelope. "This is from K.O."

As if it were nothing, she gently took it from me. "Thank you. Harold is a good man. Don't ever forget that."

For a period of time, while Dad was in prison, Harold took on the responsibility of getting money together to pay for the lawyers whenever my father was up for parole. My mother would place one phone call when it was time. That's all she needed to do. Harold always came through, no matter what.

One time I had to pick up the money at K.O.'s place up in Bayonne, New Jersey. The office was in the back of a long, dark, hole in the wall bar. The door was half open, so I knocked and began to enter.

Harold jumped out of his chair and rushed towards me. "Get the fuck out of here! Feds are coming! Take the money and run like hell! If anything happens to you, your father will never forgive me. Go out through the bathroom window!"

I grabbed the money and shoved it everywhere I could think of: my coat pockets, pants pockets, down my pants, inside my shirt, my socks. K.O. blocked the entire doorway with his body. He was so big, they couldn't even see me, never mind get to me. He held his ground there long enough for me to get the hell out of there!

I ran into the bathroom and jumped through the window. I banged into the ledge and money was flying everywhere. Within seconds, I heard. "Hands Up! Against the wall!" I heard some shots being fired. I was maybe thirty seconds ahead of it.

I had my brother-in-law's car that day. I parked it down the street. I ended up in a backyard and got lost. It took me a few hours to finally find it. When I did, I started to wonder how much money I had dropped and lost in the dark. I was lucky I got out of there with my life, never mind the money.

Yet, all Harold was worried about was my dad finding out not only about what happened, but that I was even near the place. It was supposed to be off-limits to me. He knew if word got to my father, he was in big trouble and would have to answer to someone.

He called me a few days later. "Did you make it?"

"Yeah I made it. I have no idea how much money I dropped, though."

"Fuck the money. If you need more tell me. Please don't tell your dad," he pleaded in a tone I'd never heard before.

"Tell my dad what?"

End of conversation. My father never found out about the incident.

My brief personal relationship with K.O. only lasted four years and ended when he went to prison in 1961. Being behind bars did not stop Harold from continuing to check in to make sure things were okay. He would call regularly.

"I'm in the Warden's office sitting in his chair with my feet up on his desk. I'm just calling to see how everything is."

No matter where Harold was whether it was home, on the road or in the joint, he always found a way to reach out and see how things were. Sometimes he'd talk to me for an hour on the warden's phone and tell me stories. At one point, he wound up serving some time with Dad at Trenton State Prison. He and my father were inseparable.

At the time, my father had curly hair and he was very particular about combing it. He was obsessed with making sure he always looked classy, even in prison garb.

One day, Harold saw my father coming out of the shower and ran up to him. Unlike all other prisoners, the warden allowed him to shower alone because of how he kept the peace between the inmates. "Hey Charlie! How ya doin?" Then K.O. did the unthinkable – he rubbed my father's head and messed up his hair.

My father yelled at him. "You son of a bitch!"

"I ran like hell and stayed away from him for two months," K.O. told me. "I couldn't walk near him. I thought he was going to throw me off the tier. And we were best friends!"

He towered over my father in stature but was deathly afraid of his power.

"So, what happened," I asked him. "How did you make up?"

"First, I had to get word to him that I wanted to apologize. I couldn't just go up to him."

"You were that scared?"

"Chuck, you have no idea."

"Did you ever get to apologize?"

"I told him I was sorry and didn't mean anything by it."

"What did he say?"

"Nothing. Absolutely nothing. With your dad, over means over. And once it's over, it's never talked about it again."

Boy, wasn't that the truth!

Unfortunately, Harold got move around so many times while he was in prison that we lost track of him. I tried to find him a few times to no avail.

"Chuck, you're not going to believe this!" Elyse proclaimed one morning, as she read the newspaper on the patio by the pool.

"What?"

"Harold was released from prison."

"What?" My heart almost jumped out of my chest. "When?"

"The story says he was released from Mohawk Prison on August 12th."

This was in 2011 and Harold had been in prison since 1961. He was convicted of murdering Anthony Costellito, a teamster treasurer, while under New Jersey boss Anthony Provenzano. He was sentenced to twenty years to life and served almost fifty.

"Released to where? Where is he?"

"Would you believe he's in Florida? All it says is, 'some nice gated community.' There's nothing specific."

I couldn't comprehend how he could wind up in Florida from Mohawk Prison in Rome, New York. What were the chances of that? It was as if my father sent him down to me.

"Elyse, find him! Go on the computer. We have to see him."

Harold was named my last godfather. He was the only one left. Charlie Luciano, Longy Zwillman, Gyp DeCarlo, Willie Catone, Milty Tillinger, they were all long gone. But miraculously Harold was now in same state I was in.

Elyse discovered that he was staying at his daughter's house a few hours away from us and got me a number.

"Hello?" said the gruff, stern voice I could never forget."

"Harold?"

"Chuckie!" He shouted my name with joy.

I'm not rendered speechless too often, but at that moment, I was at a loss for words.

"How the fuck did you find me kid?"

I had never heard him so happy.

We made plans to meet up the very next day. After I hung up the phone, I held my face in my hands and cried like a baby. Eventually, I got up, went outside by my pool and looked up at the heavens with my hands held in the air. "Thank you, Dad. Thank you."

The following morning could not come fast enough. As promised, I showed up. He opened the door with the hugest smile I could ever imagine, and arms opened wide. We hugged for the longest time and both cried.

Soon we started talking about old times. He was nonstop with stories. It was like he was trying to fill in three decades of his life in a few hours. I listened. Laughed. Cried some more. It was exhilarating, and I felt my father's presence with us the entire time.

From then on, I went to see him every week. I was like a kid going to visit his favorite uncle, who always had a gift. I could not wait to talk about the old times. I thought I knew a lot about that life going way back when. Turns out, I didn't know shit! Every time we met, he had a new jaw dropping tale about someone famous or some hair-raising situation. I would just sit there mesmerized by the stories. I loved every second I spent with him and he always made me feel better when I left than I was when I got there. I'd like to think I did the same for him.

After a few years, K.O. became sickly. Age and all his years in prison had exacted a high price on him. All the newspapers had his age wrong. He was in his 90's at the time. After his daughter sold her house, they put him in an assisted living facility. He eventually passed of natural causes on November 23rd, 2014, a couple of days after I went to visit him for his birthday.

When he went, a part of me went with him.

Following his death, there were articles published about him, many unflattering and some untrue. I'm not saying they were all right or wrong. All I will say is that the Harold Konigsberg I knew and loved had a heart and used it well. I was blessed to call him a dear friend and my godfather.

Harold's return to my life was just the beginning of what would turn out to be countless occasions when I knew my dad was looking out for me.

For some reason, once I moved to Florida, I felt as close to my dad as I did when he was alive. Maybe it was because I had more time on my hands or just that I wanted and needed to feel his presence more. I was headed into the years he was when he passed. When his days began to wind down, he was so calm, yet his wisdom of the world was more apparent than ever. I still needed him. I missed him every day. I think he knew that. Maybe it was the years he missed being with me while in prison, but he began to make up for that by continuously watching over me.

35
HE STILL WATCHES OVER ME

When it comes to my last name, it's all or nothing. I am either treated like I have a deadly contagious disease, or I am received warmly with great respect. When it's the latter, chances are it's because of my dad.

I had arrived in Florida without a job or any prospects, but I was confident my golf expertise would at least land me somewhere to give lessons. I helped a couple of guys years back in New York, who landed big-time jobs at upscale courses in the West Palm area. I made some calls and got nowhere so Elyse went to see one of them herself to ask on my behalf.

The response was quick and emphatic. "Oh, no, no. We can't do that."

The favor I'd done for them had been forgotten. Clearly, I wasn't in New York City anymore.

I tenaciously pounded the pavement in search of work and finally landed at a high-end country club called St. Andrews. However, within days, word started to get around about my background and about my dad. The members of the club were having second thoughts. Some wanted me gone.

Meanwhile, Elyse was out one day running errands and stopped at a small donut shop for a cup of coffee, where she struck up a conversation with a guy named Billy Friesing. Their talk quickly turned to golf and me.

Before taking up golf, Billy had been a great baseball player. He made it to the major leagues with the Minnesota Twins. Unfortunately, after just 23 games, he blew out his knee and his MLB career came to a swift, unfortunate end.

After recovering from his injury, he poured his heart and soul into golf, his second love, and became a great player. It became his dream to own or run his own golf course. At the time, he was the manager of an executive golf course at Marina Lakes Golf Club in

Del Ray Beach.

At Elyse's behest, I went to see him at Marina Lakes. I sat in an oversized plush blue chair with bronze trim. He sat behind a large mahogany desk with a glass cover. There were golf pictures all over the walls.

"How can I help you Chuck?" he asked with a smile.

I told him what was happening at St. Andrew's.

"That guy's a friend of mine."

"You're kidding? Can he help me out?"

"If he is a friend, he will. Let me talk to him and try to set him straight."

Billy called me the next day with bad news. "Sorry Chuck. He won't help. He handed me some bullshit about it being out of his hands. I may have something else for you, though."

He went on to tell me that he'd heard all about what I did at Bethpage and how he'd followed my career. Then he said, "Besides that, your father is a legend in New York."

There it was.

Although Billy was over twenty years my junior, we had very similar backgrounds, came from the same neighborhood, hung out at the same haunts and hooked up with some familiar names. Both of our fathers were also tin-knockers – sheet metal workers– back in the day. We had so much in common, it blew me away. Ever since that conversation, we became close friends. In a heartbeat, either one of us would lay down our life for the other.

Billy spoke to his boss Shelly at Marina and they let me start giving lessons off a small piece of grass near the driving range. I jumped at the opportunity. Unfortunately, I was being charged an exorbitant amount of money to rent a piece of grass. Shelly set the rent because he owned the place. I was grateful, so I kept my mouth shut but my eyes and ears open.

Eventually, I learned a little bit about the history of the place. It turned out the original owner was a guy named Peter Vitale from Staten Island. He sold Marina Lakes to Shelly, who could not pay the monthly nut, so Peter took the place back. I saw him a few times, but never got close to him. I wanted to have a sit down with him to discuss the rent but couldn't seem to get the opportunity.

Then I started giving lessons to a guy named Anthony. He was also originally from New York City and had a lot of connections. Like so many others, he knew about my father and we became tight very quickly.

Early one morning as the dew and mist began to rise above the golf course, I sat down with Anthony before lessons and admitted that I was trying to get a sit-down with Peter. Anthony didn't hesitate to help.

We went over to a pay phone and Anthony called a friend from Staten Island. After he explained my predicament, the guy asked Anthony, "So who is this buddy of yours?"

"It's Chuck Workman."

"You mean Charlie's son?" I could hear him nearly shouting. "The kid who plays golf?"

"Yep, that's him. He's standing right next to me."

Without skipping a beat, he replied, "Just tell me what he needs. We will take care of it. No problem."

Anthony said, "I want him to stay where he is rent free for as long as he wants."

"You tell Chuck it's done."

The next morning, I was giving lessons when I noticed Peter driving towards me in a golf cart. "Chuck, I'd like to talk to you. Have breakfast with me as soon as you can."

Once my lesson was over, we sat down in the clubhouse restaurant for breakfast. The place was packed, and the smell of fresh coffee filled the air. Peter and I took a table by the window overlooking the practice green and first tee.

Peter sipped his coffee then moved it aside. "No more rent from this day on. You are now part of the family. As long as we're here, you're here."

I was stunned. First, Billy Friesing, a guy I never met before, stepped up for me. Then Anthony, who I had not known long, made a crucial call for me. Then Peter Vitale took me in as if I were family.

Somebody up there was watching over me. I didn't have a doubt it was my father. His name may have lived in infamy to some. But his reputation reverberated through time.

A few years later, Peter Vitale sold Marina Lakes. I'd had a great run there, but I needed a new place to hang my hat. Billy came with me to every club I went to check out. I got plugged into a different few clubs and taught my ass off, loving every minute of it. I didn't like the constant moving around, but I stayed on the straight and narrow, doing what I had to do.

The tough part was, I couldn't find a place that I was one-hundred percent comfortable, a place that suited my personality, where I could be myself and stay permanently.

I looked up an old golfing friend from New York named Kenny Smythe, who had moved down to Florida a few years before me. I went to his club, Boca Greens, where he was the Head Pro. We sat alone on a bench near the driving range that had about 12 tee spots and small area for private lessons.

Kenny sighed heavily and ran his hands through his thick dark hair. "My boss is really breaking my balls, Chuck. He's making my life miserable and I don't understand why."

Even though I was coming to him hoping for a job, I knew I could help him too. "Let me make some calls."

I found out I knew his boss. I also heard the place was on its way down. So, it really wasn't worth trying to keep Kenny there. I got him a spot with Billy Friesing instead and Kenny become the Head Golf Pro at Osprey Point Golf Course in Boca Raton, one of the best jobs in the area.

I realized that even though I'd gone to him looking for a new job, he was the one who needed me. Dad had always taught me that friendship goes both ways. You have to do what you can, no matter what position you're in.

Sometimes I would forget how much my father taught me about true friendship until a funny incident would crop up and remind me.

Like the time when I had to go to the doctor because my foot was bothering me. I waited for over an hour in the examination room. I was at my wits end. Finally, the doctor walked in. He was white haired, muscular, and no taller than five foot three. Before he closed the door, I heard a nurse yell, "Dr. Liebler, there's a phone call for you."

I said: "If you answer that phone call we are going to have a fistfight right now!"

He turned around, smirked at me, and hollered back out the door. "Hold my calls!"

He introduced himself and started to examine my foot. Through small talk about my injury, we started to talk about golf. He asked if I played some of the local courses. I explained my background, that I'd played on the Senior Pro Tour and that I'd been at the helm of Bethpage's reestablishment.

"Who do you know from up there?" He was testing me.

"I'm good friends with Tommy Nieporte. I played with him quite a bit. As a matter of fact, he signed my tour card."

He suddenly stopped. "I have to go get an instrument. I'll be right back."

In about two minutes, the doctor came back in with a knowing look. "You really do know Tommy. I wanted to make sure you weren't full of it, so I just called him up." Then he asked, "When are we going to play golf?"

Both of us cracked up. We became great buddies and still are to this day. That's the funny thing about friendship. You never know how or when it's going to happen. But when a person is a true friend, it's a relationship that lasts a lifetime.

Though I still hadn't found a country club to call home, I started playing at the Palm Beach National Golf Club in Lake Worth, Florida. The General Manager there was a guy named Mike Dalfsthrom.

One afternoon as I was perusing their pro shop, the General Manager, Mike Dalfsthrom, popped out of his office, so I decided to introduce myself.

His eyes lit up. "I remember you from Bethpage! Pleasure to meet you. What can I do for you?"

"I really love this place. I'm looking for someplace to hang my hat one last time."

"It would be an honor. You can be our Celebrity Golf Pro."

That was that. Even though they had a pro there, Mike took me in. He was the first person to call me "The Godfather of Golf," which has stuck with me ever since. Pros seek me out for advice. Golf manufacturers ask me about their new products. Young players come to me for lessons to help kick start their careers. I am flattered and humbled. Who could ask for more?

Though my father is long departed, I never feel far from him. I know he looks out for me, as well as the entire family from beyond.

My granddaughter, who lives in Long Island, called me to say she was working at a bar in Queens and the owner told her that he was acquainted with her "relatives" and that once they found out who she was, she would always be met in the parking lot and escorted in and out of work by the bouncers, that she would be looked after.

When she told me that, I found myself once again looking up into the heavens. "Well, you feel safe, don't you?"

"Definitely! They won't even let guys hit on me while I'm bartending. There are bodyguards and bouncers around me all the time."

I had to chuckle. Three generations and over forty years removed, and my father's legacy still carries on in the form of protecting his family.

I can't tell you how many times Elyse and I go out to eat and sitting outside a restaurant are guys I know smoking cigars and hanging out. She always says hello, but then goes right inside the restaurant. However, I usually wind up being out there for twenty minutes talking to them. Everyone wants to shake my hand, give me a hug, and ask me how I am. To not return the favor when someone pays you homage is disrespectful.

Once I get into the place, Elyse always she shakes her head

lovingly. "This will never end, will it?"

"I hope not."

My life has come full circle. In my twilight years, I am surrounded by only men I trust and respect. I still give lessons and as Elyse likes to say, I find a way to make things happen. I would like to believe my dad is proud of me. I accomplished exactly what he wanted me to. I became my own man and found my way legitimately through the world of golf.

I know he has been with me and still is. I firmly believe he has put wonderful people in front of me and has protected everyone in my family in one form or another. Every time I turn around, there is a sign of that.

I know my parents did what they felt was right for me. They took care of me and always had my best interests at heart. They did the best they could. They made it their life's mission to protect me and trusted many loyal men to do the same, men most would not want to know. It started from the day I was born, carried on through dad's incarceration, through my adult life and long after he passed.

Though I am no longer involved in the New York mob life, I still have my connections. That will never die. That is my father's legacy.

Regardless of the career path he chose early in life, "Handsome" Charlie Workman was not only an honorable man, he was a man's man and he was the best father I could have had, no ifs, ands or buts. He had many favorite one-line quotes that always resonated with me.

"Family comes first."

"Do the right thing by people."

"Make sure the little guy gets an even break."

"Everyone has a right to make a living.

"If you are a friend, be a friend, good bad or indifferent."

"You can't be a stand-up guy sometimes. It has to be all the time."

In my mind, these add up to the true definition of an honorable person. If you are considered honorable, you have truly lived a life.

As my dad passed these wisdoms down to me, I hope and pray that I can pass them on to my children, my grandchildren and generations to come; the realization of what it takes to be an honorable person. If have left them with only that, then I believe I have done my job as a parent and as a friend.

It took me the better part of eighty years to realize that if I didn't actually live this life, I wouldn't believe it.

But, I did. And I wouldn't change a single thing.

It's been one hell of a ride, be it the beginning or the end

THE END

MEMORABLE PARTICIPANTS

Below, is an extraordinary list of people. Some made it into this book, some did not. However, I would like to acknowledge all of them. Each one has passed on, but they are not forgotten. They all both knew me or my father and were special to us in some way. Thank you all for being in our lives.

Sammy "the Handkerchief: Money carrier for Charlie Luciano.

Mike Wassell: Managing partner of Singapore Hotel and the Aztec Hotel for Meyer Lansky. Originally from Ireland.

Bobby Riggs: Tennis Pro & hustler

Harvey St. Jean: Part owner of Bayshore Country Club, ran it for Meyer Lansky

Allie Zack: Boxing promoter

Danny Kapilow: Pro Boxer. Head of a Teamsters local. Second biggest Teamster next to Jimmy Hoffa

Little "Ganging" Harry Davidoff: Head of the Teamsters local at John F. Kennedy Airport

Joe "Stretch": Captain in the Gambino family

Bobby Leavy: Head of the International Longshoremen's Association

Joe "Socks" Lonza: Head of the New York Fish Market and Dock Workers Union

Benny "the Lug": Banger and head breaker for the Amalgamator's Union

Frankie Faske: Owned Montrose Motors after dad went to prison. Owned Buddy Hackett

Little Morgy: Worked at Montrose motors and ran the craps game down the basement

Willy Catone: Powerful Gambino underboss. One of my Godfathers

Willie Rudini: Underboss to Rusty Roselli of the Bonanno Crime Family

Big Julie Weintraub: Junket kid to Las Vegas

John Del Mastro: Captain of the Colombo Crime Family

Bob Reith: Pro Golfer

Jan Murray: TV personality

Jim Durante: Singer and Entertainer

Dean Martin: Singer and Entertainer

Bo Winniger: PGA Tour Player. Golf Pro at Desert Inn Las Vegas

Buddy Hackett: Comedian and entertainer

Glenn Teal: Pro Golfer Englewood Country Club, New Jersey

Marty Tolomao: Pro golfer Twin Brooks Country Club, New Jersey

Dominick Rapone: Builder Long Island

George Fazio: PGA Tour Player. Famous golf course designer

Joe Moresco: Pro Golfer. President of the PGA

Fatso Marco: Gangster under Gyp DeCarlo. Was on the Milton Berle TV Show

Maury O'Conner: Golf Pro New Jersey

Harry Serio: President Teamsters 478 in New Jersey

Jack Kiefer Sr: PGA Tour Player

Charlie Sifford: PGA Tour Player

Lee Myles: Entrepreneur Lee Myles Transmission

Al Silverstein: Owner Down and Zeir Fabric Firm

Elliott Satnick: Owner Alorana Coats

Yanni Satnick: Owner Trinity Trucking

John Sheridan: Long Island States Park Commissioner. Signed my Bethpage contract

Gene Bartholomeu: LPGA Tour player. Golf Student of mine

Cindy Rarick: LPGA Tour Player

Frank Kurnitz: Prince of Harlem

Red Cerse: Bahamas

Red Levine: Boss East Side New York. Killed Salvatore Maranzano

Skinny D'Amato: Frank Sinatra's manager

Carmine DeSapio: Political Boss Bronx, New York

Tom Nieporte: PGA Tour player who signed my tour card. Won Bob Hope and Bing Crosby Tournaments.

Dave "The Fireman": Golf Hustler in Miami & Las Vegas

Mortimer Zinc: Head of New Jersey Parole Board

Jimmy Demeret: PGA Tour Player. Golf Pro at Concord Hotel. Three Time Masters Champ. My golf teacher

John Revolta: PGA Tour Player. My golf teacher from Chicago

Hunky Friedman "The Hunk": Friend of dad's. Bookmaker East Side New York

Acky Ackalites: Irish gangster. Big Boss in New York

Cardinal Spellman: Dear friend to me and other boys in the 40's and 50's

Porky Oliver: PGA Tour player Chicago. Great hustler and money player

John Bess: Owned Timber Point Country Club, Long Island New York

Craig Workman: My son, who I lost in 1988

Mickey Cohen: Gangster. Boss of Las Vegas and California. Helped me with my son

Joe Louis: World Heavyweight Boxing Champ. "The Champ". Played golf with me at Engineers with Teddy Rose & Charlie Sifford

Sugar Ray Robinson: World Boxing Champion in three different weight classes. Good golfer not as good as he thought. Best fight I ever saw was him against Joey Maxim.

Art Silverstrone: Sr. PGA Tour Player. Golf hustler. Good friend

Sal Silverstone: Art's son worked as my assistant for 10 years at Bethpage

"Wild Bill" Melhorn: PGA Tour Player. 1930's and 40's. Great champion played at Bayshore in Miami

Tommy Bolt: PGA Tour Player; U.S. Open Champion. Good friend of mine. Came to Bethpage. Known as "Terrible Tommy" due to his temper

Harry Sokol: Criminal Lawyer who handled dad's case in the 1940's. Became great friends until the day he died

Nick DeGennaro: Lawyer; Played a lot of golf together. He never won. Perry Cuomo's Manager

Joe (Joseppie): Owner of Angelina's Restaurant Oyster Bay Long Island. Very dear friend of the family.

Tommy "Brown" Lucchese: Boss of Luchese Crime Family. Also known as "Three Fingers". Got me into Hofstra University

Tony Provenzano: New Jersey Boss, Friend, Golfing Buddy. Teamster official. Accused of killing Hoffa, but he didn't

Tony Ricabone: Boss of Staten Island from the 1950's through the 1970's.

Paul Grossinger: Owner of Grossinger's Hotel in Monticello, New York. Childhood friend of dads.

Vince "Vinnie Blue Eyes" Malloy: Mob Boss; loved golf

Tony "Tony Boy" Boiardo: Friend of Gyp's; my golf partner on many occasions; owned a flower shop; always wore a flower on his lapel.

"Little Augie" Passano: Boss of New York; was at Sands Beach Club all the time; was killed with Alan Drakes wife

Perry Como: Singer and Entertainer

Anthony "Tony Ducks" Carollo: Lucchese Captain; Great guy

Funzi Terrie: Boss of Bonanno Family

Mike Miranda: Boss of Genovese Family

"Fat Tony" Salerno: On the Mafia Commission; friend of dad's

Toots Shor: Famous Restauranteur in New York. Loved my dad.

Ken Venturi: PGA Tour Player. US Open Champion. First Pro at Charter Oaks. Greatest Golf Color Commentator in my opinion.

Tony Roache: Number one tennis pro in US. Tennis Pro at Charter Oaks at my request

Willie Masconi: World Billiards Champion. Gave lessons at Charter Oaks at my request.

Parker Brothers: Owners of the Concord Hotel & Country Club

Cab Calloway: Famous Singer. Got his start through my dad at the Cotton Club while dad was part owner.

Frank Costello: Prince of the City. Original Boss of New Jersey. Helped form the Commission. Charlie Luciano's right-hand man

Frank Erickson: Biggest book maker in the United States

Jan Arden: Singer

Jimmy Roselli: Famous singer; loved dad.

Milton Berle: Comedian & Entertainer; Friend of ours

Bob Hope: Comedian & Entertainer; One of the largest groups in entertainment history

Frank Sinatra: The Chairman of the Board; Old Blue Eyes;

Harold K.O. Konigsberg: Banger with Gyp DeCarlo in New Jersey. My last Godfather

Whitey Liebowitz: Jewish Gangster

Ray "Gyp" DeCarlo: Dear friend of dad; the Real Boss of New Jersey. Independent Boss. One of my Godfathers. Had an everlasting influence on my life

Rocky Graziano: World Middleweight Boxing Champion; Dear Friend

Ken Smyth: PGA Golfer and friend

Jake LaMotta: World Middleweight Boxing Champ; Owner of nightclubs in Florida.

Frank Lesnick: Owner of record Shackamaxon Golf Club

Bill Friesing: Former MLB Player. Golf Pro. Dear Friend

Peter Vitale: Owner of Golf Course I taught at in Florida

Al Wolfson: President. Charter Oaks CC, and dear Friend

Jack Mahoney: Night club owner. Hustling mentor. Dear Friend

Carl Simone: Owner Charter Oaks then Fox Run CC

Lenny Malinaro: Great golfer, gambler and friend

Frank Kurnitz: Prince of Harlem, great friends to dad and me

Benzo: Dad's driver and partner

Saul Orlinsky: Dad's boyhood friend stepped out back into Garment Center

Julie Bernstein: Saul's partner S.O. Textile. Got dad back into Garment Center. Long time childhood friend of dad's

Lou Fugazie: Owner Diner's Club

Spunky: Dad's friend from east side who took me to all the baseball games.

Jewie: Gave me my first TV set. Died in Sing Sing

Mendy Red: Boxing Promoter from the East Side. Dear friend of ours

Milty Tillinger: Powerful Jewish mobster. Great friend. One of my godfathers.

Frankie Gold: Union official and friend.

Georgie "the Sailor": Gangster good friend of mine and dads

Mike Borsuk: Pro golfer and playing partner of mine

Davey Marr: PGA player, Golf Analyst, Good friend of mine.

Tom Strafaci: PGA Tour Player, dear friend; he knew the score

Larry Leber: Golf friend, killed in house Westbury

Meyer Lansky: Mobster mastermind. Original Boss. Luciano's right-hand man. Helped create the Commission and the Combination Mob. Boss of all Jewish Gangsters

Joe Bonanno: Boss of the Bonanno Family. On the original Commission. Original golf handler. Took me to my first lessons

Al "A" Anastasia: High Ranking Boss. Genovese Family. Head of Murder Incorporated. Dear friend of ours. Original golf handler. Bought me my first sets of clubs and equipment.

Trigger Mike Coppola: Boss of Bayshore County Club Miami

Kassinia Golf Course: Where my odyssey began

Uncle Red: Mom's brother. Always took care of me. Best athlete I ever saw.

Howard Palestine: Owner of Commack Country Club, Long Island

Eddie DiMattia: PGA Player. Pro at Commack Country Club. Good friend and mentor.

Tony Roache: Tennis pro and friend

Mike Maranda: Boss and good tennis player

Bob Murphy: PGA player. Winner of the Westchester Classic

Jimmie Nichols: The great one-armed golfer. Played on the PGA tour.

Charlie "Lucky" Luciano: Boss of Bosses; Creator of the Commission and Combination Mob. Dear friend of dad's. My first Godfather. Named after him. Even from afar, he watched out for me and made sure I was kept on the straight and narrow.

Quinton Grey: PGA Pro; Touring Partner; Dear Friend

Harry Serio: Teamsters Official

Guys I knew along the way who were killed for one reason or another

Big Bob the Lawyer: Mob Lawyer

Harvey St. Jean: Mob Lawyer

Jackie Boy: Mobster up and coming

Marty Deavey: Union Official

Tex Riddle: Golfer Bethpage

Albert Anastasia: Boss of Genovese Family after Vito Genovese, formerly the Luciano Family

Joey Gallo: Mobster. Hit Man

Little Augia Pissano: Mafia Captain in Queens, NY. Killed Janet Drake, who was at the wrong place at the wrong time married to Alan Drake at the time.

SPECIAL THANK YOU

Brett Ellen Block has been a champion of this project since its inception. She was the first person I called, when this book idea was proposed to me.

She has played numerous instrumental roles in not only helping bring this unique opportunity to fruition but making sure it reads in a way that grips the reader from beginning to end.

As she has been, since we first met, well over 7 years ago, all through this project she has been a: mentor, guide, teacher, coach, voice of reason, query expert, proposal expert, industry expert, editor and most of all a dear trusted friend.

Words cannot do justice as to how grateful Chuck and I for everything she has done to help make this book a reality. She went well above and beyond the call of duty. You can find her at www.querylettercoach.com.

To my "New Jersey Buddy" Thank you!

~ Peter Cimino

OUR STORY
HOW CHUCK WORKMAN AND PETER CIMINO BECAME "THE COMBINATION"

By Peter Cimino

I met Chuck through a friend of his on Linked In. All this man told me was, "I have a friend who wants to tell his story."

I knew exactly what he meant – that friend had ties to the mob.

I agreed to an introduction phone call but still wasn't given Chuck's name.

During that first call, within seconds, I was completely blown away. I immediately knew the man on the other end of the line was the real deal.

At first, I did not inquire who he was. I figured he would tell me in his own time.

Finally, he asked, "You haven't asked who I am?"

I politely replied. "When you are ready to tell me, you will."

"Does the name Chuck Workman mean anything to you?"

I answered honestly. "Not off the top of my head."

He came back with, "Come on! You have a whole library of Mafia books, I know you do. How about Charlie "the Bug" Workman?"

Then it hit me like a butt end of a gun to the back of my head. I almost dropped the phone. Calmly and respectfully, I answered. Yes, he was a hit man for the mob. He whacked Dutch Schultz."

"That's exactly right. I am his son." Chuck answered.

As he started talking about his relationships with the most famous and dangerous gangsters this country has ever known, I was hooked.

Unbeknownst to me Chuck had already spoken to several well-known authors. However, he turned them all down. We spoke quite a few times about how he wanted the project done.

In the end, I made a solemn vow. "This is your story. It will be told in first person (your voice), in your own words. I do not want or need any creative license."

This turned out to be exactly what he wanted to hear, but what no other author had been willing to commit to. I learned this was the very reason Chuck had declined to work with other writers. They all wanted creative license to exaggerate and expand on stories. Chuck wanted no part of that and quite honestly, I clearly understood why. He didn't need it. I wanted what he wanted. The truth. There are too many books out there that take liberties. They are misleading. He wanted no part of that.

During our conversations, Chuck said a few things to me that I will never forget.

"For someone who was never part of that life, you truly understand it. You don't have this dramatized perception. You realize there were other sides to those guys, sides that no one talks about."

"I have to tell you, you are a true man of honor and you were born well after your time."

From that moment on, we both believed our partnership was meant to be. The rest, as they say is history.

His perspective of the mob, his father and his own life are so extraordinary that they read like something straight out of a crime novel. As he puts it, "This is the truth. It's real. It's what happened and how I feel. Period. I have no motive to lie or make things up like other guys have done. I tell it like it is."

In this book, he does just that. He does what he does best - tell amazing stories with conviction and brutal honesty. I do what I do best - mold those stories into a book that comes to life, flows and leaves the reader wanting more.

Over the years, during the evolution of this project, we have become very close. I look up to him like an uncle and heed his many words of wisdom. We speak the same language, which has made this incredible relationship enjoyable and educational. We have developed a wonderful mutual respect. We both have each other's best interests at heart.

The journey from the beginning to the end of this book has been: challenging, painstaking and at times arduous. Yet, at the same time it has been a lot of fun with so many incredible laughs. We have in fact created our own stories, especially during my trips to Florida, when we worked together.

A while back, in honor of the Combination Mob, which was an arm of the Sicilian Mafia , allowing other ethnicities (especially Jews and Irish), to play a major role in the mob operations led by Charlie Luciano and Meyer Lansky and the original Commission, we decided to name ourselves, The Combination. It is just our way of confirming we understand each other, we want the same things and will stop at nothing to get there. And we stand side by side, shoulder to shoulder the whole way.

I am not only honored and privileged to be the vehicle for Chuck to tell his life story, but to call him

UPDATE ON THE AUTHORS

Chuck Workman

Today, Chuck lives a relatively busy, but quiet life in the West Palm area of Florida. He remains in the game that helped create his legacy and that he loves so much: golf. He still gives lessons, is very popular and is in high demand. He is often approached by representatives in the golf industry, be it manufacturers, course designers, club owners etc. for advice. "I still know a thing or two." He says with a wink.

He plays a few holes whenever he is able and jokingly says, "I only play for money."

Chuck is still an entrepreneur. He uses his vast web of connections to put the right people together to create business deals – something that comes natural to him. "I still get a huge kick out of it when something comes together."

Like his father, he lends a helping hand to many who need it, asking for nothing in return. "I think that's just part of my dad's legacy carrying on in me. When I feel it's the right thing to do I think back to many things my father taught me. Everyone deserves a chance. A friend is always a friend. Everyone deserves the right to make a living."

And to this day, on a regular basis Chuck meets someone new who either had ties or a family member who had ties to his father.

"Are you Charlie Workman's kid?"

"That's right."

"I will never forget what your father did...."

Peter Cimino

Born and raised in northeast New Jersey (Haledon via Garfield), Peter is a proud New Jerseyan who now lives in the western suburbs of Chicago. "As my dad always tells me. You can take the man out of New Jersey, but you can never take the New Jersey out of the man." He says.

From a young age, Peter became fascinated with the mafia. "It was all around. I read the newspaper all the time -- especially Jerry Capeci's weekly column in the Daily News. I just seemed to gain a keen sense of things and looked at it a little differently."

He is regarded as mob aficionado, due to his extensive library of gangster books, movies, videos and materials. His specialty is the early years, late 1920's through 1960's.

As a result, this is what Peter mostly writes about. His first novel, "The Four Corners: A Sicilian Story" is a dramatic, fictionalized chronicle based on his own family, set in the New Jersey town (Garfield), where his family settled after coming over from Italy. It is an historical, true-to-life, prohibition era mobster tale, using real people, places and events. The main character was inspired by his grandfather. "I took my grandfather's popularity, kindness, keen sense of business and charisma and combined these with how I think I would have acted back in that time."

Peter also wrote a short story titled, "Lucky Says Hello", a teaser-sequel to the Four Corners. Both are available through Amazon.

Respected author Elyse Draper wrote: "Peter has a genuine talent for creating real characters; not only characters that smack of reality, but ones people develop an attachment to. His talents are remarkable. It is only a matter of time before his work is on the New York Times BSL."

Peter's other passion is baseball. He is a high-level instructor and owner of the National School of Baseball & Softball, L.L.P. "Teaching this great game is my passion and my sanctuary. There is nothing like it." He has taught over 500 baseball and softball students, worked with over 50 teams and five major organizations.

The discover more about Peter's writings, please visit www.peterciminoauthor.com

To check out his baseball and softball organization visit www.nationalschoolofbaseball.com

www.ingramcontent.com/pod-product-compliance
Lightning Source LLC
Chambersburg PA
CBHW071853290426
44110CB00013B/1128